AT HOME
with the WORD
2 0 0 0

Sunday Scriptures and Reflections

Martin F. Connell

Roberta R. Glisson
David Philippart
Marie B. Picard
James Runyon
Mary Peifer

Reprinting from *At Home with the Word 2000*

A parish or an institution may purchase a license to reprint the Reflections (and their discussion questions), the Practices of Faith, Hope and Charity, the Prayer of the Season or the holy day boxes from *At Home with the Word 2000*. Please see page 158 for details.

If a parish or institution wishes to reproduce some or all of the scripture texts, a license must be acquired from the copyright owners (see below). When writing to copyright owners, state clearly which texts you wish to use, the number of copies to be made, and how often you'll be using the copies. There may be a license fee.

Acknowledgments

The Sunday scripture pericopes contained herein are from the *New Revised Standard Version of the Bible*, copyright 1989 by the Division of Christian Education of the National Council of Churches of Christ in the U.S.A. All rights reserved. Used by permission. Text emendations © 1995 Augsburg Fortress. Used by permission.

Most Roman Catholic parishes proclaim the Sunday scriptures using the readings from the *Lectionary for Mass, Volume 1: Sundays, Solemnities and Feasts of the Lord,* copyright 1998, 1997, 1970 by the Confraternity of Christian Doctrine, Washington, D.C. For information on reprint permission, write: Confraternity of Christian Doctrine, 1312 Massachusetts Avenue NW, Washington DC 20005.

The English translation of the *Salve, Regina* from *A Book of Prayers* © 1993, International Committee on English in the Liturgy, Inc. (ICEL); the English translation of Psalm 24, 51, 63, 65, 91, 98, 100, 118, 126, 131, and 147 and the Canticle of Mary, Canticle of Zechariah, and Canticle of Simeon from the *Liturgical Psalter* © 1995, ICEL. Used by permission. All rights reserved. For reprint permission, write: ICEL, 1522 K Street NW, Suite 1000, Washington DC 20005-1202.

The Prayers of the Season were written by Gabe Huck. The holy day commentaries were written by Peter Mazar.

The art in this book is by Annika Nelson. The design is by Jill Smith. The editor was David A. Lysik, and Audrey Novak Riley was the production editor. Typesetting was by Karen Mitchell, in Palatino and Universe. The book was printed and bound by Bawden Printing of Eldridge, Iowa.

AT HOME WITH THE WORD 2000 © 1999 Archdiocese of Chicago: Liturgy Training Publications, 1800 North Hermitage Avenue, Chicago IL 60622-1101; 1-800-933-1800; orders@ltp.org; fax 1-800-933-7094. All rights reserved.

ISBN 1-56854-291-7

AHW00

How to Use At Home with the Word

This book invites you to be at home with God's word, to live *with* the Sunday scriptures in order to live *by* them.

SCRIPTURE READINGS These are the heart of *At Home with the Word.* You may want to read the scriptures before going to church, or, better yet, use this book to return to the Sunday scriptures again and again throughout the week.

Because the Sunday readings of many other Christian churches are the same as those proclaimed in Catholic communities, *At Home with the Word* has highlighted the scriptures we share. There are two minor changes that result. First, there may be a few more verses in the reading here than you'll hear proclaimed in the Sunday assembly. Also, when Roman Catholic churches observe a particular feast on a given Sunday that is not celebrated by other Christian communities, there will be two sets of readings.

REFLECTIONS Martin F. Connell is an assistant professor of theology at Saint John's University in Collegeville, Minnesota. His reflections invite us to explore scripture as it is presented in the context of our Sunday liturgies.

The reflections offer background information and perhaps new things to consider. Households or small groups may share the readings and reflection weekly.

This is Year B, the year of the Gospel according to Mark. Throughout Ordinary Time we will be reading most often from this gospel. See Professor Connell's essay on the Liturgical Year and the Gospel of Mark on pages 8 – 11.

PRACTICE OF FAITH Roberta R. Glisson writes from her experience of faith and family as a mother and grandmother. She lives in Glenalden, Pennsylvania. David Philippart is an editor at LTP. He has ministered in parishes in Buffalo, New York, and has written widely on liturgy in Christian life. Occasional contributions by Christine Kenny-Sheputis.

PRACTICE OF HOPE Marie B. Picard is a recent graduate of the master of arts program in liturgical studies at the University of Notre Dame. She lives in Cleveland, Ohio, with her family.

PRACTICE OF CHARITY James Runyon is director of the Christian Service program at Notre Dame High School in Peoria, Illinois. Mary Peifer is a parish nurse. They met and married while living and working at St. Joseph Catholic Worker House in Rock Island, Illinois.

WEEKDAY READINGS Some people may want to read more than the Sunday scriptures. For each week, we've listed the verses of the books of the Bible from which the first readings for daily Mass are taken.

At Home with the Word also includes:

MORNING, EVENING AND NIGHT PRAYER These simple patterns of prayer for the home take five or ten minutes and are meant to be repeated every day. Don't be afraid of repetition; that's one way to learn.

SEASONAL PSALMS AND PRAYERS Each season is introduced by a page that includes an acclamation, a psalm and a short prayer. Repeating a single psalm throughout a season is a fine way to learn the psalms by heart.

SUNDAY AND FRIDAY PSALMS AND PRAYERS Sunday is our day of feasting, Friday our day of fasting. Both days need extra prayer and acts of discipleship. Here are psalms, a Lord's Day poem by Henry Baker and a prayer for Fridays from the U.S. bishops' letter *The Challenge of Peace.*

CALENDAR
TABLE OF CONTENTS

The Lectionary and At Home with the Word

by Martin F. Connell

WHAT IS A LECTIONARY? A lectionary is an ordered selection of readings, chosen from both testaments of the Bible, for proclamation in the assembly gathered for worship. Lectionaries have been used for Christian worship since the fourth century. At different times and in different places before the invention of the printing press in the fifteenth century, the orders of the readings varied a bit. The variety from church to church often reflected the different issues that were important to the local communities of the time.

For the four centuries from the Council of Trent (1545–1563) to the Second Vatican Council (1963–1965), the readings in most Catholic churches were basically the same from year to year and were proclaimed in Latin, an ancient language that many Catholics did not understand. The use of the language of the people in the liturgy and the revision of the lectionary after Vatican II have had tremendous effects on the accessibility of the Bible for Catholics. The Bible is again a vibrant source of our faith and tradition.

THE THREE-YEAR LECTIONARY CYCLE The lectionary issued by the church after the Second Vatican Council appeared in 1970. The most exciting feature of the lectionary was its basic plan. This three-year plan incorporates a fuller selection of readings from the books of the Bible. Each of the first three gospels — Matthew, Mark and Luke — corresponds with one year: Matthew for Year A, Mark for Year B and Luke for Year C. The Sunday lectionary cycle, therefore, takes three years to complete. This liturgical year, 2000, is Year B, which begins on the First Sunday of Advent, November 28, 1999.

YEAR B: THE GOSPEL OF MARK You will find that most of the gospel readings proclaimed in your Sunday assembly this year and printed in *At Home with the Word 2000* are from the Gospel of Mark. This gospel will be proclaimed on most Sundays from the First Sunday of Advent, to the celebration of Christ the King, November 26, 2000. The introduction to the liturgical year and the Gospel of Mark on pages 8–11 and the commentaries on the gospel each week will help you recognize and appreciate the contribution of this gospel to our faith.

THE GOSPEL OF JOHN You might ask: What about the Fourth Gospel? The Gospel of John is not excluded from proclamation during the three-year cycle. Though it does not have a year during which it is highlighted, the Gospel of John punctuates certain seasons and times of the year.

The readings from Year A on the third, fourth and fifth Sundays of Lent are from the Gospel of John, and they are proclaimed every year in parishes celebrating the RCIA. These three wonderful stories from the Gospel of John — the woman at the well (on the third Sunday), the man born blind (on the fourth Sunday) and the raising of Lazarus (on the fifth Sunday) — are important texts to accompany the celebration of the scrutinies in the process of Christian initiation.

During Years B and C, you will find two sets of readings on these Sundays in *At Home with the Word:* one set for churches celebrating the scrutinies of the RCIA and one set for parishes that are not having the initiation process during that particular liturgical year.

The Gospel of John also appears for the Mass of the Lord's Supper on Holy Thursday and for the long passion reading on Good Friday. And on most of the Sundays of Easter — during the fifty days from Easter Sunday until Pentecost — the Gospel of John is proclaimed at the liturgy.

THE DIFFERENCE BETWEEN THE BIBLE AND THE LECTIONARY The shape of the lectionary comes from the ancient church practice of *lectio continua,* a Latin term which describes the successive reading through books of the Bible from Sunday to Sunday. You can see such a *lectio continua* in practice if you flip through *At Home with the Word* and, for example, consider the gospel texts assigned to the Sundays from the Thirteenth Sunday in Ordinary Time, July 2, to the Sixteenth Sunday in Ordinary Time, July 23, and from the Twenty-second Sunday in Ordinary Time, September 3, to the Feast of Christ the King, November 26. Though not every verse is included, you will notice that through these Sundays we move from chapter 5 of Mark to chapter 13.

You will find, moreover, that the first readings often will echo some image, character or idea in the gospel, as is the church's intention. The second reading often stands on its own and comes from a letter of Paul or some other letter of the New Testament. You will notice, for example, that the second readings from July through November take us through Second Corinthians, Ephesians, James and Hebrews.

UNITY WITH OTHER CHRISTIAN CHURCHES IN THE WORD OF GOD The basic plan of the lectionary for Catholics is universal. The readings proclaimed in your church on a particular Sunday are the same as those proclaimed in Catholic churches all over the globe. The lectionary is one of the main things that makes our liturgy so "catholic," or universal.

But as time has passed, other Christian churches have adopted the Catholic lectionary also. So not only are the readings the same as those in other Catholic churches, but the revision of the Roman Catholic lectionary has been so well received that other churches have begun to follow its three-year lectionary cycle.

Catholics and their neighbors who attend other Christian churches often hear the same word of God proclaimed and preached in the Sunday gathering. Even though you may not talk about the Sunday readings with you neighbors and therefore haven't realized that your readers read the same lections and your preachers preach on the same scriptural texts, this is really a remarkable change when you consider how very far apart from one another Catholic and Protestant churches were before the Second Vatican Council.

The slight difference between the readings you'll find in *At Home with the Word 2000* and what is proclaimed on Sunday is a result of our efforts to highlight the scriptures shared by many Christian churches. The major parts of the readings will be secure, but there might be a few verses tacked on in *At Home with the Word* at the beginning or end of a reading to match those in the Revised Common Lectionary, which is used in many non – Catholic Christian churches. As always, when the page with the readings is short on space, a shorter version of a reading or two will be printed and the full citation will be provided at the end so that you can check out the fuller text in your Bible.

At the bottom of each right-hand column on the odd-numbered pages, you will find citations for the readings of the daily liturgy. When a reading is from the same book of the Bible as the reading from the day before, you will find only the citation of chapter and verse. When the book of the Bible changes from one day to the next, the full citation will be given.

We hope that your celebration of the liturgy in your parish is deepened by the preparation you will find in this book. Have a wonderful liturgical year being "at home with the Word" of God.

The Liturgical Year and the Gospel of Mark

by Martin F. Connell

Our experience of Christian faith is shaped fundamentally by baptism, anointing with oil (called chrism) and thereafter by our participation in the celebration of the eucharist Sunday after Sunday. Our bodies, emotions, minds and hearts are formed by what we see and hear in the eucharistic liturgy; by the words, familiar or not, that we say; by how our bodies move during the liturgy; by our association with other baptized Christians in the assembly — however great or tiny — gathered in fellowship around the table of the Lord week after week. Two basic influences on the content of the Sunday liturgy by which we are formed in faith are the liturgical year and the lectionary.

THE LITURGICAL YEAR The basic outline of the liturgical year has been in place since the earliest centuries of Christianity. Each liturgical year has three basic spans: the first extends from the Three Days of Easter (Holy Thursday through Easter Sunday) back into the Forty Days of Lenten preparation and forward into the Fifty Days of the Easter season, the seven weeks from Easter Sunday to Pentecost. The second span goes from the celebration of the memory of Jesus' birth at Christmas back into the four weeks of Advent anticipation and forward into the Christmas season, with its feasts of the Holy Family, Epiphany and the Baptism of the Lord. The third span, "Ordinary Time," fills in the two spaces — one short, one long — between the other two. The shorter span goes from mid-January until the Sunday before Ash Wednesday, and the longer one stretches out for more than half the year, from Pentecost at the beginning of summer until the following Advent.

MATTHEW, MARK AND LUKE The two spans of Ordinary Time are part of a larger three-year cycle (years A, B and C) of gospel readings of the lectionary. Almost all the gospel readings in Ordinary Time of Year A come from the first gospel of the New Testament, the Gospel of Matthew. Almost all the gospel readings in Ordinary Time of Year C come from the Gospel of Luke. And many, though not all (see "The Gospel of John" below), of the gospel readings in Ordinary Time of Year B, this liturgical year, come from the Gospel of Mark.

Though these three gospels share many stories about Jesus of Nazareth, each has a unique slant on the life of Jesus, a view colored by the resurrection experience of the particular early church community for which that gospel was written. Each community experienced the risen Lord in the celebration of the eucharist according to the aggregation of individuals who belonged to it and according to the culture in which that experience took place.

This three-year cycle of readings for Ordinary Time began after the Second Vatican Council, and the year from Advent 1999 until just before Advent 2000 is Year B. During it we will discover the unique narration of the life of Jesus according to the Gospel of Mark.

The Gospel of John Even though the fourth gospel does not have a liturgical year during which is it proclaimed as do the other three gospels, it contributes many gospel readings during particular seasons of the year, especially the Forty Days of Lent and the Fifty Days of Easter.

Also, because the Gospel of Mark is relatively short, merely 16 chapters, and thus not long enough to fill the whole year, Year B also draws from chapter 6 of the Gospel of John, on the eucharist. The Gospel of John will therefore be proclaimed from the Seventeenth (July 30, 2000) through the Twenty-first (August 27) Sunday in Ordinary Time.

JESUS IN THE GOSPEL OF MARK The influence of the Gospel of Mark on Christian tradition cannot be overestimated. Scholars posit that this gospel was the earliest written of the four in the New Testament. And because 80% of the Gospel of Mark was used by the author of the Gospel of Matthew, and 65% of Mark was used by the author of the Gospel of Luke, the impact of the portrait of Jesus in Mark is vast and deep. The Gospel of Mark is indeed the text by which we have come to know what a "gospel" actually is.

In spite of its impact, the contribution of the Gospel of Mark usually goes unrecognized. This is because the gospel itself is rather short, and we mentally supplement its spare narrative with stories we know from the other three gospels. For example, the Gospel of Mark has Jesus appear first as an adult proclaiming repentance. There is no scene in Mark of Jesus as an infant with magi and shepherds, but our imaginations add characters, stories and teachings that its author had not included. The Gospel of Mark has no sermon on the mount (as in Matthew); no parable of the good Samaritan or the prodigal son (as in Luke); no woman at the well, no man born blind, no raising of Lazarus (as in John). The Gospel of Mark is arresting in its uniquely spare version of the life and ministry of Jesus of Nazareth.

Also "missing" from the original version of the Gospel of Mark is, believe it or not, a resurrection account. Open a Bible to Mark 16:8. Most Bibles have a note at the bottom of the page telling us that verses 16:9 – 20 were added later. The account originally ended at 16:8 — with an empty tomb and the fearful disciples fleeing! As such issues are made clear, we realize that Mark, which seemed to be a gospel just like the others, actually gives us a very different portrait of Jesus.

In spite of some of these oddities, Jesus in this gospel is a Savior we can relate to. His divinity is not so overwhelming that we forget the humanity he shared with us. In fact, in one scene of the gospel, we discover that Jesus had to perform a miracle twice before it actually worked! After wiping saliva on a blind man's eyes and laying hands on him, Jesus asks him, "Can you see anything?" The man responds, "I can see people, but they look like trees, walking." Jesus gives it another shot, and the man sees clearly (8:22 – 26). Mark's Jesus is a savior who worked very hard at ministering to the people seeking him out, yet also a savior who sought solitude when the burdens of ministry were too great.

The Messianic Secret One of the enigmatic characteristics of the Gospel of Mark is what biblical scholars call its "messianic secret." Again and again in this gospel, we find Jesus telling people he has healed and demons he has expelled not to tell anyone about who he is or what he has done. He even commands his own disciples to be silent about his identity.

This messianic secret is puzzling because we expect that Jesus would have wanted others to know how the presence of God and the nearness of God's reign changed the lives of those touched by them. Yet it fits in with the gospel's overall theology, in which the saving and healing presence of Jesus would only be fully realized on the cross. Only then would his followers and those whose lives he had touched understand who he was and why he had come.

AN OUTLINE OF THE GOSPEL OF MARK

PROLOGUE   1:1 – 13

Proclamation of John the Baptist (1:1 – 8)
  "Prepare the way of the Lord."

Baptism and temptation of Jesus (1:9 – 13)
  "You are my Son, the Beloved."

REVELATIONS, MINISTRY AND EARLY ACCUSATIONS IN GALILEE   1:14 — 3:5

Call of the first disciples (1:16 – 20)

Healing a man with an unclean spirit (1:21 – 28)
  "What is this? A new teaching — with authority!"

Healing at Simon's house, cleansing of a leper (1:29 – 45)

Healing of a paralytic (2:1 – 12)
  "Why does this fellow speak in this way?"
  "It is blasphemy!" "We have never seen anything like this."

Call of Levi (2:13 – 17)
  "Why does he eat with tax collectors and sinners?"

Teaching about fasting, and the Sabbath (2:18 – 28)

MISCOMPREHENSIONS, ACCUSATIONS AND REJECTION IN GALILEE   3:1 — 6:6

Healing of a man with a withered hand (3:1 – 6)

Appointment of the Twelve (3:13 – 19)

Miscomprehensions (3:20 – 35)
  "He has gone out of his mind."
  "By the ruler of the demons he casts out demons."

Parables and explanations (4:1 – 34)

Jesus calms a storm (4:35 – 41)
  "Who this is this, that even the wind and the sea obey him?"

Three healing miracles (5:1 – 43)

Rejection of Jesus at Nazareth (6:1 – 6)
  "Where did this man get all this?"
  "And they took offense at him."

MISUNDERSTANDING BY DISCIPLES, BELIEF BY OTHERS   6:7 — 8:21

Feeding the five thousand (6:30 – 44)
  "Are we to go and buy two hundred denarii worth of bread, and give it to them to eat?"

The Syrophoenician woman's faith (7:24 – 30)

Cure of a deaf man in the Decapolis (7:31 – 37)

The demand for a sign (8:11 – 21)
  "Do you not yet understand?"

ON THE WAY TO JERUSALEM   8:22 — 10:52

Jesus foretells his death and resurrection (8:31 — 9:1)

Jesus again foretells his passion (9:30 – 32)

A third time Jesus foretells his passion (10:32 – 34)

JESUS IN JERUSALEM   11:1 — 13:37

Triumphal entry, and cleansing of the Temple (11:1 – 19)

Controversies over authority, tax and resurrection of the dead (11:27 — 12:27)

Discourse on the end times (13:1 – 37)

Passion, death and burial (14:1 — 15:47)
  "Truly this man was God's Son."

EPILOGUE   16:1 – 8

Visit of Mary Magdalene, Mary the mother of James, and Salome to the empty tomb; encounter with the angel
  "And they said nothing to anyone, for they were afraid."

APPENDIX — LATER ENDINGS; APPEARANCES OF THE RISEN CHRIST   16:9 – 20

Appearances to Mary Magdalene and to two disciples (16:9 – 13)

Commissioning of the disciples, and the ascension (16:14 – 19)
  "Go into all the world and proclaim the good news."

A Passion Account with a Long Introduction
Because the cross casts a long backward shadow over the whole of the Gospel of Mark, some scholars have described this gospel as a "passion account with a long introduction." Indeed, about halfway through the gospel, at the end of chapter 8, Jesus first foretells his own passion and tells his followers that they too must "take up their cross." Predictions of his passion punctuate the narrative from this point until the abandonment, betrayal, arrest, denial and finally the death of Jesus, a passion account that is a major piece of the whole gospel, and which in retrospect colors all of the events of the earlier chapters.

Discipleship in the Gospel of Mark In this gospel Jesus regularly reminds his followers of the high cost of discipleship. In this way the gospel is engaging for those of us who believe but still find life difficult and perplexing.

The twelve disciples in the gospel are not portrayed in a very favorable light. Again and again they do not grasp the actions or words of Jesus, and their repeated misunderstandings are accentuated by their fear. The disciples share in Jesus' ministry of healing, exorcising and teaching, but they do not understand fully who he is, even though they are his closest companions. This uncomplimentary portrait of the twelve is capped with Judas' betrayal (14:43 – 45), Peter's denial (14:66 – 72) and the flight of the disciples after Jesus' arrest (14:50).

Outsiders in the Gospel of Mark The disciples are not much help to Jesus, uncomprehending and cowardly as the gospel tells us they are, but other people in the gospel step up to help Jesus in his times of need. There is the Syrophoenician woman who persuades Jesus to heal her daughter even though at first he would not minister to her because she was a Gentile (7:24 – 30). There is the woman who, in the house of Simon the leper, anoints Jesus' head and prepares his body for burial (14:3 – 9). There is the passerby from north Africa, Simon of Cyrene, who is pressed into ser-vice to help Jesus carry the cross (15:21). There are the many women who, after the disciples have fled, stand by faithfully, looking at the suffering Jesus on the cross from a distance (15:40 – 41). And there is Joseph of Arimathea, a member of the council, who asks Pilate for the body of Jesus and sees to its proper burial when it is taken down from the cross (15:42 – 46).

Because we ourselves are far from the time and place of the life of Jesus, we can take heart from the role of these outsiders in the Gospel of Mark. Their faithfulness and its effects in the paschal mystery invite us to be open to the life of God in our own lives, and to be attentive in our own world to the presence of God and how we can be instruments of God's presence today.

BIBLIOGRAPHY
Raymond E. Brown, "The Gospel according to Mark," chapter 7 of his *An Introduction to the New Testament* (New York: Doubleday, 1997): 126 – 170.
Paul J. Achtemeier, "Mark, Gospel of," *Anchor Bible Dictionary*, volume 4 (New York: Doubleday, 1992): 541 – 559.
R. A. Guelich, "Mark, Gospel of," *Dictionary of Jesus and the Gospels* (Downers Grove, IL: InterVarsity Press, 1992): 512 – 525.
F. J. Matera, *What Are They Saying about Mark?* (New York: Paulist, 1987).

M O R N I N G
p r a y e r

This order of prayer may be said upon waking or before or during breakfast.

O Lord, open my lips,
and my mouth shall declare your praise.

The Sign of the Cross

In the name of the Father
and of the Son
and of the Holy Spirit.

Psalm 63

God, my God, you I crave;
my soul thirsts for you,
my body aches for you
like a dry and weary land.
Let me gaze on you in your temple:
a vision of strength and glory.

Your love is better than life,
my speech is full of praise.
I give you a lifetime of worship,
my hands raised in your name.
I feast at a rich table,
my lips sing of your glory.

On my bed I lie awake,
your memory fills the night.
You have been my help,
I rejoice beneath your wings.
Yes, I cling to you,
your right hand holds me fast.

Let those who want me dead
end up deep in the grave!
They will die by the sword,
their bodies food for jackals.
But let the king find joy in God.
All who swear by truth be praised,
every lying mouth be shut.

*One of the seasonal psalms throughout this book
may be prayed instead of Psalm 63.*

The Canticle of Zechariah

Praise the Lord, the God of Israel,
who shepherds the people and sets them free.

God raises from David's house
a child with power to save.
Through the holy prophets
God promised in ages past
to save us from enemy hands,
from the grip of all who hate us.

The Lord favored our ancestors
recalling the sacred covenant,
the pledge to our ancestor Abraham,
to free us from our enemies,
so we might worship without fear
and be holy and just all our days.

And you, child, will be called
Prophet of the Most High,
for you will come to prepare
a pathway for the Lord
by teaching the people salvation
through forgiveness of their sin.

Out of God's deepest mercy
a dawn will come from on high,
light for those shadowed by death,
a guide for our feet on the way to peace.

The Lord's Prayer

*You may join hands with others or hold your
hands with palms facing upward while praying the
Lord's Prayer.*

EVENING
prayer

This order of prayer may be said before or after dinner.

O God, come to my assistance.
O Lord, make haste to help me.

The Lighting of a Candle

*A candle may be lit to welcome the evening
while saying:*

Jesus Christ is the light of the world,
a light no darkness can overcome.

Psalm 141:1–5, 8

Hurry, Lord! I call and call!
Listen! I plead with you.
Let my prayer rise like incense,
my upraised hands, like an evening sacrifice.

Lord, guard my lips,
watch my every word.
Let me never speak evil
or consider hateful deeds,
let me never join the wicked
to eat their lavish meals.

If the just correct me,
I take their rebuke as kindness,
but the unction of the wicked
will never touch my head.
I pray and pray
against their hateful ways.

Lord my God, I turn to you,
in you I find safety.
Do not strip me of life.

The Canticle of Mary

I acclaim the greatness of the Lord,
I delight in God my savior,
who regarded my humble state.
Truly from this day on
all ages will call me blest.

For God, wonderful in power,
has used that strength for me.
Holy the name of the Lord!
whose mercy embraces the faithful,
one generation to the next.

The mighty arm of God
scatters the proud in their conceit,
pulls tyrants from their thrones,
and raises up the humble.
The Lord fills the starving,
and lets the rich go hungry.

God rescues lowly Israel,
recalling the promise of mercy,
the promise made to our ancestors,
to Abraham's heirs for ever.

Intercession and Lord's Prayer

*At day's end we offer our petitions in Jesus' name.
We make intercession for our church, our world,
our parish, our neighbors, our family and friends
and ourselves. We seal all our prayers with the
Lord's Prayer. In conclusion, those present may
exchange the sign of peace.*

This order of prayer may be said before going to sleep.

May Almighty God give us a restful night and a peaceful death.

Psalm 131

Lord, I am not proud,
holding my head too high,
reaching beyond my grasp.

No, I am calm and tranquil
like a weaned child
resting in its mother's arms:
my whole being at rest.
Let Israel rest in the Lord,
now and for ever.

The Canticle of Simeon

Lord, let your servant
now die in peace,
for you kept your promise.

With my own eyes
I see the salvation
you prepared for all peoples:

a light of revelation for the Gentiles
and glory to your people Israel.

Invocation to Mary

The final prayer of the day is customarily to Mary.

Hail, holy Queen, Mother of mercy,
our life, our sweetness, and our hope!
To you we cry, the children of Eve;
to you we send up our sighs,
mourning and weeping in this land of exile.
Turn, then, most gracious advocate,
your eyes of mercy toward us;
lead us home at last
and show us the blessed fruit
of your womb, Jesus:
O clement, O loving, O sweet Virgin Mary.

The Sign of the Cross

*We end the day the way we began it,
with the sign of the cross.*

May the almighty and merciful Lord,
the Father and the Son and the Holy Spirit,
bless and keep us. Amen.

The wedding feast of the Lamb has begun,
and his bride is prepared to welcome him.

Psalm 100

Shout joy to the Lord, all earth,
serve the Lord with gladness,
enter God's presence with joy!

Know that the Lord is God,
our maker to whom we belong,
our shepherd, and we the flock.

Enter the temple gates,
the courtyard with thanks and praise;
give thanks and bless God's name.

Indeed the Lord is good!
God's love is for ever,
faithful from age to age.

Prayer of the Day

On this day, the first of days,
God the Father's name we praise;
Who, creation's Lord and spring,
Did the world from darkness bring.

On this day the eternal Son
Over death the triumph won;
On this day the Spirit came
With the gift of living flame.

God, the blessed Three in One,
May thy holy will be done;
In thy word our souls are free.
And we rest this day with thee.

**Sunday is our weekly feast day,
our celebration of creation,
liberation and resurrection.**

FRIDAY
p r a y e r

Friday is our weekly fast day, our day of special prayer, fasting and almsgiving.

Lord, by your cross and resurrection
 you have set us free.
You are the savior of the world.

Psalm 51:3 – 6, 12 – 13

Have mercy, tender God,
forget that I defied you.
Wash away my sin,
cleanse me from my guilt.

I know my evil well,
it stares me in the face,
evil done to you alone
before your very eyes.

Creator, reshape my heart,
God, steady my spirit.
Do not cast me aside
stripped of your holy spirit.

Prayer of the Day

All praise be yours, God our Creator,
as we wait in joyful hope
for the flowering of justice
and the fullness of peace.

All praise for this day, this Friday.
By our weekly fasting and prayer,
cast out the spirit of war, of fear and mistrust,
and make us grow hungry
 for human kindness,
thirsty for solidarity
 with all the people of your dear earth.

May all our prayers, our fasting and our deeds
be done in the name of Jesus. Amen.

ADVENT

Maranatha! Come, Lord Jesus!

God owns this planet
and all its riches.
The earth and every creature
belong to God.

God set the land on top of the seas
and anchored it in the deep.

Who is fit to climb God's mountain
and stand in his holy place?

Whoever has integrity:
not chasing shadows,
not living lies.

God will bless them,
their savior will bring justice.
These people long to see the Lord,
they seek the face of Jacob's God.

Stretch toward heaven, you gates,
open high and wide.
Let the glorious sovereign enter.

Who is this splendid ruler?
The Lord of power and might,
the conqueror of chaos.

Stretch toward heaven, you gates,
open high and wide.
Let the glorious sovereign enter.

Who is this splendid ruler?
The Lord of heaven's might,
this splendid ruler is God.

— *Psalm 24*

In the long nights of December,
we call you God of Jacob
because our ancestor Jacob
    wrestled all night long with you
and won your blessing
    and the name Israel.
Remember Jacob
who saw the ladder in the sky
and all your angels going up and down,
Jacob, who was the child
of Rebekah and Isaac,
the husband of Leah and Rachel,
the father of Joseph and Judah
and of all the tribes.
These are the tribes
that climb your mountain,
seek your face.
These are the tribes of Joseph and Mary
with whom we stand and reach up
like high, open gates
that wait for you to enter, God of Jacob,
wait for your gentleness and justice
to save us.

— *Prayer of the Season*

READING I *Isaiah 63:16–17, 19; 64:3–9*

For you are as a father to us,
 though Abraham does not know us
 and Israel does not acknowledge us;
you, O LORD, are as a father to us;
 our Redeemer from of old is your name.
Why, O LORD, do you make us stray from your ways
 and harden our heart, so that we do not fear you?
Turn back for the sake of your servants,
 for the sake of the tribes that are your heritage.
We have long been like those whom you do not rule,
 like those not called by your name.
When you did awesome deeds
  that we did not expect,
 you came down, the mountains quaked
  at your presence.
From ages past no one has heard,
 no ear has perceived,
no eye has seen any God besides you,
 who works for those who wait for you.
You meet those who gladly do right,
 those who remember you in your ways.
But you were angry, and we sinned;
 because you hid yourself we transgressed.
We have all become like one who is unclean,
 and all our righteous deeds are like a filthy cloth.
We all fade like a leaf,
 and our iniquities, like the wind, take us away.
There is no one who calls on your name,
 or attempts to take hold of you;
for you have hidden your face from us,
 and have delivered us into the hand
  of our iniquity.
Yet, O LORD, you are as a father to us;
 we are the clay, and you are our potter;
 we are all the work of your hand.
Do not be exceedingly angry, O LORD,
 and do not remember iniquity forever.
 Now consider, we are all your people.

READING II *1 Corinthians 1:3–9*

Grace to you and peace from God, our Father, and the Lord Jesus Christ. I give thanks to my God always for you because of the grace of God that has been given you in Christ Jesus, for in every way you have been enriched in Christ, in speech and knowledge of every kind—just as the testimony of Christ has been strengthened among you—so that you are not lacking in any spiritual gift as you wait for the revealing of our Lord Jesus Christ. He will also strengthen you to the end, so that you may be blameless on the day of our Lord Jesus Christ. God is faithful, by whom you were called into the communion of the Son of God, Jesus Christ our Lord.

GOSPEL *Mark 13:24–37*

Jesus said: "In those days, after that suffering, the sun will be darkened, and the moon will not give its light, and the stars will be falling from heaven, and the powers in the heavens will be shaken. Then they will see 'the Son-of-Man coming in clouds' with great power and glory. Then the Son-of-Man will send out the angels, and gather his elect from the four winds, from the ends of the earth to the ends of heaven.

"From the fig tree learn its lesson: as soon as its branch becomes tender and puts forth its leaves, you know that summer is near. So also, when you see these things taking place, you know that he is near, at the very gates. Truly I tell you, this generation will not pass away until all these things have taken place. Heaven and earth will pass away, but my words will not pass away.

"But about that day or hour no one knows, neither the angels in heaven, nor the Son, but only the Father. Beware, keep alert; for you do not know when the time will come. It is like someone going on a journey, who leaving home and putting the slaves in charge of their own work, commands the doorkeeper to be on the watch. Therefore, keep awake—for you do not know when the lord of the house will come, in the evening, or at midnight, or at cockcrow, or at dawn, or else, coming suddenly, the lord may find you asleep. And what I say to you I say to all: Keep awake."

REFLECTION

This Sunday is the beginning of a new liturgical year. That this beginning, according to the church's measurement of time, is slightly out of sync with the secular year alerts us immediately to our *outsider* status as Christians: We are *in* the world but not *of* the world. That we measure and appraise time differently is a fundamental clue to the contrary stance that we as Christians sometimes need to maintain toward other measurements and values of the world.

The gospel passage wakes us up suddenly to the different stance baptism gives us and to what the church wants us to bear in our hearts at this beginning. It comes from chapter 13 of the Gospel of Mark, perhaps the most ominous part of the message of this gospel. Jesus speaks of the destruction of buildings, "wars and rumors of wars," earthquakes, famines, trials, beatings, betrayals, all accompanying the end of time.

The passage reveals that only the Father knows when this will happen. So in these days and weeks before the beginning of a new millennium, let us be wary of people and groups suggesting that the wrath of God will be revealed at the turn of the millennium. The scriptures tell a wholly different story: Jesus advises us to "keep awake," for we do not know, just as he as a human being did not know, when the end of time will be.

Inspired by the teachings of the church and by our local assembly gathered for the proclamation of the scriptures, for the breaking of the bread and the pouring of the wine, we will choose to live our lives steadily, ever vigilant for the presence of Christ, as much in each 24-hour day as at the end of the world.

■ **Do you mark the beginning of the liturgical year with as much celebration and anticipation as you do New Year's Eve? How might you observe the beginning of the church's year this week? Getting together socially with other members of the Sunday worshiping community might be a good start.**

■ **In what ways do you and your parish "keep awake"? How are you keeping vigil in your life for the coming of Christ?**

PRACTICE OF FAITH

BE PREPARED. "Live each day as if it were your last." How often we have heard this maxim. This can be burdensome, if we focus on the thought that each new day may be our last. Perhaps we should say, "Live each day as if we were going to meet Jesus for dinner." We would want to be at our best.

We should be prepared to meet Jesus any time, anywhere — and especially in our interactions with one another. We do not know the day or time of Christ's coming but we have opportunities to meet him each day — at home, at work, in the classroom, in all the facets of our lives. Advent is a time of joyous preparation for the coming of the Lord. Let us prepare to welcome each other as a preparation for welcoming Christ when at last he comes. (RG)

PRACTICE OF HOPE

WAIT FOR THE LORD. "Be vigilant, keep awake." The Lord may come at any time. We begin this new church year with the same theme with which we ended the last year — eager expectation for the end of time and the coming of Christ. The hours Mark names as when the master of the house might come — evening, midnight, cockcrow, dawn — eventually became times of prayer for the church. Christians would gather for prayer at these times in part to signify their readiness to meet the Lord.

When you are expecting a visit from someone you love, there is anticipation and preparation. If they are to come in the night, you do not sleep until they arrive. You stay awake; you pray for their safety. Imagine being that excited about the coming of Christ. How much anticipation, preparation and prayer shall we gather for the Lord's coming? (MP)

PRACTICE OF CHARITY

SHARING YOUR GIFTS. Advent can be hurried through, dismissed as the time between the two big holidays of Thanksgiving and Christmas. Busyness and business conspire to rob Advent of its rich traditions. But this season demands its due! Advent calls for reflection and committed action. We are challenged to look within for honest self-assessments, plans for improvement and new beginnings. Relationships need attention too. Justice, "love's minimum," demands that we be concerned with the well-being of every person we encounter. During this season of new beginnings, reflect on your gifts, talents and skills. Make a commitment to share a gift with someone you know well and with someone who is a stranger to you.

WEEKDAY READINGS (Mo) Isaiah 2:1 – 5; (Tu) Romans 10:9 – 18; (We) Isaiah 25:6 – 10; (Th) 26:1 – 6; (Fr) 29:17 – 24; (Sa) 30:19 – 21, 23 – 26

READING I *Isaiah 40:1–5*

Comfort, O comfort my people,
says your God.
Speak tenderly to Jerusalem,
    and cry to the city
that it has served its term,
    that its penalty is paid,
that it has received from the LORD's hand
    double for all its sins.
A voice cries out:
"In the wilderness prepare the way of the LORD,
    make straight in the desert a highway
        for our God.
Every valley shall be lifted up,
    and every mountain and hill be made low;
the uneven ground shall become level,
    and the rough places a plain.
Then the glory of the LORD shall be revealed,
    and all people shall see it together,
    for the mouth of the LORD has spoken."

[Complete reading: Isaiah 40:1–11]

READING II *2 Peter 3:8–15a*

Do not ignore this one fact, beloved, that with the Lord one day is like a thousand years, and a thousand years are like one day. The Lord is not slow concerning the promise, as some think of slowness, but is patient with you, not wanting any to perish, but all to come to repentance.

But the day of the Lord will come like a thief, and then the heavens will pass away with a loud noise, and the elements will be dissolved with fire, and the earth and everything that is done on it will be disclosed. Since all these things are to be dissolved in this way, what sort of persons ought you to be in leading lives of holiness and godliness, waiting for and hastening the coming of the day of God, because of which the heavens will be set ablaze and dissolved, and the elements will melt with fire?

But, in accordance with God's promise, we wait for new heavens and a new earth, where righteousness is at home. Therefore, beloved, while you are waiting for these things, strive to be found by God at peace, without spot or blemish; and regard the patience of our Lord as salvation.

GOSPEL *Mark 1:1–8*

The beginning of the good news of Jesus Christ, the Son of God.
As it is written in the prophet Isaiah,
    "See, I am sending my messenger ahead of you,
    who will prepare your way;
    the voice of one crying out in the wilderness:
    'Prepare the way of the Lord,
    make straight the paths of the Lord.'"
John the baptizer appeared in the wilderness, proclaiming a baptism of repentance for the forgiveness of sins. And people from the whole Judean countryside and all the people of Jerusalem were going out to him, and were baptized by him in the river Jordan, confessing their sins. Now John was clothed with camel's hair, with a leather belt around his waist, and he ate locusts and wild honey. He proclaimed, "After me one who is more powerful than I is coming, the thong of whose sandals I am not worthy to stoop down and untie. I have baptized you with water; but the one who is coming will baptize you with the Holy Spirit."

Wednesday, December 8, 1999

THE IMMACULATE CONCEPTION OF THE VIRGIN MARY

Genesis 3:9–15, 20 *Eve is "the mother of the living."*

Ephesians 1:3–6, 11–12 *God chose us before the world began.*

Luke 1:26–38 *I am the servant of the Lord.*

Sin means separation from God. We believe Mary was never separated from God from the moment of her conception in her mother's womb. On this Advent feast of Mary, her "yes" undoes Eve's "no." Mary is our new Eve, the mother of the living God.

REFLECTION

Last Sunday was the beginning of the new liturgical year, and this Sunday brings us the beginning of the Gospel of Mark. (For how the gospels are distributed over the course of the three liturgical years, see pages 8 – 11.) The Gospel of Mark can be an odd text for believers, not for what it contains, but for what is absent.

In today's gospel reading, for example, we hear the very first verses of Mark's gospel, but we do not find what we might expect: There are no shepherds and no infant John the Baptist (they're only in Luke), no wise men (only in Matthew), and no exalted proclamation of "In the beginning was the Word" (it's only in John). Rather, the beginning of Mark's gospel opens with an *adult* John the Baptist, who has emerged from the wilderness to proclaim a baptism of repentance.

John the Baptist appears as a prophetic figure, as the fulfillment of the sometimes fiery and frightening prophets of the Old Testament tradition. That is why he is portrayed as "clothed with camel's hair" and eating "locusts and wild honey." His ascetic demeanor marks him as someone to be taken seriously, as one who prepares the way of the Lord.

His place in this Sunday's liturgy can lead us to think back to our own initiation into the Christian faith. If you were baptized in early childhood, before you were old enough to make your own decision to join the church, you can write to the parish where you were baptized for a copy of your baptism certificate. Having that certificate will make your entrance into the church feel more concrete, placing your own step into salvation in time and space, as John the Baptist did for Jesus. You might find out some interesting details about the parish in the process. Perhaps you can supplement this by investigating the news of the world at that time.

■ **What kinship do you feel with those who are initiated into your parish community each year?**

■ **Have you thought about becoming involved in your parish's process of initiation? As the liturgical year begins, consider increasing your participation in the parish's welcoming of new members.**

PRACTICE OF FAITH

A PROMISE KEPT. A savior had been eagerly anticipated for centuries and the signs were becoming clearer. The people had been told by the prophets of the signs that would tell them that the time had come. God had promised them that a savior would be born who would teach them the way of life. God was to send a shepherd to the people who would comfort, feed, guard and love them. God would send a savior who would teach a new way, which if followed would create a new, more loving order. When we follow Christ, we are following that long-promised savior. Our faith bridges the gap between past and present, and we see Christ as the promised shepherd of God's people. Live your faith so that others will know that the promise made so long ago has been kept. (RG)

PRACTICE OF HOPE

THE MESSENGER OF HOPE. John was the son of Zachariah, priest of the temple, and Elizabeth, kinswoman of Mary the mother of Jesus. We can imagine that they were a family who knew the scriptures, were strong in their faith and deeply attached to it. But what an unimaginable future was in store for John!

"Who will go if not I; who will speak, if not I?" John took up the message of a baptism of repentance for the forgiveness of sins. He did so because of his vision of the coming of the Messiah and of the kingdom of God. John is the great prophet who delivered the age-old message of repentance as a fresh, new hope. This Advent, share his courage! (MP)

PRACTICE OF CHARITY

MODERN-DAY PROPHETS. My friend Chuck is a gadfly. He is annoyingly concerned with injustice, confrontational in speech, passionate in his convictions and determined to make this world a better place. In other words, he is a modern-day prophet. Whether he is speaking about dicing onions at the soup kitchen, or organizing a protest of the latest city council decision adversely affecting the homeless, Chuck lives his charism of prophecy, and he has paid dearly for his outspoken commitment to the "least of his brothers and sisters." Family relationships have been strained, friendships have been lost, and career advancements have long ago disappeared, yet he perseveres. "What else would God have me do?" he says. Consider the women and men of your community who challenge the acceptable and comfortable views. Pray for their steadfast commitment.

WEEKDAY READINGS (Mo) Isaiah 35:1 – 10; (Tu) 40:1 – 11; (We) Immaculate Conception, see box; (Th) Isaiah 41:13 – 20; (Fr) 48:17 – 19; (Sa) Sirach 48:1 – 4, 9 – 11

READING I *Isaiah 61:1–4, 8–11*

The spirit of the Lord GOD is upon me,
    because the LORD has anointed me;
the LORD has sent me to bring good news
        to the oppressed,
    to bind up the brokenhearted,
to proclaim liberty to the captives,
    and release to the prisoners;
to proclaim the year of the LORD'S favor,
    and the day of vengeance of our God;
    to comfort all who mourn;
to provide for those who mourn in Zion —
    to give them a garland instead of ashes,
the oil of gladness instead of mourning,
    the mantle of praise instead of a faint spirit.
They will be called oaks of righteousness,
    the planting of the LORD, to display
    the glory of God.
They shall build up the ancient ruins,
    they shall raise up the former devastations;
they shall repair the ruined cities,
    the devastations of many generations.

For I the LORD love justice,
    I hate robbery and wrongdoing;
I will faithfully give them their recompense,
    and I will make an everlasting covenant
    with them.
Their descendants shall be known
    among the nations,
    and their offspring among the peoples;
all who see them shall acknowledge
    that they are a people whom the LORD has blessed.
I will greatly rejoice in the LORD,
    my whole being shall exult in my God;
for God has clothed me with the garments
        of salvation,
    and has covered me with the robe
        of righteousness,
as a bridegroom decks himself with a garland,
    and as a bride adorns herself with her jewels.
For as the earth brings forth its shoots,
    and as a garden causes what is sown in it
        to spring up,
so the Lord GOD will cause righteousness
    and praise
    to spring up before all the nations.

READING II *1 Thessalonians 5:16–24*

Rejoice always, pray without ceasing, give thanks in all circumstances; for this is the will of God in Christ Jesus for you. Do not quench the Spirit. Do not despise the words of prophets, but test everything; hold fast to what is good; abstain from every form of evil.

May that very God of peace sanctify you entirely; and may your spirit and soul and body be kept sound and blameless at the coming of our Lord Jesus Christ. The one who calls you is faithful, and will do this.

GOSPEL *John 1:6–8, 19–28*

There was a man sent from God, whose name was John. He came as a witness to testify to the light, so that all might believe through him. He himself was not the light, but he came to testify to the light.

This is the testimony given by John when the Judeans sent priests and Levites from Jerusalem to ask him, "Who are you?" John confessed and did not deny it, but confessed, "I am not the Messiah." And they asked him, "What then? Are you Elijah?" He said, "I am not." "Are you the prophet?" He answered, "No." Then they said to him, "Who are you? Let us have an answer for those who sent us. What do you say about yourself?" John said, "I am the voice of one crying out in the wilderness, 'Make straight the way of the Lord,'" as the prophet Isaiah said.

Now they had been sent from the Pharisees. They asked him, "Why then are you baptizing if you are neither the Messiah, nor Elijah, nor the prophet?" John answered them, "I baptize with water. Among you stands one whom you do not know, the one who is coming after me, the thong of whose sandal I am not worthy to untie." This took place in Bethany across the Jordan where John was baptizing.

REFLECTION

Today's gospel reading, like last Sunday's, focuses on baptism by John the Baptist. This week, however, the church draws not from the Gospel of Mark but from John, providing us with a theology of light for this season of anticipation. Though last Sunday's and this Sunday's gospel readings each concentrate on John the Baptist, their portraits of him differ, as do their portraits of Jesus later in the narratives.

The Gospel of Mark is the earliest of the four gospels in the New Testament, probably composed sometime near the year 70. The Gospel of John is the latest, coming about a quarter-century after Mark. Because the churches' appreciation of who Jesus was increases as time passes, then and now, we find a more exalted understanding in today's reading from the Gospel of John than we found in last week's reading from Mark.

The Gospel of John is clear about the Baptist, that "he himself was not the light, but he came to testify to the light," who was Jesus. This theology of light is a foreshadowing of the words of Jesus himself later in the Gospel of John, where he says, "I am the light of the world" (8:12). Already in this wintry season of Advent, we see lights going up all over to mark the coming feast of Christmas. As we see them, let us recall the theology of light in the Gospel of John and take responsibility for doing our own part in realizing the good news of Jesus Christ in our world. As members of the church and the presence of Christ in the world today, we need to accept our responsibility to indeed be a "light of the world," bearing gospel values into a sometimes barren and resistant world.

■ **What are some of the main impediments to your being a "light" of the world?**

■ **Does the church provide you with enough training and inspiration to let your light shine before others?**

■ **What might you do uniquely this Advent to light up a path and "prepare the way of the Lord"?**

PRACTICE OF FAITH

REMAIN OPEN. In today's first reading, Isaiah exults in all that God has done for him and he is mindful of the gratitude and praise due God. Paul echoes these ideas — "give thanks in all circumstances." John tells the priests and Levites that Jesus is among them at that very moment, but that they fail to recognize him.

Children, even small children, are aware of the beauty and goodness of God's creation. Encourage that awareness by pointing out to them the richness of the autumn colors, the beauty of softly falling snow and the sight of white clouds lazily floating across an azure sky. Turn your shared awareness into a prayer of thanksgiving. In pausing to give thanks you are not only recognizing the past activity of the Lord but are keeping yourself open to future encounters. (RG)

PRACTICE OF HOPE

TESTIFYING TO CHRIST. During the season of Advent, Christians are not preparing merely to celebrate the birthday of Jesus, as a past event at that. We know the whole gospel: Jesus was born, suffered, died and was raised. We always celebrate the whole of Christ's existence whenever we remember a single event of his life.

At this point in Advent, we turn from reflecting on the last days and the second coming of Christ to remembering the first coming when Jesus lived among us. In our life experiences, in our faith and baptism, we come to know this Christ who is with us still. John testified to the one coming after him; we testify that that One is standing now in our midst. (MP)

PRACTICE OF CHARITY

JUBILEE 2000. Ancient Jewish law called for a Jubilee Year every 50th year. In Jubilee Years, the ultimate fresh beginning, slaves were to be freed and ancestral lands returned to their original owners. Both social and economic equilibrium were to be preserved by these acts of justice and mercy. The powerless and the poor were assured that their condition would not be permanent or inherited by succeeding generations.

As we near the year 2000, religious leaders around the globe are calling for a new Year of Jubilee. A primary focus: forgiving the debts of the poorest nations of the world, and freeing them from the heavy interest payments that are a terrible burden to their people. For more information, contact Jubilee 2000/USA, 222 E. Capitol Street NE, Washington DC 20003-1036; 202-783-3566.

WEEKDAY READINGS (Mo) Numbers 24:2 – 7, 15 – 17; (Tu) Zephaniah 3:1 – 2, 9 – 13; (We) Isaiah 45:6 – 8, 18, 21 – 25; (Th) 54:1 – 10; (Fr) Genesis 49:2, 8 – 10; (Sa) Jeremiah 23:5 – 8

READING I *2 Samuel 7:1–11, 16*

Now when David the king was settled in his house, and the LORD had given him rest from all his enemies around him, the king said to the prophet Nathan, "See now, I am living in a house of cedar, but the ark of God stays in a tent." Nathan said to the king, "Go, do all that you have in mind; for the LORD is with you."

But that same night the word of the LORD came to Nathan: Go and tell my servant David: Thus says the LORD: Are you the one to build me a house to live in? I have not lived in a house since the day I brought up the people of Israel from Egypt to this day, but I have been moving about in a tent and a tabernacle. Wherever I have moved about among all the people of Israel, did I ever speak a word with any of the tribal leaders of Israel, whom I commanded to shepherd my people Israel, saying, "Why have you not built me a house of cedar?"

Now therefore thus you shall say to my servant David: Thus says the LORD of hosts: I took you from the pasture, from following the sheep to be prince over my people Israel; and I have been with you wherever you went, and have cut off all your enemies from before you; and I will make for you a great name, like the name of the great ones of the earth. And I will appoint a place for my people Israel and will plant them, so that they may live in their own place, and be disturbed no more; and evildoers shall afflict them no more, as formerly, from the time that I appointed judges over my people Israel; and I will give you rest from all your enemies. Moreover the LORD declares to you that the LORD will make you a house. Your house and your kingdom shall be made sure forever before me; your throne shall be established forever.

[Complete reading: 2 Samuel 7:1–5, 8b–12, 14a, 16]

READING II *Romans 16:25–27*

Now to God who is able to strengthen you according to my gospel and the proclamation of Jesus Christ, according to the revelation of the mystery that was kept secret for long ages but is now disclosed, and through the prophetic writings is made known to all the Gentiles, according to the command of the eternal God, to bring about the obedience of faith—to the only wise God, through Jesus Christ, be the glory forever! Amen.

GOSPEL *Luke 1:26–38*

In the sixth month the angel Gabriel was sent by God to a town in Galilee called Nazareth, to a virgin woman engaged to a man whose name was Joseph, of the house of David. The virgin's name was Mary. And the angel came to her and said, "Greetings, favored one! The Lord is with you." But she was much perplexed by the angel's words and pondered what sort of greeting this might be.

The angel said to her, "Do not be afraid, Mary, for you have found favor with God. And now, you will conceive in your womb and bear a son, and you will name him Jesus. He will be great, and will be called the Son of the Most High, and the Lord God will give to him the throne of his ancestor David. He will reign over the house of Jacob forever, and of his dominion there will be no end." Mary said to the angel, "How can this be, since I am a virgin?" The angel said to her, "The Holy Spirit will come upon you, and the power of the Most High will overshadow you; therefore the child to be born will be holy; he will be called Son of God. And now, your relative Elizabeth in her old age has also conceived a son; and this is the sixth month for her who was said to be barren. For nothing will be impossible with God."

Then Mary said, "Here am I, the servant of the Lord; let it be with me according to your word."

Then the angel departed from her.

R E F L E C T I O N

On this last Sunday of Advent, as we near the solemnity of Christmas, the church turns from the Gospel of Mark, the guiding text and portrait of Jesus for this liturgical Year B, whose portrait of Jesus begins in his adulthood, and chooses from the Gospel of Luke. This Lukan reading is the same text proclaimed for the feast of the Annunciation (March 25). The angel Gabriel appears and announces the good news, perplexing though it is, to the virgin Mary.

Some of the angel's words to Mary are familiar to Catholic readers for, in an older translation, they are the first half of the prayer "Hail Mary." It is tempting to sentimentalize these readings about the annunciation to Mary and the nativity of Jesus, seeing them as telling of God's actions in human life only in the past. Yet the presence of God in the world and in the church has not faded, and the challenge for us as believers is to discover God's presence and God's gifts in our lives today.

We might object, thinking that the message of God is not nearly as clear to us in our lives as it was to those in New Testament times or in the time of Jesus. Yet, following the example of Mary, who was "much perplexed by the angel's words," we must strive to discern what the Lord's will for us is and respond as she did: "Let it be with me according to your word."

The example of Mary, and of many whom we meet in scripture, makes it clear that being given such a divine mission does not mean that we will fully understand. Though we may feel that we are stumbling toward our mission, brows furrowed in puzzlement, we can set out to make whatever meager contribution we can, trusting that God and the church will guide our way.

■ **What good news has been brought to you, O highly favored daughter or son of God, during this Advent season? Might you not find the life of God in your own days as did Mary, that is, as no one has discovered it before?**

■ **What ways do you use to discern the Lord's will for you? Who or what do you turn to for guidance?**

PRACTICE OF FAITH

GOOD DECISIONS. The good news is brought to Mary that the Savior's coming is imminent. But Mary must freely choose to cooperate with God. This birth will not be forced on her. In allowing free choice, God takes the chance that we will make the wrong choice. But Mary does not. She chooses wisely, allows God's grace to flourish and provides us with an example of good decision-making.

Young people often have difficult choices to make. If you are a parent, teach good decision-making skills to your sons and daughters early in their childhood. Teach them to act like Mary — to listen attentively, to ask questions, and to bring their needs to the Lord. They will make good decisions and, like Mary, will help God's grace flourish in our world. (RG)

PRACTICE OF HOPE

ADVENT DISCIPLES. Mary's consent to the angel's announcement meant that God's covenant with David would be fulfilled. Luke's gospel focuses on how this mystery came about in Jesus as the final stage of salvation history. Mary was the highly favored disciple who had the trust and the courage to follow the Holy Spirit.

The angel's words presented an open-ended promise, like a marriage promise, a baptismal promise or religious vows. Mary could not have envisioned what Jesus' life would be like, or that the messiah of whom the angel spoke would become a suffering servant. But here at the beginning she gracefully stepped out of her fears and her own plans and into the future offered by God. (MP)

PRACTICE OF CHARITY

TEMPLES OF THE SPIRIT. As a first-year nursing student I came into the report room one winter morning and found that I had been assigned to care for a thirteen-year-old new mother and her baby son. The nursing staff gasped and shook their heads as they discussed this woman-child. I had a daughter the same age and I could not begin to fathom what the girl might be going through. What fears and anxieties were running through her mind? Had anyone said to her, "Do not be afraid; I am with you"?

Instead of being a head shaker, get involved with groups that work to prevent teen pregnancy through education. City and county health departments are a great place to start. Take a program to your church. Promote self-respect in youth. Instill in young women and men the fact that they are indeed temples of the Holy Spirit.

WEEKDAY READINGS (Mo) Isaiah 7:10 – 14; (Tu) Song of Songs 2:8 – 14 or Zephaniah 3:14 – 18; (We) 1 Samuel 1:24 – 28; (Th) Malachi 3:1 – 4, 23 – 24; (Fr) 2 Samuel 7:1 – 5, 8 – 12, 14, 16; (Sa) Christmas

CHRISTMASTIME

The Lord our God comes, comes to rule the earth!

Sing to the Lord a new song,
the Lord of wonderful deeds.
Right hand and holy arm
brought victory to God.

God made that victory known,
revealed justice to nations,
remembered a merciful love
loyal to the house of Israel.
The ends of the earth have seen
the victory of our God.

Shout to the Lord, you earth,
break into song, into praise!
Sing praise to God with a harp,
with a harp and sound of music.
With sound of trumpet and horn,
shout to the Lord, our king.

Let the sea roar with its creatures,
the world and all that live there!
Let rivers clap their hands,
the hills ring out their joy!

The Lord our God comes,
comes to rule the earth,
justly to rule the world,
to govern the peoples aright.

—Psalm 98

When people witness deeds like these—
mercy winning victories
and justice welcomed
        in the public places—
then the earth itself will be an orchestra
and all creatures a choir,
and we shall sing together a song
that announces you,
God of poor shepherds and stargazers.
Rehearse us now in that Christmas song:
Like those shepherds may we know where
        to look,
like the magi may we know
        when to listen to the powerful
and when to mere dreams.
Come, Lord, and lift us up in song.

—Prayer of the Season

READING I *Isaiah 9:1–7*

There will be no gloom for those who were in anguish. In the former time the LORD brought into contempt the land of Zebulun and the land of Napthali, but in the latter time the LORD will make glorious the way of the sea, the land beyond the Jordan, Galilee of the nations.

> The people who walked in darkness
>   have seen a great light;
> those who lived in a land of deep darkness —
>   on them light has shined.
> You have multiplied the nation,
>   you have increased its joy;
> they rejoice before you
>   as with joy at the harvest,
>   as people exult when dividing plunder.
> For the yoke of their burden,
>   and the bar across their shoulders,
>   the rod of their oppressor,
>   you have broken as on the day of Midian.
> For all the boots of the tramping warriors
>   and all the garments rolled in blood
>   shall be burned as fuel for the fire.
> For a child has been born for us,
>   a son given to us;
> authority rests upon his shoulders;
>   and he is named
>   Wonderful Counselor, Mighty God,
>   Everlasting Father, Prince of Peace.
> His authority shall grow continually,
>   and there shall be endless peace
>   for the throne and dominion of David,
>   to establish and uphold it
> with justice and with righteousness
>   from this time onward and forevermore.

The zeal of the LORD of hosts will do this.

READING II *Titus 2:11–14*

The grace of God has appeared, bringing salvation to all, training us to renounce impiety and worldly passions, and in the present age to live lives that are self-controlled, upright, and godly, while we wait for the blessed hope and the manifestation of the glory of our great God and Savior, Jesus Christ.

It is Jesus Christ who gave himself for us to redeem us from all iniquity and purify for himself a people of his own who are zealous for good deeds.

GOSPEL *Luke 2:1–14*

In those days a decree went out from Emperor Augustus that all the world should be registered. This was the first registration and was taken while Quirinius was governor of Syria. All went to their own towns to be registered. Joseph also went from the town of Nazareth in Galilee to Judea, to the city of David called Bethlehem, because he was descended from the house and family of David. He went to be registered with Mary, to whom he was engaged and who was expecting a child. While they were there, the time came for her to deliver her child. And she gave birth to her firstborn son and wrapped him in bands of cloth, and laid him in a manger, because there was no place for them in the inn.

In that region there were shepherds living in the fields, keeping watch over their flock by night. Then an angel of the Lord stood before them, and the glory of the Lord shone around them, and they were terrified. But the angel said to them, "Do not be afraid; for see — I am bringing you good news of great joy for all the people: to you is born this day in the city of David a Savior, who is the Messiah, the Lord. This will be a sign for you: you will find a child wrapped in bands of cloth and lying in a manger." And suddenly there was with the angel a multitude of the heavenly host, praising God and saying,

> "Glory to God in the highest heaven,
>   and on earth peace among those
>   whom God favors!"

R E F L E C T I O N

The gospel for Christmas Midnight Mass is one of the most familiar Christian stories: "She gave birth to her firstborn son and wrapped him in swaddling clothes, and laid him in a manger, because there was no place for them in the inn." It is perhaps made more famous each year not by its proclamation at the midnight liturgy but by Linus' proclamation of the story on the echoing school stage in the "Charlie Brown Christmas Special."

What is imperative on hearing Luke's story of the birth of Jesus is hearing what is in *this* story, and not adding details from the Gospel of Matthew. In Matthew, Joseph (not Mary) is the protagonist of the story, and the visitors are not smelly shepherds but exotic traveling magi from the East. Although we casually merge the Matthean and Lukan infancy narratives when we arrange our nativity sets by the Christmas tree — everybody gets in there, magi, sheep, cows, shepherds, lambs — the portraits of the family of Jesus are quite different in the first and the third gospels. (The gospels of Mark and John do not have infancy stories.)

The narrative from Luke, with its decree for a world census, emphasizes the universality of the miraculous birth. Surely the evangelist Luke could not have imagined that this emphasis of his gospel would have come true to the degree that it has, now nearly two millennia after the life of Jesus!

Spreading the good news of the gospel and the church may seem to be the work of missionaries in far-away places where Christians are in the minority. But each of us, as baptized Christians, is called to spread the "good news of great joy for all the people." As you celebrate Christmas, thank God for your own faith and think about how you might give this gift to someone during the Christmas season.

■ **What does the universal dimension of Christ's coming mean? In a world with people of so many varied religious beliefs, what are we saying when we proclaim the universality of Christianity?**

■ **In what ways do you spread the good news of the gospel?**

PRACTICE OF FAITH

GOD AMONG US. The shepherds were called to rejoice and worship, and they did just that. But did the event change their lives? Did the angels' announcement or the visit with the Holy Family make a difference in the shepherds' relationship with God? We have no idea, but we hope it did. A wise woman once said to me about new babies, "They bring so much love with them." It is a wonderful thing that through our humanity God fills our world with beauty and love. All we need to do is teach ourselves and our children to be aware of the life around us, to take joy in it and to share it with our one another. (RG)

PRACTICE OF HOPE

OUR TIMELESS SONG. In the carefully crafted and multi-layered text of this midnight gospel, Luke tells of the birth of Jesus the Christ. The angel of the Lord proclaimed to the shepherds this good news of great joy. The news is the mystery of redemption, the same message the disciples proclaimed after Christ's resurrection. It is the message proclaimed through the ages by all the disciples of the Lord. Today and every day, we join the angels in proclaiming the good news, the word of God.

A multitude of the heavenly host joined the angel, praising God, singing "Glory to God in the highest heaven." This song was sung by the multitude of disciples when Jesus entered Jerusalem; it is an early canticle of the church; it is the praise offered through the ages by all the disciples of the Lord. It is the timeless song of angels and disciples. (MP)

PRACTICE OF CHARITY

LIVE YOUR LIGHT. The winter solstice (December 21) has now passed; the longest night of the year has come and gone. From here on we will notice more and more sunlight slicing through our windowpanes in the wintry late afternoons. We have been a people in darkness waiting for the light. Our waiting is over; our Advent is now complete. Remember that first night of Advent when the light of a solitary candle pierced the darkness of our gathering space. Oh, how it lit the faces around the table! Tonight is the night for lights! Not only ceiling lights, votives and tall wax candles, but the light that is within you — the light of Christ's love. Share it with everyone you meet. Bless one of your candles and dedicate it to new changes, new promises, new hopes and dreams for a new millenium.

READING I *Genesis 15:1–6; 21:1–3*

The word of the Lord came to Abram in a vision, "Fear not, Abram, I am your shield; your reward shall be very great." But Abram said, "O Lord God, what will you give me, for I continue childless, and the heir of my house is Eliezer of Damascus?" And Abram said, "Behold, you have given me no offspring; and a slave born in my house will be my heir." And the Lord brought Abram outside and said, "Look toward heaven, and number the stars, if you are able to number them." Then the Lord said to him, "So shall your descendants be." And Abram believed the Lord; and the Lord reckoned it to him as righteousness.

The Lord visited Sarah as had been said, and the Lord did to Sarah as had been promised. And Sarah conceived, and bore Abraham a son in his old age at the time of which God had spoken to him. Abraham called the name of his son who was born to him, whom Sarah bore him, Isaac.

[Revised Common Lectionary: Isaiah 61:10 — 62:3]

READING II *Hebrews 11:8, 11–12, 17–19*

By faith Abraham obeyed when he was called to go out to a place which he was to receive as an inheritance; and he went out, not knowing where he was to go. By faith Sarah herself received power to conceive, even when she was past the age, since she considered faithful the one who had promised. Therefore from one man, and him as good as dead, were born descendants as many as the stars of heaven and as the innumerable grains of sand by the seashore.

By faith Abraham, when he was tested, offered up Isaac, and he who had received the promises was ready to offer up his only son, of whom it was said, "Through Isaac shall your descendants be named." He considered that God was able to raise the dead; hence, figuratively speaking, Abraham did receive Isaac back.

[Revised Common Lectionary: Galatians 4:4–7]

GOSPEL *Luke 2:22–25a, 26, 28–32, 36, 38–40*

When the time came for their purification according to the law of Moses, Mary and Joseph brought Jesus up to Jerusalem to present him to the Lord (as it is written in the law of the Lord, "Every firstborn male shall be designated as holy to the Lord"), and they offered a sacrifice according to what is stated in the law of the Lord, "a pair of turtledoves or two young pigeons."

Now there was a man in Jerusalem whose name was Simeon. It had been revealed to him by the Holy Spirit that he would not see death before he had seen the Lord's Messiah. Simeon took Jesus in his arms and praised God, saying,

"Lord, now you are dismissing your servant in
   peace, according to your word;
for my eyes have seen your salvation,
   which you have prepared in the presence of
   all peoples,
a light for revelation to the Gentiles
   and for glory to your people Israel."

There was also a prophet, Anna. She began to praise God and to speak about the child to all who were looking for the redemption of Jerusalem.

When the parents had finished everything required by the law of the Lord, they returned to Galilee, to their own town of Nazareth. The child grew and became strong, filled with wisdom; and the favor of God was upon him.

[Complete reading: Luke 2:22–40]

Saturday, January 1, 2000

MARY, MOTHER OF GOD

Numbers 6:22–27 *The Lord's face shines on you!*

Galatians 4:4–7 *You are no longer slaves but children of God.*

Luke 2:16–21 *Mary pondered these things in her heart.*

Our merry Christmastime unfolds with the blessing of the new year, with the astonishing good news of peace on earth and with the treasures that Mary pondered within her heart.

R E F L E C T I O N

Because the Gospel of Mark—the gospel for this liturgical year—has no stories of Jesus' early years to be proclaimed on this feast of the Holy Family, the church again turns to the Gospel of Luke for a gospel passage. This Sunday we find a holy man, Simeon, "righteous and devout" (2:25), who is held out as an example of someone close to death. Yet the Holy Spirit had assured him that "he would not see death before he had seen the Lord's Messiah."

In faith we are as close to salvation as Simeon, for like him we have seen the Messiah. At baptism we became members of the body of Christ; indeed we were engrafted into his saving body. And by the grace of God we find ourselves still part of this one saving body around the one table of the Lord.

In the middle of the gospel we find a few verses that have a rich tradition in the liturgy of the church. Simeon's praise of God (2:29 – 32) has been the canticle for the church's Night Prayer for centuries (see page 16). This beautiful prayer anticipates both a peaceful night of sleep and the inevitable coming of death for each of us. Perhaps you might commit Simeon's prayer to memory so that you and your family may enjoy peaceful nights of rest and welcome the end of life when it comes, as the words of Simeon and the tradition of the church prompt us to do. This prayer will join you to the many other baptized who pray Simeon's words just before going to bed.

■ **Simeon was an old man, close to death, when he offered his song of praise, a song that has enriched the lives of many throughout the ages. In what ways do you value the contributions of today's senior citizens? How do you think our society treats its elders?**

■ **How have you prepared for your own death? What do you feel are some things you still need to do before you may die in peace? When will you do them?**

PRACTICE OF FAITH

SIMEON'S SONG. This version of Simeon's song of praise may be sung to the tune of "O God Our Help in Ages Past." Try singing it this week before you go to sleep:

Lord, bid your servant go in peace
Your word has been fulfilled.
These eyes have seen salvation's dawn,
The child so long foretold.
This is the Savior of the world,
The gentiles' promised light,
God's glory dwelling in our midst,
The joy of Israel. (DP)

PRACTICE OF HOPE

OUR CHILDREN. Today's gospel passage gives us a broad outline of a simple yet splendid family life. It tells us much of what we know of Jesus' life before his public ministry. Jesus grew up in the midst of his family, and in that good environment, he became strong and filled with wisdom. His parents Mary and Joseph were good teachers who shared their faith with him as they guided him into maturity. Jesus' life with Mary and Joseph is an ideal of family life for us to follow as best we can. (MP)

PRACTICE OF CHARITY

LET THE CHILDREN COME. Ian felt that his parents did not understand him. Julie's father was drunk every weekend and took out his anger on her. Evading immigration officers has been Pierre's primary concern since he arrived from Haiti four years ago. Tia's pimp abandoned her after her third arrest for solicitation at the age of fifteen. These teens and thousands more with similar stories of alienation and abuse are the invisible face of urban homelessness. Homeless adolescents, estranged from family, often become victims of exploitation. Large cities are not the only places where youths suffer homelessness. A task force in Peoria, Illinois, estimated that during a six-month period, more than 600 young people were homeless there. What is your community's situation? Are your local leaders aware of your city's homeless children? Are you part of the solution? For more information on youth homelessness, contact Covenant House, 346 W. 17th Street, New York NY 10011-5002.

WEEKDAY READINGS (Mo) 1 John 1:1 – 4; (Tu) 1:5 — 2:2; (We) 2:3 – 11; (Th) 2:12 – 17; (Fr) 2:18 – 21; (Sa) Mary, Mother of God (see box)

READING I *Isaiah 60:1–6*

Arise, shine; for your light has come,
    and the glory of the LORD has risen upon you.
For darkness shall cover the earth,
    and thick darkness the peoples;
but the LORD will arise upon you,
    and the glory of the LORD will appear over you.
Nations shall come to your light,
    and rulers to the brightness of your dawn.
Lift up your eyes and look around;
    they all gather together, they come to you;
your sons shall come from far away,
    and your daughters shall be carried
    on their nurses' arms.
Then you shall see and be radiant;
    your heart shall thrill and rejoice,
because the abundance of the sea
        shall be brought to you,
    the wealth of the nations shall come to you.
A multitude of camels shall cover you,
    the young camels of Midian and Ephah;
    all those from Sheba shall come.
They shall bring gold and frankincense,
    and shall proclaim the praise of the Lord.

[Revised Common Lectionary: Sirach 24:1–12 or Jeremiah 31:7–14]

READING II *Ephesians 3:1–6*

This is the reason that I Paul am a prisoner for Christ Jesus for the sake of you Gentiles — for surely you have already heard of the commission of God's grace that was given me for you, and how the mystery was made known to me by revelation, as I wrote above in a few words, a reading of which will enable you to perceive my understanding of the mystery of Christ.

In former generations this mystery was not made known to humankind, as it has now been revealed to his holy apostles and prophets by the Spirit: that is, the Gentiles have become heirs with us, members of the same body, and sharers in the promise in Christ Jesus through the gospel.

[Revised Common Lectionary: Ephesians 1:3–14]

GOSPEL *Matthew 2:1–12*

In the time of King Herod, after Jesus was born in Bethlehem of Judea, magi from the East came to Jerusalem, asking, "Where is the child who has been born king of the Jews? For we observed his star at its rising, and have come to pay him homage."

When King Herod heard this, he was frightened, and all Jerusalem with him; and calling together all the chief priests and scribes of the people, he inquired of them where the Messiah was to be born. They told him, "In Bethlehem of Judea; for so it has been written by the prophet:

"'And you, Bethlehem, in the land of Judah,
    are by no means least among the rulers
        of Judah;
    for from you shall come a ruler
    who is to shepherd my people Israel.' "

Then Herod secretly called for the magi and learned from them the exact time when the star had appeared. Then he sent them to Bethlehem, saying, "Go and search diligently for the child; and when you have found him, bring me word so that I may also go and pay him homage."

When they had heard the king, they set out; and there, ahead of them, went the star that they had seen at its rising, until it stopped over the place where the child was. When they saw that the star had stopped, they were overwhelmed with joy.

On entering the house, they saw the child with Mary his mother; and they knelt down and paid him homage. Then, opening their treasure chests, they offered him gifts of gold, frankincense, and myrrh.

And having been warned in a dream not to return to Herod, they left for their own country by another road.

[Revised Common Lectionary: John 1:(1–9) 10–18]

R E F L E C T I O N

The word "epiphany" comes from ancient Greek for "appearance." For centuries, the appearance at the heart of the feast of Epiphany has been the revelation of the infant Messiah to the "wise men" from the East, as this narrative is proclaimed today from the Gospel of Matthew. (As it does for all the stories of the infancy and childhood of Jesus, the church turns to the Gospels of Matthew and Luke during Year B, for the Gospel of Mark has none. See "The Liturgical Year and the Gospel of Mark," pages 8–11.) But in earlier times, different churches emphasized different manifestations on this feast: some told the story of the magi (as we do today), some the story of the water turned into wine at the wedding feast of Cana (from John 2), some the baptism of Jesus (which was eventually moved to next Sunday), some the Transfiguration, and some—before Christmas was fixed as December 25 in Rome and Africa in the fourth century—marked the birth of Jesus.

What this conjunction of narratives from the early church offers us as believers is a lesson about the incarnation and manifestation of the presence of God in the world: It happens in different ways in different times and in different places. Each of us, then, has an obligation to discern the appearance of God in our lives. The Christian tradition assures us that God is present when we celebrate the sacraments, when we gather as an assembly, as church. But because we do not live in church, we are called to seek and find God in the out-of-the-way places of our lives and our world.

It would be terrific if we could find a map or clock telling us where and when God is in the world. It would be nice to be strolling in the neighborhood and come across a few magi, or a woman changing water into wine, or a man's clothes becoming dazzling white. But the church's tradition teaches us that the presence of God is also found in the less spectacular. Be alert for it where it may be found.

■ **Where would you go right this minute to find a manifestation of the presence of God? Why would you go there? What would the manifestation be like?**

PRACTICE OF FAITH

INTO THE HOUSE. Notice how the magi found Jesus "on entering the house." The door to your house is the door to where God lives! You can bless your house—and all who enter it this new year—by inscribing a prayer above your front door. With a piece of chalk or lump of coal, inscribe this above the doors to your home:

20 + C + M + B + 00

Legend has it that the letters stand for the names of the magi—Caspar, Melchior and Balthasar. Blessing your doorways in January is appropriate. The Latin word *janua* means portal or doorway, and January is the doorway to the coming year of faith. (DP)

PRACTICE OF HOPE

SEARCHERS. We know the story of the magi who were searching for the king of the Jews. Their journey ended when they beheld the infant Jesus. Long ago, adult candidates for baptism were enrolled on the feast of the Epiphany. This is an appropriate time to encourage those who might be searching for God. We pray to be like the magi, to elude the powers of evil, to be drawn into one company and to be enlightened by the king of kings. (MP)

PRACTICE OF CHARITY

RECONCILIATION. Traditionally, the pope delivers a message of peace on January 1. Twenty-five years ago, Pope Paul VI chose to discuss reconciliation as the means to peace in the world. "It is our clear duty, then, to strain every muscle as we work for the time when all war can be completely outlawed by international consent. Peace must be born of mutual trust between the nations rather than imposed on them through fear of one another's weapons. For government officials, who must simultaneously guarantee the good of all their own people and promote the universal good, depend on public opinion and feeling to the greatest possible extent. It does no good to work at building peace so long as feelings of hostility, contempt and distrust, as well as racial hatred and unbending ideologies, continue to divide people and place them in opposing camps." Make it your resolution this new year to be an instrument of reconciliation and peace.

WEEKDAY READINGS (Mo) 1 John 3:22 — 4:6; (Tu) 4:7 – 10; (We) 4:11 – 18; (Th) 4:19 – 5:4; (Fr) 5:5 – 13; (Sa) 5:14 – 21

READING I *Isaiah 55:1–3a, 6–11*

Everyone who thirsts,
   come to the waters;
and you that have no money,
   come, buy and eat!
Come, buy wine and milk
   without money and without price.
Why do you spend your money
   for that which is not bread,
   and your labor for that which does not satisfy?
Listen carefully to me, and eat what is good,
   and delight yourselves in rich food.
Incline your ear, and come to me;
   listen, so that you may live.
Seek the LORD while the LORD may be found,
   call upon God while God is near;
let the wicked forsake their way,
   and the unrighteous their thoughts;
let them return to the LORD, who will have
   mercy on them,
   and to our God, who will abundantly pardon.
For my thoughts are not your thoughts,
   nor are your ways my ways, says the LORD.
For as the heavens are higher than the earth,
   so are my ways higher than your ways
   and my thoughts than your thoughts.
For as the rain and the snow
   come down from heaven,
and do not return there
   until they have watered the earth,
making it bring forth and sprout,
   giving seed to the sower and bread to the eater,
so shall my word be that goes out from my mouth;
   it shall not return to me empty,
but it shall accomplish that which I purpose,
   and succeed in the thing for which I sent it.
*[Complete reading: Isaiah 55:1–11; Revised Common
Lectionary: Genesis 1:1–5]*

READING II *1 John 5:1–9*

Everyone who believes that Jesus is the Christ has
been born of God, and everyone who loves the parent loves the child. By this we know that we love the
children of God, when we love God and obey God's
commandments. For the love of God is this, that we
obey the commandments, which are not burdensome,
for whatever is born of God conquers the world.
And this is the victory that conquers the world, our
faith. Who is it that conquers the world but the one
who believes that Jesus is the Son of God? This is the
one who came by water and blood, Jesus Christ, not
with the water only but with the water and the
blood. And the Spirit is the one that testifies, for the
Spirit is the truth. There are three that testify: the
Spirit and the water and the blood, and these three
agree. If we receive human testimony, the testimony
of God is greater; for this is the testimony of God
that God has testified to the Son.
[Revised Common Lectionary: Acts 19:1–7]

GOSPEL *Mark 1:4–11*

John the baptizer appeared in the wilderness, proclaiming a baptism of repentance for the forgiveness
of sins. And people from the whole Judean countryside and all the people of Jerusalem were going out
to him, and were baptized by him in the river Jordan,
confessing their sins. Now John was clothed with
camel's hair, with a leather belt around his waist,
and he ate locusts and wild honey.

He proclaimed, "After me the one who is more
powerful than I is coming, the thong of whose sandals I am not worthy to stoop down and untie. I have
baptized you with water; but the one who is coming
will baptize you with the Holy Spirit."

In those days Jesus came from Nazareth of Galilee
and was baptized by John in the Jordan. And just as
Jesus was coming up out of the water, he saw the
heavens torn apart and the Spirit descending like a
dove on him. And a voice came from heaven, "You are
my Son, the Beloved; with you I am well pleased."

R E F L E C T I O N

It is thought that this time of year began to be associated with baptism back in ancient Egypt, where the rising and falling of the Nile River determined the annual agricultural cycles and the people's celebrations, Christian or not. The Christian observance of the baptism of Jesus set forth the idea that Jesus was baptized not because he was in need of something, but so that he would consecrate the waters of baptism.

We — gathered as the body of Christ in the Sunday assembly, week after week, year after year — can participate in this celebration of the baptism of the Lord because it was our own baptism that made us members of the assembly, that brought us into the light of faith. "Baptism," says the introduction to the *Rite of Christian Initiation of Adults*, "is the door to life and to the kingdom of God"; in it we "enter into fellowship with the Father, Son, and the Holy Spirit," "are engrafted in the likeness of Christ's death," and we "pass from the death of sin into life."

As Christians, we recall with gravity the life of the historical Jesus. But our baptisms call us further: We need to accept the life of the risen Christ in our midst, and our vocations to incarnate God's presence in the world as Jesus did (though more perfectly than any of us).

As the passage from the Gospel of Mark proclaimed on this Sunday reminds us, when we came up out of the waters of baptism, the heavens opened and the Spirit descended. And, as at the baptism of Jesus, a voice from heaven announced and continues to announce: "You are my beloved; with you I am well pleased."

■ **It can be difficult for us to imagine ourselves and accept ourselves as children of God. Yet if we are to trust the church, this is who we are, brought ever more deeply into the life of God as we share in the bread and cup each Sunday. What are the main impediments to your accepting who you are in the life of God? In the life of the church?**

■ **What steps can you make toward discovering yourself as the person God wants you to be?**

PRACTICE OF FAITH

WATER AND SPIRIT. Do you know the date of your baptism? If not, find out. Ask a relative, or write to the parish that baptized you. Write the date of your baptism on your new calendar for this year, and celebrate the anniversary by participating in the eucharist and spending some time reflecting on your Christian mission — your part in spreading God's love.

When Jesus was baptized, he came out of the water and heard a heavenly voice say, "You are my Son, the Beloved; with you I am well pleased." Listen for this message this week whenever you "come out of the water" — the shower, the snow or rain, the sudsy kitchen sink. (DP)

PRACTICE OF HOPE

BAPTIZED INTO CHRIST'S LIFE. At our church, the baptismal font stands under a stained glass window depicting Jesus' baptism. We go to the font often for baptisms, crowding together, inviting the children to draw near. Last winter, a couple who had moved away brought back their first child to be baptized. Sadly, the infant became ill and died soon thereafter. Her funeral was on a June afternoon, and while our eyes were full of tears, sunlight came streaming into the church through the windows.

The parents thanked everyone, asking to be remembered in prayer whenever light shined in through the windows. I would venture to say that we remember them, sunlight or not, whenever we gather at our baptismal font. For we professed our belief that we are baptized into Christ's life *and* death. We hope to share in Christ's glory. (MP)

PRACTICE OF CHARITY

WATERS OF LIFE. In the midst of a severe drought or during a torrential rain, we are reminded of the power of water. Most of us in wealthier nations are carelessly wasteful of water, a precious resource. How do you conserve water? Some practical suggestions include: limit showers to five minutes using a low-flow nozzle; wash only full loads of laundry; fill a one-gallon plastic jug and place it in your toilet tank to reduce the volume of each flush; resist using lawn sprinklers. Water scarcity particularly affects regions with hot, arid climates. Villages in developing nations depend on their life-sustaining communal wells. The International Development Research Centre works to help such communities establish clean water supplies. Contact them at IDRC, PO Box 8500, Ottawa ON K1G 3H9, Canada.

WEEKDAY READINGS (Mo) 1 Samuel 1:1 – 8; (Tu) 1:9 – 20; (We) 3:1 – 10, 19 – 20; (Th) 4:1 – 11; (Fr) 8:4 – 7, 10 – 22; (Sa) 9:1 – 4, 17 – 19; 10:1

WINTER ORDINARY TIME

God speaks, the ice melts; God breathes, the streams flow.

Jerusalem, give glory!
Praise God with song, O Zion!
For the Lord strengthens your gates
guarding your children within.
The Lord fills your land with peace,
giving you golden wheat.

God speaks to the earth,
the word speeds forth.
The Lord sends heavy snow
and scatters frost like ashes.

The Lord hurls chunks of hail.
Who can stand such cold?
God speaks, the ice melts;
God breathes, the streams flow.

God speaks his word to Jacob,
to Israel, his laws and decrees.
God has not done this for others,
no others receive this wisdom.

Hallelujah!

—*Psalm 147:12–20*

Shall we praise you, hail-hurling God,
in winter's splendor,
in the grace of snow
that covers with brightness
and reshapes both your creation and ours?
Or shall we curse the fierce cold
that punishes homeless people
and shortens tempers?
Blessed are you
in the earth's tilt and course.
Blessed are you in the sleep of winter
and in the oncoming Lenten spring.
Now and then and always,
fill these lands with peace.

—*Prayer of the Season*

READING I *1 Samuel 3:1–10, 19*

Now the boy Samuel was ministering to the Lord under Eli. The word of the Lord was rare in those days; visions were not widespread. At that time Eli, whose eyesight had begun to grow dim so that he could not see, was lying down in his room; the lamp of God had not yet gone out, and Samuel was lying down in the temple of the Lord, where the ark of God was. Then the Lord called, "Samuel! Samuel!" and he said, "Here I am!" and ran to Eli, and said, "Here I am, for you called me." But Eli said, "I did not call; lie down again." So Samuel went and lay down.

The Lord called again, "Samuel!" Samuel got up and went to Eli, and said, "Here I am, for you called me." But Eli said, "I did not call, my son; lie down again." Now Samuel did not yet know the Lord, and the word of the Lord had not yet been revealed to him.

The Lord called Samuel again, a third time. And he got up and went to Eli, and said, "Here I am, for you called me." Then Eli perceived that the Lord was calling the boy. Therefore Eli said to Samuel, "Go, lie down; and if the Lord calls you, you shall say, 'Speak, Lord, for your servant is listening.'" So Samuel went and lay down in his place.

Now the Lord came and stood there, calling as before, "Samuel! Samuel!" And Samuel said, "Speak, for your servant is listening."

As Samuel grew up, the Lord was with him and let none of his words fall to the ground.

READING II *1 Corinthians 6:12–20*

"All things are lawful for me," but not all things are beneficial. "All things are lawful for me," but I will not be dominated by anything. "Food is meant for the stomach and the stomach for food," and God will destroy both one and the other. The body is meant not for fornication but for the Lord, and the Lord for the body. And God raised the Lord and will also raise us up by divine power.

Do you not know that your bodies are parts of the body of Christ? Should I therefore take parts of the body of Christ and make them parts of a prostitute? Never! Do you not know that whoever is united to a prostitute becomes one body with that prostitute? For it is said, "The two shall be one flesh." But anyone united to the Lord becomes one spirit with the Lord. Shun fornication! Every sin that a person commits is outside the body; but the fornicator sins against the body itself. Or do you not know that your body is a temple of the Holy Spirit within you, which you have from God, and that you are not your own? For you were bought with a price; therefore glorify God in your body.

GOSPEL *John 1:35–42*

The next day John again was standing with two of his disciples, and as he watched Jesus walk by, he exclaimed, "Look, here is the Lamb of God!" The two disciples heard him say this, and they followed Jesus. When Jesus turned and saw them following, he said to them, "What are you looking for?" They said to him, "Rabbi" (which translated means Teacher), "where are you staying?" He said to them, "Come and see."

They came and saw where Jesus was staying, and they remained with him that day. It was about four o'clock in the afternoon. One of the two who heard John speak and followed him was Andrew, Simon Peter's brother. Andrew first found his brother Simon and said to him, "We have found the Messiah" (which is translated Anointed). He brought Simon to Jesus, who looked at him and said, "You are Simon son of John. You are to be called Cephas" (which is translated Peter).

[Revised Common Lectionary: John 1:43–51]

R E F L E C T I O N

First Corinthians 6:16 is among my favorite sentences in the whole Bible. Paul is upbraiding the wayward Christians of Corinth for their behavior, their sexual behavior in particular. He asks, "Do you not know that whoever is united to a prostitute becomes one body with her?"

Christian sexual morality is often characterized as prohibitive and restrictive because, we think, the behaviors themselves are bad, wrong or obstacles to our experience of the presence of God. But here Paul tells the Corinthians that the sexual experience of "two becoming one" is not so restrictive; it can happen even with a prostitute! How can this be?

What Paul is highlighting is the absolute generosity of God, that the experience of God is unconstrained, available in many places — even in paid sex, a situation that most of us Christians two millennia later would assume excludes God's presence. But the church teaches that sex should happen in marriage, and it does so (at least based on Paul's letter here) not because God is found only in sex celebrated between persons committed to one another in love, but because it happens elsewhere too. Like Paul, the church wants its members to "glorify God in your body" because "your body is a temple of the Holy Spirit." Let us be attentive to Paul's writing as well as to the church's sacramental and moral teachings when we assess how much we indeed give praise to God in our bodies.

■ The *Rite of Marriage* teaches that "Christian couples, therefore, nourish and develop their marriage by undivided affection, which wells up from the fountain of divine love, while, in a merging of human and divine love, they remain faithful in body and in mind, in good times as in bad." How does sex in marriage qualify and ennoble the way God is present in the world and in the church?

PRACTICE OF FAITH

AGNES. Friday we remember Agnes, a young woman (perhaps thirteen) who was killed during Diocletian's persecution of Christians in the fourth century. In art, Agnes is shown holding a lamb, a symbol of her innocence — and a visual pun. Agnes sounds like *agnus*, the Latin word for lamb. (In today's gospel, John calls Jesus *"Agnus Dei"* — Lamb of God.) If you have a lamb-shaped cake mold for Easter, get it out and bake a cake this week in honor of Agnes. (DP)

PRACTICE OF HOPE

FOLLOWING THE BAPTIST. John the Baptist was completely selfless, completely the prophet. He set things in motion, pushed the boat away from shore, so to speak, and the boat gathered speed. First, he prophesied about Jesus to the priests and Levites. *The next day,* he baptized Jesus; *the next day* he sent two of his own disciples after Jesus. Andrew got Peter to come along. *The next day,* Jesus went to Galilee and found Philip, Philip found Nathaniel, and *"on the third day"* there was a wedding in Cana at which Jesus first revealed his glory.

Our best hope for the church in the coming years is that we take our cue from John the Baptist, the courageous prophet. We must talk about Jesus in a world seeking repentance, identify him as Messiah to inquirers, and invite friends to follow him. Jesus will do everything else. (MP)

PRACTICE OF CHARITY

LIVE THE DREAM. Every year on the third Monday in January, our nation commemorates the life of Dr. Martin Luther King, Jr., and the contributions he made to civil rights, racial justice, peace and nonviolence. This day is not like every other day: the mail is not delivered; many schools are not in session; most government workers get the day off.

Are we, our churches and communities, living out King's challenge? He exhorted us: "Let us not seek to satisfy our thirst for freedom by drinking from the cup of bitterness and hatred. Again and again we must rise to the majestic heights of meeting physical force with soul force." King had a dream that helped pave the way for the Civil Rights Act of 1964. Here we are, 36 years later, still struggling with hatred and prejudice. Look into your soul; what force is there? Live the dream not just in words but in action.

WEEKDAY READINGS (Mo) 1 Samuel 15:16 – 23; (Tu) 16:1 – 13, (We) 17:32 – 33, 37, 40 – 51; (Th) 18:6 – 9; 19:1 – 7; (Fr) 24:3 – 21; (Sa) 2 Samuel 1:1 – 4, 11 – 12, 19, 23 – 27

READING I   *Jonah 3:1–5, 10*

The word of the Lord came to Jonah a second time, saying, "Get up, go to Nineveh, that great city, and proclaim to it the message that I tell you." So Jonah set out and went to Nineveh, according to the word of the Lord. Now Nineveh was an exceedingly large city, a three days' walk across. Jonah began to go into the city, going a day's walk. And he cried out, "Forty days more, and Nineveh shall be overthrown!" And the people of Nineveh believed God; they proclaimed a fast, and everyone, great and small, put on sackcloth.

When God saw what they did, how they turned from their evil ways, God had second thoughts about the calamity that God had said would be done to them; and God did not do it.

READING II   *1 Corinthians 7:29–31*

Brothers and sisters, the appointed time has grown short; from now on, let even those who are married be as though they were not, and those who mourn as though they were not mourning, and those who rejoice as though they were not rejoicing, and those who buy as though they had no possessions, and those who deal with the world as though they had no dealings with it. For the present form of this world is passing away.

GOSPEL   *Mark 1:14–20*

Now after John was arrested, Jesus came to Galilee, proclaiming the good news of God, and saying, "The time is fulfilled, and the dominion of God has come near; repent, and believe in the good news."

As Jesus passed along the Sea of Galilee, he saw Simon and his brother Andrew casting a net into the sea — for they were fishermen. And Jesus said to them, "Follow me and I will make you fish for human beings." And immediately they left their nets and followed him. As Jesus went a little farther, he saw James son of Zebedee and his brother John, who were in their boat mending the nets. Immediately Jesus called them; and they left their father Zebedee in the boat with the hired men, and followed him.

R E F L E C T I O N

The absence of infancy and childhood stories about Jesus in the Gospel of Mark has sent us to the other gospels quite a bit since November 28, when the liturgical year began. But now, beginning this Sunday and continuing over the next nine weeks, we will hear a large portion of Mark's gospel, and thereby start to discover this text's unique portrait of Jesus. (This might be a good time to read or review "The Liturgical Year and the Gospel of Mark" on pages 8 – 11.)

This Sunday's passage reveals the first words of Jesus in Mark. (Jesus' first spoken words are different in each gospel: See Matthew 3:15, Mark 1:15, Luke 2:49, John 1:38. His last words before death on the cross are also different, though similar in Matthew and Mark: See Matthew 27:46, Mark 15:34, Luke 23:46, John 19:28 – 30.) Today, we hear Jesus' words, "The time is fulfilled."

In ancient Greek there are two words that we translate as "time": *chronos* and *kairos*. The former, *chronos*, means time as a clock would measure it, strictly quantitative: Each minute is the same *quantity* of time no matter what happens during one. The latter word, *kairos*, is a qualitative measure of time, a word for time that is pregnant with meaning.

In the gospel today, when Jesus says that "the time is fulfilled," the Greek word used by the evangelist is *kairos*. The evangelist wrote this for his community because he wanted the members to measure and appreciate their lives not according to the ways of the world or the ways of science, but according to the ways of God. *Now* is the time to change, Jesus says here; the kingdom is at hand.

■ **How tied are you to watches, clocks, alarms, buzzers, bells and other indicators of the *quantitative* measure of time?**

■ **Is there any time that you leave free for considering and experiencing the *quality* of your life — that is, the gifts that God has given you in the people you love and the pleasures you enjoy with them?**

PRACTICE OF FAITH

FISH FOR HUMAN BEINGS. More and more parishes invite adults who have not been baptized to consider becoming Christian. The *catechumenate* is the group of unbaptized people in a parish preparing for baptism. Individuals are called *catechumens,* an old Greek name that means "people who learn by word of mouth." The catechumens are cared for by catechists (those who teach "by word of mouth") and by sponsors.

It seems too simple, but many an unbaptized adult decides to become a Christian because someone *asks* him or her. Do you know someone who has not been baptized? Do you know someone who is searching for meaning in life? Find out if your parish has an inquiry group. Invite the unbaptized person you know to attend, and go with him or her. (DP)

PRACTICE OF HOPE

THE APPOINTED TIME. The poorest countries of our world live under a crushing debt of over \$250 billion owed to rich nations and financial institutions. An organization known as Jubilee 2000 believes that the start of this new millennium should be a time to give hope to people living in poverty by putting behind us the mistakes made by both lenders and borrowers, and by canceling this heavy debt. Part of the Jubilee 2000 campaign includes presenting a petition with as many signatures as possible to the leaders of the United States and of the wealthy G8 nations. Contact Jubilee 2000/USA at 222 East Capitol Street NE, Washington DC 20003-1036; or visit their Web site at www.j2000usa.org; or call 202-783-3566. Now is the appointed time to break the chains of debt.

PRACTICE OF CHARITY

FOLLOW ME. Tim is proud of the fact that he owns exactly 100 items. If he gets one more item than that, he gives another thing away. Gayle and Dan live in a remote rural area subsisting on a meager income while living "off the land." Chuck bikes instead of driving, weaves his own clothing, grows organic food, and makes hand tools and fine furniture. "Live simply, that others may simply live" is not just a motto; these people live it every day.

Materialism and consumerism are rampant in our world. We have been brainwashed by a "buy-me-and-be-happy" mentality. You can start to change your life today — but start small. Keep a log of every cent you spend. After a month, look for trends and areas where you could improve. Go from there. Always set aside a percentage for tithing.

WEEKDAY READINGS (Mo) 2 Samuel 5:1 – 7, 10; (Tu) Acts 22:3 – 16 or 9:1 – 22; (We) 2 Timothy 1:1 – 8 or Titus 1:1 – 5; (Th) 2 Samuel 7:18 – 19, 24 – 29; (Fr) 11:1 – 10, 13 – 17; (Sa) 12:1 – 7, 10 – 17

READING I *Deuteronomy 18:15–20*

The Lord your God will raise up for you a prophet like me from among your own people; you shall heed such a prophet. This is what you requested of the Lord your God at Horeb on the day of the assembly when you said: "If I hear the voice of the Lord my God any more, or ever again see this great fire, I will die." Then the Lord replied to me: "They are right in what they have said. I will raise up for them a prophet like you from among their own people; I will put my words in the mouth of the prophet, who shall speak to them everything that I command. Anyone who does not heed the words that the prophet shall speak in my name, I myself will hold accountable. But any prophet who speaks in the name of other gods, or who presumes to speak in my name a word that I have not commanded the prophet to speak — that prophet shall die."

READING II *1 Corinthians 7:32–35*

I want you to be free from anxieties. The unmarried man is anxious about the affairs of the Lord, how to please the Lord; but the married man is anxious about worldly affairs, how to please his wife, and his interests are divided. And the unmarried woman or virgin is anxious about the affairs of the Lord, how to be holy in body and spirit; but the married woman is anxious about worldly affairs, how to please her husband. I say this for your own benefit, not to lay any restraint upon you, but to promote good order and to secure your undivided devotion to the Lord.

[Revised Common Lectionary: 1 Corinthians 8:1–13]

GOSPEL *Mark 1:21–28*

Jesus and his disciples went to Capernaum; and when the sabbath came, he entered the synagogue and taught. They were astounded at his teaching, for he taught them as one having authority, and not as the scribes.

Just then there was in their synagogue a man with an unclean spirit, and he cried out, "What have you to do with us, Jesus of Nazareth? Have you come to destroy us? I know who you are, the Holy One of God." But Jesus rebuked the spirit, saying, "Be silent, and come out of him!" And the unclean spirit, convulsing him and crying with a loud voice, came out of the man. They were all amazed, and they kept on asking one another, "What is this? A new teaching — with authority! He commands even the unclean spirits, and they obey him."

At once his fame began to spread throughout the surrounding region of Galilee.

Wednesday, February 2, 2000

THE PRESENTATION OF THE LORD

Malachi 3:1–4 *The Lord whom you seek will come to the temple.*

Hebrews 2:14–18 *He became like us in every way.*

Luke 2:22–40 *Simeon took the child in his arms.*

The light of Christmas shone feebly at first, increasing to shine brightly from a star at Epiphany. Today this light is placed in our arms. Like old Simeon, we are hand in hand with God.

REFLECTION

In the Gospel of Mark, Jesus is intent on keeping his divine identity hidden. Scripture scholars call this the "messianic secret," for what Jesus seeks to hide is that he is the savior, the Messiah, the "holy one of God."

Today's reading is the first appearance of this secret. When Jesus commands the unclean spirit to come out of the man in the synagogue, the spirit recognizes Jesus immediately: "I know who you are, the Holy One of God." It is hard to know what the gospel writer sought to accomplish when he had Jesus hide his identity rather than proclaim it. Some scholars have suggested that there might have been some kind of political or social or even physical threat to the community of Mark's gospel. To ease the burden on the consciences of those who had hidden their Christian identities in order to avoid harm, the author of the Gospel of Mark has Jesus himself hiding his true identity.

All of us Christians, at some time or other in our lives, find ourselves having to sacrifice something for our faith. Now that Christianity is a world religion — unlike the first century, when the Gospel of Mark was written — our sacrifices are not as severe as they probably were for Christians in the first centuries. Nevertheless our faith has a price in our lives. The tradition urges us to care for the poor, the lonely, the abandoned, the sick, the dying, the imprisoned, the widowed, the outcast, but there are times when we resist making the sacrifice of time and thought and energy.

■ **What, in your experience of the church and of the risen Christ, is the greatest motivator? Is it worship? Preaching? The proclamation of the scriptures? Childhood faith traditions?**

■ **When are you most inclined to hide your faith? To have your own "messianic secret"?**

PRACTICE OF FAITH

CANDLES AND THROATS. Wednesday is the solemnity of the Presentation of the Lord. We remember that Mary and Joseph took their firstborn son to the Temple to consecrate him to God. When they arrived, the prophets Simeon and Anna recognized the baby as the light of the world. So today the church gives thanks to God for candles, which remind us of Chirst's light. Even if you cannot attend Mass to get blessed candles, light candles at dinner Wednesday night. Did you learn Simeon's song last month (see page 35)? Sing it before you go to bed on Wednesday.

Thursday, we remember the bishop and martyr Blase, who once saved someone from choking. With the blessed candles of the Presentation held in the shape of a cross, we touch each other's throats and pray that God keeps us well this winter. (DP)

PRACTICE OF HOPE

TEACHERS. In his home synagogue, Jesus taught on the Sabbath. Those who were present listened intently, silent in their focus on Jesus. Then a man with an unclean spirit could not stand the intensity and voiced his pain and confusion. Jesus healed the man with words of authority. Jesus' words proclaimed the works of God in history, and his healing works confirmed his words about God's love. (MP)

PRACTICE OF CHARITY

HOMELESS PROBLEM? "Birdman" would sit on the edge of his bed flapping his arms and batting his eyelids at an impossible rate. Without his medications, his behavior was bizarre. He frightened most people, including the other homeless men who were sheltered at St. Joseph Catholic Worker House. His plight was the direct result of the "de-institutionalization" of the mentally ill, which occurs around the country. Without adequate support and regular access to necessary medications, tens of thousands of men and women have become homeless, living on the streets. Resolving "Birdman's" problem took much time and an extraordinary coordination of social services, which he never could have accomplished alone. Blame is meaningless. We all need to ask ourselves and our institutions to put human dignity and basic needs as the highest priority. The homeless are persons, not problems.

WEEKDAY READINGS (Mo) 2 Samuel 15:13 – 14, 30; 16:5 – 13; (Tu) 18:9 – 10, 14, 24 – 15, 30 — 19:3; (We) Presentation, see box; (Th) 1 Kings 2:1 – 4, 10 – 12; (Fr) Sirach 47:2 – 11; (Sa) 1 Kings 3:4 – 13

READING I *Job 7:1–4, 6–7*

Job spoke to his friends: "Do not human beings have a hard service on earth, and are not their days like the days of a labourer? Like a slave who longs for the shadow, and like labourers who look for their wages, so I am allotted months of emptiness, and nights of misery are apportioned to me. When I lie down I say, 'When shall I rise?' But the night is long, and I am full of tossing until dawn. My days are swifter than a weaver's shuttle, and come to their end without hope. Remember that my life is a breath; my eye will never again see good."

[Revised Common Lectionary: Isaiah 40:21–31]

READING II *1 Corinthians 9:16–23*

If I proclaim the gospel, this gives me no ground for boasting, for an obligation is laid on me, and woe to me if I do not proclaim the gospel! For if I do this of my own will, I have a reward; but if not of my own will, I am entrusted with a commission. What then is my reward? Just this: that in my proclamation I may make the gospel free of charge, so as not to make full use of my rights in the gospel.

For though I am free with respect to all, I have made myself a slave to all, so that I might win more of them. To the Jewish people I became as a Jew, in order to win the Jewish people. To those under the law I became as one under the law (though I myself am not under the law) so that I might win those under the law. To those outside the law I became as one outside the law (though I am not free from God's law but am under Christ's law) so that I might win those outside the law. To the weak I became weak, so that I might win the weak. I have become all things to all people, that I might by all means save some. I do it all for the sake of the gospel, so that I may share in its blessings.

GOSPEL *Mark 1:29–39*

As soon as Jesus and the disciples left the synagogue, they entered the house of Simon and Andrew, with James and John. Now Simon's mother-in-law was in bed with a fever, and they told him about her at once. Jesus came and took her by the hand and lifted her up. Then the fever left her, and she began to serve them.

That evening, at sundown, they brought to Jesus all who were sick or possessed with demons. And the whole city was gathered around the door. And he cured many who were sick with various diseases, and cast out many demons; and he would not permit the demons to speak, because they knew him.

In the morning, while it was still very dark, Jesus got up and went out to a deserted place, and there he prayed. And Simon and his companions hunted for him. When they found him, they said to him, "Everyone is searching for you." Jesus answered, "Let us go on to the neighboring towns, so that I may proclaim the message there also; for that is what I came out to do." And he went throughout Galilee, proclaiming the message in their synagogues and casting out demons.

R E F L E C T I O N

In the first reading, Job complains to his friends that his days fly by faster than a weaver's shuttle. Think of the needle of a sewing machine racing up and down faster than the eye can see. This speed of Job's days is certainly echoed in what we hear about Jesus' activities in today's gospel reading. Jesus — moving from town to town, preaching the good news and casting out demons — is a bundle of energy in Mark. Within a few verses we find him healing "all who were sick or possessed." Indeed, "the whole city was gathered around the door" looking for his attention!

We find Jesus entering the house of Peter (Simon) and Andrew, and there is the mother of Peter's wife sick in bed with a fever. The interesting thing is not the cure, but that upon being healed, the mother-in-law immediately began to serve. (The original Greek word for her service is *diakonein,* the same word that is the origin of the church's ministry of "deacon" today.) So, when we find gifts of God in our lives today, we give thanks to God, knowing that the gift is not an end in itself but to be given back to God in service.

Next, we notice that Jesus' fame is beginning to spread like wildfire. It's not even the end of chapter 1 of the Gospel of Mark and already everyone is looking for Jesus. Just as last week, now we find another instance of Jesus' wanting to keep his identity hidden: "He would not permit the demons to speak." As our progress through the gospel continues through this liturgical year, we will discover that the more Jesus tries to keep his identity hidden, the more his fame and popularity with the crowds spread.

■ **The portrait of Jesus in the Gospel of Mark is sometimes at odds with the way Jesus is portrayed by the other three gospel writers. Does Mark's Jesus seem odd to you? What particular characteristics strike you as different from the Jesus portrayed in other parts of the New Testament?**

PRACTICE OF FAITH

TURN TO GOD. The Risen Christ no longer physically walks among us healing and teaching. But when we bring our needs, pains and sorrows to God in prayer, we will find healing. In the first reading, Job speaks of this life as if it were nothing but a great disappointing burden. How often do we feel the same? How often does everything seem to be going wrong at once? It can happen: bills pile up, a child's grades plummet, work becomes drudgery, a family member becomes seriously ill. We can sulk and scowl and moan "Why me?" — or we can turn to God, who we know is waiting for us. After discussing our problems with God — maybe crying or shouting in anger — our strength to deal with them one at a time will grow. Things may get better — or they may not. But whatever happens, God's grace is always there for us to draw on. (RG)

PRACTICE OF HOPE

CASTING OUT DEMONS. Many large American cities average more than one murder a day. During the 1990s, several larger cities saw more than 1,000 of their inhabitants murdered each year. But more recently, it is reported that there are fewer incidents of violent crime, including fewer murders, in our cities. Whether this is due to tougher gun laws, community policing or improved opportunities for economic advancement, it seems that at least some demons of violence are being cast out.

PRACTICE OF CHARITY

REHABILITATION OF THE SPIRIT. Seventeen years ago, New York Theological Seminary began a wonderful experiment in the renewal of the human spirit. Few would expect to find a seminary program behind the walls of legendary Sing Sing Prison, and even fewer would expect it to be successful. But nearly 250 men have already graduated from the program, with many taking human service jobs upon their release from prison. The recidivism rate is low, the lowest of any education program within the prison's walls. A few men have gone on to advanced theology studies and ordination. Those with longer sentences apply their training to teaching, counseling and working with prisoners with AIDS. Graduates have said that the program's greatest benefit is its belief in a person's ability to overcome evil and do good. The originators of this program have enthusiastically embraced the view of the apostle Paul that we must "become all things to all people, so that some may be saved."

WEEKDAY READINGS (Mo) 1 Kings 8:1–7, 9–13; (Tu) 8:22–23, 27–30; (We) 10:1–10; (Th) 11:4–13; (Fr) 11:29–32; 12:19; (Sa) 12:26–32; 13:33–34

READING I *Leviticus 13:1–2, 44–46*

The LORD spoke to Moses and Aaron, saying: "When a person has on the skin of the body a swelling or an eruption or a spot, and it turns into a leprous disease on the skin of the body, that person shall be brought to Aaron the priest or to one of his sons the priests. "A person who has the leprous disease shall wear torn clothes and let the hair of the head be dishevelled and shall cover the upper lip and cry out, 'Unclean, unclean.' A person shall remain unclean as long as the disease persists; and being unclean, that peson shall live alone with a dwelling outside the camp."

[Revised Common Lectionary: 2 Kings 5:1–14]

READING II *1 Corinthians 10:31—11:1*

Whether you eat or drink, or whatever you do, do everything for the glory of God. Give no offense to Jews or to Greeks or to the church of God, just as I try to please everyone in everything I do, not seeking my own advantage, but that of many,so that they may be saved. Be imitators of me, as I am of Christ.

[Revised Common Lectionary: 1 Corinthians 9:24–27]

GOSPEL *Mark 1:40–45*

A man with leprosy came to Jesus begging him, and kneeling said to Jesus, "If you choose, you can make me clean." Moved with pity, Jesus stretched out his hand and touched him, and said to him, "I do choose. Be made clean!" Immediately the leprosy left him, and he was made clean. After sternly warning him Jesus sent him away at once, saying to him, "See that you say nothing to anyone; but go, show yourself to the priest, and offer for your cleansing what Moses commanded, as a testimony to them." But the man went out and began to proclaim it freely, and to spread the word, and people came to Jesus from every quarter.

R E F L E C T I O N

Of the many laws of the Old Testament observed in the time of Jesus, those with the most severe social consequences dealt with people with skin diseases: lepers. The examinations performed by the Jewish priests and the rites of purification performed by the leprous persons themselves were precisely and rigidly prescribed, and excluded the person with leprosy from society. Some of these laws are in the first reading this Sunday. (There are longer and more detailed regulations of this sort elsewhere in the Bible; see, for example, the Book of Leviticus, chapters 13 – 14.)

Key to understanding today's gospel passage is that skin disease was thought to spread readily: "He is unclean. He shall live alone. His dwelling shall be outside the camp" (Leviticus 13:46). Persons with leprosy were to tear their clothing and dishevel their hair so that all would recognize and avoid them. The law even dictated that they were to cry out "Unclean, unclean" whenever they were out in public.

At first glance, the gospel can seem to be merely one more of the many cures that Jesus performed in his public ministry. But on a deeper level, it deals with the social exclusion of the sick. Consider: Jesus' culture would have thought Jesus leprous as well after he touched the man who had leprosy. The gospel writer is clear: "Jesus stretched out his hand and *touched* him." Jesus was willing to suffer the social consequences of the touch.

Again, we find the Markan messianic secret: "See that you say nothing to anyone," Jesus sternly commands. And, as before, in spite of this charge, the news of the cure spread, and "Jesus could no longer go into a town openly."

■ **It is easy to ignore the idea that scripture passages about leprosy and people with leprosy have meaning for us in the church today. "Another time, another place," we think. But often our own sick are removed from society in many ways, some obvious and some more subtle. Do you think that the sick are to be set apart? What do you think the consequences of this social exclusion of the sick and dying might be?**

PRACTICE OF FAITH

VALENTINE. One legend has it that Valentine was a third-century Roman priest and physician who sent letters of love, solidarity and encouragement to Christians suffering persecution. The practice of sending cards on his feast day, February 14, may have developed in imitation of this practice. While the modern St. Valentine's Day is more concerned with the sales of chocolates, roses and tokens of romantic love, expressions of solidarity and encouragement still have a place in our practice of faith. Most of us know someone who could benefit from our concern and support: members of our family or parish who are grieving or ill, friends who are bearing hardships, children who feel neglected. Take some time to send them a surprise greeting, letting them know of your interest and affection.

PRACTICE OF HOPE

GOD CHOOSES TO HEAL US. The plea of the man with leprosy carries a hint of an attitude toward God that plagues Christianity even today. The man's "If you choose" echoes a perception of God as a capricious God whom we must please, or a cruel God who might punish us or not forgive us. As if God would choose not to heal; as if Jesus, looking at the man, would say, "No, not today." The man sparked deep feelings in Jesus. Imagine the strength and compassion with which Jesus touched him and spoke the words: "I do choose. Be made clean."

Read today's responsorial psalm, Psalm 32. We must ask for forgiveness, not keep silence or be closed to understanding like a horse or mule. God always chooses our good, covers over our sin, surrounds us with steadfast love whenever we trust. (MP)

PRACTICE OF CHARITY

HEART HEALTH. February is national "Healthy Heart" month. Reports abound that obesity and heart disease are on the rise, particularly in younger people. We live in a land of plenty. A walk through a grocery store reveals a multitude of choices. It is easy to reach for quick-to-prepare, high-fat foods.

Be kind to your heart! Eat more fresh vegetables and fruit, pasta and whole grains. Begin an exercise program. Heart health also involves our spiritual sense. Make time daily to hear God's voice. Do a kind-hearted deed today. Visit a friend or fellow parishioner in a nursing home. Oddly enough, most nursing home residents rarely get fresh fruit. Make a big fruit salad and bring two forks!

WEEKDAY READINGS (Mo) James 1:1 – 11; (Tu) 1:12 – 18; (We) 1:19 – 27; (Th) 2:1 – 9; (Fr) 2:14 – 24, 26; (Sa) 3:1 – 10

READING I *Isaiah 43:18–25*

The LORD said:
"Do not remember the former things,
   or consider the things of old.
I am about to do a new thing;
   now it springs forth, do you not perceive it?
I will make a way in the wilderness
   and rivers in the desert.

"I will give drink to my chosen people,
   the people whom I formed for myself
so that they might declare my praise.

"Yet you did not call upon me, O Jacob;
   but you have been weary of me, O Israel!
You have burdened me with your sins;
   you have wearied me with your iniquities.

"I, I am the one
   who blots out your transgressions
   for my own sake,
and I will not remember your sins."

READING II *2 Corinthians 1:18–22*

As surely as God is faithful, our word to you has not been "Yes and No." For the Son of God, Jesus Christ, whom we proclaimed among you, Silvanus and Timothy and I, was not "Yes and No"; but in him it is always "Yes." For in him every one of God's promises is a "Yes." For this reason it is through him that we say the "Amen," to the glory of God. But it is God who establishes us with you in Christ and has anointed us, by putting his seal on us and giving us his Spirit in our hearts as a first installment.

GOSPEL *Mark 2:1–12*

When Jesus returned to Capernaum, it was reported that he was at home. So many gathered around that there was no longer room for them, not even in front of the door; and he was speaking the word to them. Then some people came, bringing to Jesus a paralyzed man, carried by four of them. And when they could not bring him to Jesus because of the crowd, they removed the roof above him; and after having dug through it, they let down the mat on which the paralysed man lay. When Jesus saw their faith, he said to the man, "My child, your sins are forgiven." Now some of the scribes were sitting there, questioning in their hearts, "Why does this fellow speak in this way? It is blasphemy! Who can forgive sins but God alone?" At once Jesus perceived in his spirit that they were discussing these questions among themselves; and he said to them, "Why do you raise such questions in your hearts? Which is easier, to say to the paralyzed man, 'Your sins are forgiven,' or to say, 'Stand up and take your mat and walk'? But so that you may know that the Son of Man has authority on earth to forgive sins" — he said to the man who was paralyzed — "I say to you, stand up, take your mat and go to your home." And he stood up, and immediately took the mat and went out before all of them; so that they were all amazed and glorified God, saying, "We have never seen anything like this!"

R E F L E C T I O N

This gospel story of the paralyzed man being lowered down to Jesus has always amused me. Each time I hear that the four friends "removed the roof" when they could not get through the crowd to bring their paralyzed friend close to Jesus, I scratch my head and think, "They did what?"

I've wondered about the untold parts of the story, like whether the owners of the house were there and what they thought about the four friends deciding to climb up and take off the roof so they could get their friend to the front of the line. After telling us that the friends tore through the roof, the gospel writer tells us that Jesus saw their faith and forgave the paralytic's sins. If I had been the writer, verse 5 would have read, "So the homeowners jumped up and yelled, 'Hey, who do you think you are, tearing through our roof like that?'"

Faith has practical consequences in all areas of our life — physical, emotional, social, economic, intellectual and spiritual. Many gospel stories, especially in Mark, are so terse that we get very few details about the many practical effects of faith and salvation. In story after story, we hear of the crowds following Jesus, people changing their lives because of their encounters with Jesus or simply because of witnessing another person's encounter with him.

What we do not hear about, however, are the consequences. For example, when people who met Jesus decided to change their lives, what did they say to their family members when they came home for dinner that night? What were the many consequences of their decision to follow Jesus?

■ **Enthusiastic religious faith is usually short-lived. A "life of faith" is not the same as a "religious experience." Both are necessary for us to keep our commitment to the church and to keep it lively. Where does your faith lie on the continuum between a "life of faith" and discrete "religious experiences"? To which side might you attend in order to keep your faith both steady and lively?**

PRACTICE OF FAITH

MARDI GRAS. Lent is approaching — Ash Wednesday is a little more than two weeks away — and it is not too early to start thinking about Mardi Gras (Tuesday, March 7). Mardi Gras is the day of indulgence before Ash Wednesday, but it need not exist just for its own sake. It can help set the stage for the reconciliation and growth that Lent offers.

Plan a menu of favorite foods, and play your favorite dance music. Have family members make costumes or masks that exaggerate some bad habit or demon that each would like to subdue this Lent. As you eat, drink, sing and dance, share your hopes for personal change by Easter. Invite everyone to write their resolution on slips of paper. Then burn the slips at the end of the day in anticipation of Wednesday's ashes.

PRACTICE OF HOPE

AMAZING GRACE. Long curly brown hair framed a handsome face with a dazzling smile. But his dark blue eyes told another story. Mike abused drugs and alcohol. One sultry July evening in a dark dirty bar, someone pulled a knife. In no time at all, a stranger lay dead at Mike's feet. Mike was sentenced to 26 years in prison. Clearly admitting his guilt, Mike sought to redeem himself. In prison, he completed his high school equivalency requirements and became an optical technician. Through letters of encouragement from friends and family, and from an awakening within his own heart and soul, Mike found a dwelling place for God. He was changed.

PRACTICE OF CHARITY

THEN SOME PEOPLE CAME. It has been about 19 years since the first cases of AIDS were diagnosed in the United States, and it is estimated that more than 400,000 people have died of AIDS in this country. The Centers for Disease Control and Prevention estimate that there were more than 21,000 AIDS deaths in 1997, more than 271,000 persons living with AIDS, and more than 100,000 living with HIV infection in the United States.

Organizations founded to meet the needs of people living with HIV/AIDS continue to do their good work, and continue to need our help. Volunteers are always needed to provide rides, deliver hot meals, run errands, pay pastoral visits and get involved in advocacy efforts on behalf of people living with HIV/AIDS. Check your telephone directory and find an organization that you can assist. Become one of those people who come and do what it takes to help someone in need.

WEEKDAY READINGS (Mo) James 3:13 – 18; (Tu) 1 Peter 5:1 – 4; (We) James 4:13 – 17; (Th) 5:1 – 6; (Fr) 5:9 – 12; (Sa) 5:13 – 20

READING I *Hosea 2:14–20*

The LORD says this concerning Israel, his people: "I will allure her, and bring her into the wilderness, and speak tenderly to her. There she shall respond as in the days of her youth, as at the time when she came out of the land of Egypt.

"On that day, says the LORD, you will call me, 'My husband,' and no longer will you call me, 'My Baal.' For I will remove the names of the Baals from your mouth, and they will be mentioned by name no more. I will make for you a covenant on that day with the wild animals, the birds of the air, and the creeping things of the ground; and I will abolish the bow, the sword, and war from the land; and I will make you lie down in safety.

"I will take you for my wife forever; I will take you for my wife in righteousness and in justice, in steadfast love, and in mercy. I will take you for my wife in faithfulness; and you shall know the LORD."

READING II *2 Corinthians 3:1–6*

We do not need, as some do, letters of recommendation to you or from you, do we? You yourselves are our letter, written on our hearts, to be known and read by all; and you show that you are a letter of Christ, prepared by us, written not with ink but with the Spirit of the living God, not on tablets of stone but on tablets of human hearts. Such is the confidence that we have through Christ toward God. Not that we are competent of ourselves to claim anything as coming from us; our competence is from God, who has made us competent to be ministers of a new covenant, not of letter but of spirit; for the letter kills, but the Spirit gives life.

GOSPEL *Mark 2:13–22*

Jesus went out again beside the sea; the whole crowd gathered around him, and he taught them. As Jesus was walking along, he saw Levi son of Alphaeus sitting at the tax booth, and said to him, "Follow me." And Levi got up and followed him.

And as Jesus sat at dinner in Levi's house, many tax collectors and sinners were also sitting with Jesus and his disciples — for there were many who followed him. When the scribes of the Pharisees saw that he was eating with sinners and tax collectors, they said to his disciples, "Why does he eat with tax collectors and sinners?" When Jesus heard this, he said to them, "Those who are well have no need of a physician, but those who are sick; I have come to call not the righteous but sinners."

Now John's disciples and the Pharisees were fasting; and people came and said to Jesus, "Why do John's disciples and the disciples of the Pharisees fast, but your disciples do not fast?" Jesus said to them, "The wedding guests cannot fast while the bridegroom is with them, can they? As long as they have the bridegroom with them, they cannot fast. The days will come when the bridegroom is taken away from them, and then they will fast on that day.

"No one sews a piece of unshrunken cloth on an old cloak; otherwise, the patch pulls away from it, the new from the old, and a worse tear is made. And no one puts new wine into old wineskins; otherwise, the wine will burst the skins, and the wine is lost, and so are the skins; but one puts new wine into fresh wineskins."

R E F L E C T I O N

This Sunday's second reading is from the Second Letter of Paul to the Corinthians. Many of us are familiar with passages from First Corinthians — "Love is patient, love is kind," "Your body is God's temple," "Do this in remembrance of me" — but the second letter to the same community is not as widely known. In the first letter Paul was indicting the Corinthian church for practices he found problematic; between that letter and the second, he has heard back from them about what they find problematic about him! So the second letter is his self-defense: "I wrote you out of much distress . . . and with many tears, not to cause you pain" (2:4), he says, just before the passage we find today.

Perhaps you will find the second reading more real if you know someone who recently applied for a job or to college. It is likely that the job seeker or student-to-be needed letters of recommendation to accompany their application. And you know that the applicant can be full of anxiety during the nerve-racking wait to hear the employer's or admission committee's decision.

Paul knows this kind of anxiety, and he employs the image of the "letter of recommendation" poetically when he writes: "You are a letter of Christ, prepared by us, written not with ink but with the Spirit of the living God." Simply and beautifully put, and an important image for us to commit to memory when we think of our own place in the church today. For we are still "letters," bearing the message and word of the living God; it is the Holy Spirit who animates us and gives us the words to communicate both in speech and in action. Be such a "letter of recommendation" for your family, for those you love, for those in your church, for the world.

■ **If you are a letter of recommendation for the church community in which you celebrate the eucharist, what does your letter say?**

■ **How does the eucharistic assembly bring to life the power of your witness to the world?**

PRACTICE OF FAITH

EXAMPLES. As adults, we do our best to set good examples for the children whose lives we influence. We also encourage older children to set a good example for younger siblings.

When two of our daughters were very young, three and five, the family was enjoying a Sunday out. In the course of the day we bought each girl a balloon and wound the strings around their wrists so the balloons would not drift off. Of course, the little one's balloon did. Trying to offer some comfort, her big sister said, "Come on, we'll both hold my string and when I count to three we'll let it go. We'll share our balloons with the world." And they did. Keep alert for ways to act generously in your daily contacts with others. It is more than just a nice thing to do; it is an expression of faith in the goodness of our God and each other.

PRACTICE OF HOPE

REJOICE. Our family recently took a vacation. Everyone came along and we took great joy in being together. There was forgiving, healing of old wounds and adjusting again to everyone's different ways and favorite activities. We went on outings and hikes, and went together to a different restaurant each night. Our festive dinners were a fine culmination of each day spent together.

Jesus told his questioners that while the bridegroom is with them, the guests do not fast, they rejoice. In probably all cultures, rejoicing usually includes sharing a meal in an atmosphere of joy, trust and mutual forgiveness. In the same way, as church, we disciples rejoice at every eucharist. We have a festive meal and draw new hope from our time together. (MP)

PRACTICE OF CHARITY

REND YOUR HEARTS. Fasting as a means of worship and protest has a long history. Native American peoples found their visions through self-denial, and ancient Israelites saw periodic fasting as a sacrifice that God demanded. In 1983, when the American Catholic bishops published *The Challenge of Peace: God's Promise and Our Response,* a pastoral letter on war and peace, they promoted regular Friday fasting coupled with acts of service as signs of penance. Mohandas Gandhi, Dick Gregory and others committed to justice and peace stand as examples of the transforming power fasting has on the person and society. Examine your life today. What can you do without? What impact will this sacrifice have on your conversion? How can you stand with others in prayer and protest?

WEEKDAY READINGS (Mo) 1 Peter 1:3 – 9; (Tu) 1:10 – 16; (We) 1:18 – 25; (Th) 2:2 – 5, 9 – 12; (Fr) 4:7 – 13; (Sa) Jude 17:20 – 25

READING I *Deuteronomy 5:12–15*

The LORD says this:

"Observe the sabbath day and keep it holy, as the LORD your God commanded you. Six days you shall labor and do all your work. But the seventh day is a sabbath to the LORD your God; you shall not do any work — you, or your son or your daughter, or your male or female slave, or your ox or your donkey, or any of your livestock, or the resident alien in your towns, so that your male and female slave may rest as well as you. Remember that you were a slave in the land of Egypt, and the LORD your God brought you out from there with a mighty hand and an outstretched arm; therefore the LORD your God commanded you to keep the sabbath day."

[Revised Common Lectionary: 2 Kings 2:1–12]

READING II *2 Corinthians 4:6–11*

It is the God who said, "Let light shine out of darkness," who has shone in our hearts to give the light of the knowledge of the glory of God in the face of Jesus Christ. But we have this treasure in clay jars, so that it may be made clear that this extraordinary power belongs to God and does not come from us. We are afflicted in every way, but not crushed; perplexed, but not driven to despair; persecuted, but not forsaken; struck down, but not destroyed; always carrying in the body the death of Jesus, so that the life of Jesus may also be made visible in our bodies. For while we live, we are always being given up to death for Jesus' sake, so that the life of Jesus may be made visible in our mortal flesh.

[Revised Common Lectionary: 2 Corinthians 4:3–6]

GOSPEL *Mark 2:23 — 3:6*

One sabbath Jesus was going through the grainfields; and as they made their way his disciples began to pluck heads of grain. The Pharisees said to Jesus, "Look, why are they doing what is not lawful on the sabbath?" And Jesus said to them, "Have you never read what David did when he and his companions were hungry and in need of food? He entered the house of God, when Abiathar was high priest, and ate the bread of the Presence, which it is not lawful for any but the priests to eat, and he gave some to his companions." Then Jesus said to them, "The sabbath was made for humankind, and not humankind for the sabbath; so the Son of Man is lord even of the sabbath." Again Jesus entered the synagogue, and a man was there who had a withered hand. They watched Jesus to see whether he would cure him on the sabbath, so that they might accuse him. And Jesus said to the man who had the withered hand, "Come forward." Then Jesus said to them, "Is it lawful to do good or to do harm on the sabbath, to save life or to kill?" But they were silent. Jesus looked around at them with anger; he was grieved at their hardness of heart and said to the man, "Stretch out your hand." He stretched it out, and his hand was restored. The Pharisees went out and immediately conspired with the Herodians against Jesus, how to destroy him.

[Revised Common Lectionary: Mark 9:2–9]

Wednesday, March 8, 2000

ASH WEDNESDAY

Joel 2:12–18 *Proclaim a fast. Rend your hearts.*

2 Corinthians 5:20 — 6:2 *Now is the time to be reconciled.*

Matthew 6:1–6,16–18 *Pray, fast and give alms.*

The Spirit urges us into the desert discipline of the lenten spring. For forty days we will strip away everything that separates us from God, beginning today, as we are marked with a cross of ashes. Death and life in a single sign!

R E F L E C T I O N

The first reading, from Deuteronomy, prepares us for the conflict that Jesus will face in the gospel incident related in Mark. The Jewish law is clear: "No work may be done on the seventh day . . . on the sabbath." And the gospel reading begins by telling us that Jesus' disciples are violating the law: They were walking through standing grain *on the sabbath* and "began to pluck heads of grain." Their actions are opposed by the religious authorities, the Pharisees.

The Gospel of Mark is set up so that in the very first chapter we discover conflict between Jesus and the demons cast out of the sick (1:26, 1:34). In the next chapter we find more conflicts, this time with the Pharisees and the scribes (2:16, 2:18), leading up to today's reading with similar tension between Jesus and the Pharisees (2:24, 3:2). The scene ends with a foreshadowing of things to come: "The Pharisees went out and immediately conspired . . . against Jesus," figuring out "how to destroy him." We know the story, and we know how it will end. What is important in Mark, however, is that the threat of Jesus' destruction and death at the hands of religious authorities is introduced so early. The first threat comes from the demons, and the second from religious authorities.

At the same point in the gospels of Matthew and Luke we are still reading about Jesus' infancy! The Gospel of Mark, however, is unique; we can here see why this gospel is sometimes called "a passion account with a long introduction." Very early in the story Jesus' enemies are already plotting his death. Frightening though this is, this foreshadowing of death can also be a consolation to Christians for whom suffering and death are part of their day-to-day existence.

■ **Can you think of people in your church for whom death is an ever-present reality? What does Christian faith supply in their difficult lives? Speak with your pastor about what your church's assembly can supply in your own time of need.**

PRACTICE OF FAITH

ASHES. This Wednesday the church gathers to smear ashes on each forehead and admonish each person to believe and repent. The ashes are made by burning the remaining palms from last Palm Sunday. Just like our best intentions, the palms have become dry and dusty. Again we've wandered off course. So in Lent we find out way back to the basics: prayer, fasting, almsgiving.

An old way of showing that we were lost was to veil the statues in church in purple cloth. Images of Christ and the saints are promises of heaven; the veil reminds us that we've lost sight of our goal. At Easter the veils come off and we see more clearly our destiny. You may want to do this: Cover your cross or other religious images with a simple purple cloth until Easter. (DP)

PRACTICE OF HOPE

THE LORD'S DAY. In Jesus' day, the sabbath — intended as a day of rest in the Lord — had become a burden of legalistic observances. Jesus meant to change that when he proclaimed that the Son of Man is lord of the sabbath. Jesus in effect became the sabbath.

Christians today often confuse sabbath and Sunday. Our Sunday is not the Christian sabbath. We rest in Christ always; Christ is our sabbath. Sunday is the foretaste of our promised life. Sunday is the first day of the week, the first day of creation, the day of light, the day of resurrection, the day of the Spirit, the day of baptism, the day of the church, the day of eucharist. Whenever we gather as the church on Sunday, we are celebrating our hope for a glorious future. (MP)

PRACTICE OF CHARITY

BREAD FIRST. Jesus knew that basic human necessities were more important than religious practices or property laws. The "survival rights" — food, water, clothing and shelter — are essential and nonnegotiable. Catholic social teaching has consistently held that "in their use of things people should regard the external goods they lawfully possess as not just their own but common to others as well, in the sense that they can benefit others as well as themselves (Vatican II). "Feed the people dying of hunger," argued the early church fathers, "because if you do not feed them you are killing them." Join Bread for the World, a Christian organization dedicated to eliminating hunger: 1100 Wayne Avenue, Suite 1000, Silver Spring MD 20910; 301-608-2400.

WEEKDAY READINGS (Mo) 2 Peter 1:2–7; (Tu) 3:12–15, 17–18; (We) Ash Wednesday, see box; (Th) Deuteronomy 30:15–20; (Fr) Isaiah 58:1–9; (Sa) 58:9–14

LENT

Wash away my sin.
Cleanse me from my guilt.

You see me for what I am,
a sinner before my birth.

You love those centered in truth;
teach me your hidden wisdom.
Wash me with fresh water,
wash me bright as snow.

Fill me with happy songs,
let the bones you bruised now dance.
Shut your eyes to my sin,
make my guilt disappear.

Save me, bring back my joy,
support me, strengthen my will.
Then will I teach your way
and sinners will turn to you.

Help me, stop my tears,
and I will sing your goodness.
Lord, give me words
and I will shout your praise.

When I offer a holocaust,
the gift does not please you.
So I offer my shattered spirit;
a changed heart you welcome.

—Psalm 51:7–11, 14–19

Like a gift we only want to want,
these forty days surround us once more
and you set about washing us, God.
Scrub and scour these stubborn ashes.
Separate what we are
from what we are not
and so bring on the lenten ordeal:
the prayer by day and night,
the fast that clears our sight,
the alms that set things right.
At the end, when we have lost again,
you alone make dry bones come together
and bruised bones dance
round the cross where sinners live
now and for ever.

—Prayer of the Season

READING I *Genesis 9:8–17*

God said to Noah and to his sons with him, "As for me, I am establishing my covenant with you and your descendants after you, and with every living creature that is with you, the birds, the domestic animals, and every animal of the earth with you, as many as came out of the ark. I establish my covenant with you, that never again shall all flesh be cut off by the waters of a flood, and never again shall there be a flood to destroy the earth." God said, "This is the sign of the covenant that I make between me and you and every living creature that is with you, for all future generations: I have set my bow in the clouds, and it shall be a sign of the covenant between me and the earth. When I bring clouds over the earth and the bow is seen in the clouds, I will remember my covenant that is between me and you and every living creature of all flesh; and the waters shall never again become a flood to destroy all flesh. When the bow is in the clouds, I will see it and remember the everlasting covenant between God and every living creature of all flesh that is on the earth." God said to Noah, "This is the sign of the covenant that I have established between me and all flesh that is on the earth."

READING II *1 Peter 3:18–22*

Christ also suffered for sins once for all, the righteous for the unrighteous, in order to bring you to God. He was put to death in the flesh, but made alive in the spirit, in which also he went and made a proclamation to the spirits in prison, who in former times did not obey, when God waited patiently in the days of Noah, during the building of the ark, in which a few, that is, eight persons, were saved through water. And baptism, which this prefigured, now saves you—not as a removal of dirt from the body, but as an appeal to God for a good conscience, through the resurrection of Jesus Christ, who has gone into heaven and is at the right hand of God, with angels, authorities, and powers made subject to him.

GOSPEL *Mark 1:9–15*

In those days Jesus came from Nazareth of Galilee and was baptized by John in the Jordan. And just as Jesus was coming up out of the water, he saw the heavens torn apart and the Spirit descending like a dove on him. And a voice came from heaven, "You are my Son, the Beloved; with you I am well pleased."

And the Spirit immediately drove Jesus out into the wilderness. He was in the wilderness forty days, tempted by Satan; and he was with the wild beasts; and the angels waited on him.

Now after John was arrested, Jesus came to Galilee, proclaiming the good news of God, and saying, "The time is fulfilled, and the dominion of God has come near; repent, and believe in the good news."

R E F L E C T I O N

We have entered into the Forty Days of Lent, and the readings for this First Sunday of Lent orient us for our journey toward Easter. These Forty Days of preparation go back to the early centuries of Christianity, when it was dangerous to become a Christian. In order to make sure the adults seeking initiation were ready and their commitment to the church was firm, there was a rigorous period of preparation and scrutiny before baptism.

When, in the Middle Ages, the initiation of adults into the faith declined and most Christians were baptized as infants, the core meaning of the Forty Days was gradually lost. In recent years, the church has restored the adult initiation process, the Rite of Christian Initiation of Adults (the "RCIA"), in many parishes. Interestingly, the readings used during Lent, with their echoes of initiation, did not change, even though the ritual elements had. Two things in today's readings help us to appreciate the initiation element of this season of Lent.

First, the appearance of Noah and the flood story in the first and second readings certainly make us think "water," which makes us think "baptism"! The establishment of a covenant between Noah and God anticipates the similar covenant that will come about between God and those to be initiated into our communities at Easter.

Second, the short gospel reading from Mark gives us a paradigm for "forty days," as Jesus, before going out to his ministry in the world, goes out to the wilderness where he is tested by Satan. For those of us already initiated, the gospel reminds us that "the dominion of God has come near," and we must "repent, and believe in the good news."

Filled with the message of these readings, let us support the people in our parishes who will be baptized and let us make ourselves physically and spiritually ready for the kingdom to come.

■ **What do you think about Jesus' forty days in the desert? Why would this have preceded his ministering in the world?**

■ **What is similar about your own experience of Lent and Jesus' preparation for his work?**

PRACTICE OF FAITH

ENTER THE WILDERNESS. In Genesis, Noah and the people and animals with him endured 40 days and nights of rain. In Mark, Jesus endured 40 days and nights in the wilderness. After the rain, God made a covenant with Noah that never again would the earth be punished in such a manner. After 40 days in the wilderness, Jesus was ready to proclaim the good news of God. He became an itinerant preacher bringing God's message to everyone. Both Noah and Jesus emerged from their 40-day periods of isolation — one from the confines of the ark, the other from the hostility of the wilderness — invigorated by the covenant and relationship they had with God.

God makes a similar covenant with us in baptism. Lent's 40 days afford us the opportunity to invigorate our relationship with God through prayer, fasting and almsgiving. Find ways this Lent to enter your own wilderness. (RG)

PRACTICE OF HOPE

REPENT AND TAKE HOPE. We hear today that the Spirit drove Jesus into the wilderness. It was a time of deliberation, of facing choices. Mark tells us that Jesus came out of the wilderness focused on the central message of his preaching: The kingdom of God has come near; repent and believe the good news.

Repentance is an essential practice of Lent. Throughout this season we hear calls to reflect on our lives, to evaluate our actions and thoughts and to repent. But repentance takes time; rarely can it happen during the frantic rush of everyday life. Take that time this Lent. (MP)

PRACTICE OF CHARITY

COME BACK TO ME. In the film, "Ulee's Gold," Peter Fonda plays Ulee, a man struggling to keep his family and family beekeeping business going. Life had dealt Ulee some hard blows — his beloved wife had died of cancer, their only son was imprisoned, their daughter-in-law was strung out on drugs and two grandchildren became his to raise. In quiet determination, Ulee's faith in and love for his family perseveres. Despite past wrongs by his family, Ulee's deep strength endures. This film is an excellent resource for Lent. Though we are sinners, we can reform our lives and turn back to the God who gives us strength and loves us unconditionally. Watch this touching film during your lenten journey to Easter.

WEEKDAY READINGS (Mo) Leviticus 19:1 – 2, 11 – 18; (Tu) Isaiah 55:10 –11; (We) Jonah 3:1 – 10; (Th) Esther 14:12, 14 – 16, 23 – 25; (Fr) Ezekiel 18:21 – 28; (Sa) Deuteronomy 26:16 – 19

READING I *Genesis 22:1–2, 9, 10–13, 15–18*

God tested Abraham and said to him, "Abraham!" And he said, "Here I am." God said, "Take your son, your only son Isaac, whom you love, and go to the land of Moriah, and offer him there as a burnt offering on one of the mountains that I shall show you." When they came to the place that God had shown him, Abraham built an altar there and laid the wood in order. He bound his son Isaac, and laid him on the altar, on top of the wood. Then Abraham reached out his hand and took the knife to kill his son. But the angel of the LORD called to him from heaven, and said, "Abraham, Abraham!" And he said, "Here I am." The angel said, "Do not lay your hand on the boy or do anything to him; for now I know that you fear God, since you have not withheld your son, your only son, from me." And Abraham looked up and saw a ram, caught in a thicket by its horns. Abraham went and took the ram and offered it up as a burnt offering instead of his son.

[Complete reading: Genesis 22:1–2, 9, 10–13, 15–18]
[Revised Common Lectionary: Genesis 17:1–7, 15–16]

READING II *Romans 8:31–34*

What then are we to say about these things? If God is for us, who is against us? The very Son of God was not withheld, but was given up for all of us; will God not along with the Son also give us everything else? Who will bring any charge against God's elect? It is God who justifies. Who is to condemn? It is Christ Jesus, who died, yes, who was raised, who is at the right hand of God, who indeed intercedes for us.

[Revised Common Lectionary: Romans 4:13–25]

GOSPEL *Mark 9:2–10*

Six days later, Jesus took with him Peter and James and John, and led them up a high mountain apart, by themselves. And he was transfigured before them, and his clothes became dazzling white, such as no one on earth could bleach them. And there appeared to them Elijah with Moses, who were talking with Jesus. Then Peter said to Jesus, "Rabbi, it is good for us to be here; let us make three dwellings, one for you, one for Moses, and one for Elijah." He did not know what to say, for they were terrified. Then a cloud overshadowed them, and from the cloud there came a voice, "This is my Son, the Beloved; listen to him!" Suddenly when they looked around, they saw no one with them any more, but only Jesus.

As they were coming down the mountain, Jesus ordered them to tell no one about what they had seen, until after the Son-of-Man had risen from the dead.

So they kept the matter to themselves, questioning what the rising from the dead meant.

[Revised Common Lectionary: Mark 8:31–38]

Monday, March 20, 2000

JOSEPH, HUSBAND OF MARY

2 Samuel 7:4–5, 12–14, 16 *I will make David's throne endure.*

Romans 4:13, 16–18, 22 *He is father of us all.*

Matthew 1:16, 18–21, 24 *Joseph, Son of David, fear not!*

Near the beginning of spring, as the earth is about to awaken from its sleep, we tell the story of Joseph. In the Book of Genesis, Joseph is the "dreamer of dreams." In the Gospel of Matthew, Joseph dreams of the coming kingdom. Then he awakens to find himself the father of the king.

Saturday, March 25, 2000

THE ANNUNCIATION OF THE LORD

Isaiah 7:10–14; 8:10 *A virgin will bear a child.*

Hebrews 10:4–10 *I come to do God's will.*

Luke 1:26–38 *Rejoice, O highly favored daughter!*

Because pregnancy outside of marriage was punishable by death, Mary's "yes" to the angel was an acceptance of death. But in this death, the risen Spirit conquers death. Mary's mortal body conceives the Immortal One. The paschal victory is won.

R E F L E C T I O N

The connection between the sacrifice of Isaac and the sacrifice of Jesus on the cross is very ancient in the Christian tradition. This story makes its way into the Lenten readings by anticipating the passion of Jesus as the sacrificed "only son" of the Father.

Although the second reading does not usually have such a deep theological relation to the other two readings, this Sunday it does: "The very Son of God," says Paul in his letter to the Romans, "was not withheld, but was given up for all of us."

The gospel narrative of the transfiguration of Jesus is juxtaposed with the sacrifice of Isaac, thereby foreshadowing the glorification of Jesus in his suffering. As the Gospel of Mark tells it, the transfiguration narrative gathers up the history of Israel with the mention of Moses and Elijah. Moses is the foundational liberator of the nation Israel, a great figure in ancient Hebrew tradition. His appearance here in the Lenten season should echo in our imaginations with his role in bringing the people through the desert to freedom; as we are in the "desert" of preparation, so we anticipate our own exodus from slavery to sin into the freedom of Easter.

Also making an appearance at the transfiguration is Elijah, a prophet from the ninth century before Christ — he figures primarily in the books of 1 and 2 Kings — who in the transfiguration scene represents the whole prophetic tradition. Elijah's challenges to the people and nation of Israel are much like the challenges that call us, as individuals and church, to reform. That Jesus is placed in such company is significant. Oddly, we find even in this magnificent scene Mark's Jesus again seeking secrecy: "Jesus ordered them to tell no one about what they had seen."

■ In the transfiguration the disciples become aware of the significance of Jesus in their lives. What moments of new awareness can you remember in your life as a Christian? Did these cause a kind of transfiguration for you? How are moments of conversion and transfiguration sustained in your life of faith?

PRACTICE OF FAITH

LETTING GO. In complete obedience to God, Abraham took the son of his old age, his only son, up to the mountain as God directed. When he was told to offer his son in sacrifice to God, he was heartbroken but began the preparation for the sacrifice as God had instructed him. Abraham, steadfast in his faith, trusted God and was willing to obey even when it seemingly meant the death of his only son by his own hand.

We have an example in Abraham. Faith may well involve making sacrifices, being prepared to surrender what we consider important in our lives. Are the things in your life that seem so important really that vital? What would hold you back from making the sacrifices you feel called to make? (RG)

PRACTICE OF HOPE

OUR HOPE OF GLORY. Christians take Abraham's willingness to sacrifice his son Isaac as a symbol of Jesus' passion and death. The transfiguration of Jesus also symbolizes his passion, death and resurrection. Just before this passage in Mark, Jesus predicted his passion and death. And now Jesus stands in dazzling white clothes, speaking with the prophets. The transfiguration was a vision that summed up the paschal mystery of Christ: through his passion and death, Christ would rise in brilliant glory. The transfiguration is also an insight into our own life and death. In our rite of baptism, all who come up from the water of the font put on a white robe, symbolic of our new life in Christ. (MP)

PRACTICE OF CHARITY

SEED OF FREEDOM. James R. Brockman concludes his book, *Romero: A Life,* with an interview that Archbishop Oscar Romero gave a couple of weeks before his assassination on March 24, 1980. The words proved to be prophetic. "Martyrdom is a grace of God that I do not believe I deserve. But if God accepts the sacrifice of my life, let my blood be a seed of freedom and the sign that hope will soon be a reality. Let my death, if it is accepted by God, be for my people's liberation and as a witness of hope in the future. You may say, if they succeed in killing me, that I pardon and bless those who do it. Would, indeed, that they might be convinced that they will waste their time. A bishop will die, but God's church, which is the people, will never perish." This week visit your library or bookstore to learn more about the life and thoughts of Archbishop Romero.

WEEKDAY READINGS (Mo) Joseph, see box; (Tu) Isaiah 1:10, 16 – 20; (We) Jeremiah 18:18 – 20; (Th) 17:5 – 10; (Fr) Genesis 37:3 – 4, 12 – 13, 17 – 28; (Sa) Annunciation, see box

READING I *Exodus 20:1–17*

God spoke all these words: I am the LORD your God, who brought you out of the land of Egypt, out of the house of slavery; you shall have no other gods before me. You shall not make for yourself an idol, whether in the form of anything that is in heaven above, or that is on the earth beneath, or that is in the water under the earth. You shall not bow down to them or worship them; for I the LORD your God am a jealous God, punishing children for the iniquity of parents, to the third and the fourth generation of those who reject me, but showing steadfast love to the thousandth generation of those who love me and keep my commandments.

You shall not make wrongful use of the name of the LORD your God, for the LORD will not acquit anyone who misuses the divine name.

Remember the sabbath day, and keep it holy. Six days you shall labor and do all your work. But the seventh day is a sabbath to the LORD your God; you shall not do any work — you, your son or your daughter, your male or female slave, your livestock, or the alien resident in your towns. For in six days the LORD made heaven and earth, the sea, and all that is in them, but rested the seventh day; therefore the LORD blessed the sabbath day and consecrated it.

Honor your father and your mother, so that your days may be long in the land that the LORD your God is giving you. You shall not murder. You shall not commit adultery. You shall not steal. You shall not bear false witness against your neighbor. You shall not covet your neighbor's house; you shall not covet your neighbor's wife, or male or female slave, or ox, or donkey, or anything that belongs to your neighbor.

READING II *1 Corinthians 1:18–25*

The message about the cross is foolishness to those who are perishing, but to us who are being saved it is the power of God. For it is written, "I will destroy the wisdom of the wise, and the discernment of the discerning I will thwart." Where is the one who is wise? Where is the scribe? Where is the debater of this age? Has not God made foolish the wisdom of the world?

For since, in the wisdom of God, the world did not know God through wisdom, God decided, through the foolishness of our proclamation, to save those who believe. For Jews demand signs and Greeks desire wisdom, but we proclaim Christ crucified, a stumbling block to Jews and foolishness to Gentiles, but to those who are the called, both Jews and Greeks, Christ the power of God and the wisdom of God. For God's foolishness is wiser than human wisdom, and God's weakness is stronger than human strength.

GOSPEL *John 2:13–25*

The Passover of the Jewish people was near, and Jesus went up to Jerusalem. In the temple he found people selling cattle, sheep, and doves, and the money changers seated at their tables. Making a whip of cords, he drove all of them out of the temple, both the sheep and the cattle. He also poured out the coins of the money changers and overturned their tables. He told those who were selling the doves, "Take these things out of here! Stop making my Father's house a marketplace!" His disciples remembered that it was written, "Zeal for your house will consume me." The Judeans then said to him, "What sign can you show us for doing this?" Jesus answered them, "Destroy this temple, and in three days I will raise it up." The Judeans then said, "This temple has been under construction for forty-six years, and will you raise it up in three days?" But Jesus was speaking of the temple of his body.

After he was raised from the dead, his disciples remembered that he had said this; and they believed the scripture and the word that Jesus had spoken.

When he was in Jerusalem during the Passover festival, many believed in his name because they saw the signs that he was doing. But Jesus on his part would not entrust himself to them, because he knew all people and needed no one to testify about anyone; for he himself knew what was in everyone.

R E F L E C T I O N

On this Sunday, we find the first of several readings from the Gospel of John that appear on Sundays during the long paschal period between Ash Wednesday and Pentecost Sunday. One of the reasons that the Gospel of John appears more often in the days related to Easter is because its understanding of who Jesus was (and who Christ is) is so magnificent, so transcendent, so lofty; this theology is appropriate for the celebration of exaltation that the church observes at this time of the year. The portrait of Jesus in the Gospel of John is more exalted than those in the Gospels of Matthew, Mark and Luke, and so it is proclaimed at this time of the year.

This scene, where Jesus overturns the tables of the money changers, is familiar because it occurs in all of the gospels, yet in the other gospels it appears much later in the span of Jesus' ministry. Here in John it appears very close to the beginning of the gospel, but in Matthew, Mark and Luke it happens close to the passion. The motive of the author of John's gospel is primarily theological.

From the beginning the author seeks to establish Jesus' place at the center of faith. By placing this scene at the beginning of the gospel, the author takes the temple in Jerusalem — the center of Jewish worship and life — and lowers its significance: The portrayal of the temple as a marketplace, rather than a place of prayer, anticipates this gospel's aim of making Jesus' own body the center of worship and life. The body of Jesus here in the Gospel of John replaces the temple of Jerusalem as the place of true holiness. Jesus himself is the instrument of this shift in understanding.

■ **In the New Testament we find the body of Jesus and our own bodies described as temples. In your own life reflect on what your body, your own flesh and blood, shares with the flesh and blood of the man Jesus of Nazareth. What does this mean for you?**

PRACTICE OF FAITH

SIMPLY LOVE. One would probably expect a set of rules intended to guide us as people of faith in living a good life to be complicated. We like to cover all the bases, plan for every possible situation. But sometimes complexity is a mask for a series of excuses and exceptions. Sometimes complexity needs to give way to simplicity. This is what we see in the Ten Commandments. God kept them simple. But despite their simplicity, we do seem to have difficulty keeping the commandments. Jesus taught even more simply: Love God; love one another. Try simply loving your way through Lent. (RG)

PRACTICE OF HOPE

CLEANSING OPENNESS. I received a religious goods catalog recently and was offended by the poor quality and tastelessness of many of the advertised items. Christians deserve well-made, tasteful objects for their personal prayer and public worship spaces.

Even good quality, in quantity, can be excessive. Our parish church had accumulated much decoration over the years, and when the inside of the building was cleared out for renovation, some parishioners were not sure whether they would like the newly undecorated space. It had a certain monastic spareness about it. Now, most have come to appreciate it. What contentment to rest the eyes, to have empty space and light, like ocean or prairie. The openness seems to cleanse our minds and hearts.

How many people do you think breathed a great sigh of relief when Jesus cleansed the temple? (MP)

PRACTICE OF CHARITY

FOOLS FOR CHRIST. Chris, a former seminarian, was like other young Christians who flocked to several new Catholic Worker Houses that sprouted around the Midwest during the 1970s. Energized by the peace movement, inspired by the spirit sweeping through the post – Vatican II church, and drawn to Dorothy Day's example of service, he dedicated himself to the ideals of the Catholic Worker. Whether it was preparing soup for lunch, writing the latest leaflet to be distributed at the nearby arsenal, or helping crabby Ben to the restroom, Chris lived his faith enthusiastically. More than 20 years later, Chris no longer lives in a Worker House. He is married, has teenage children and is paying a mortgage; but his life, his work and his family are centered around the active faith he embraced years ago. What were the ideals of your youth? Can you embrace them still?

WEEKDAY READINGS (Mo) 2 Kings 5:1 – 15; (Tu) Daniel 3:25, 34 – 43; (We) Deuteronomy 4:1, 5 – 9; (Th) Jeremiah 7:23 – 28; (Fr) Hosea 14:2 – 10; (Sa) 6:1 – 6

READING I — *Exodus 17:2–7*

The people quarreled with Moses, and said, "Give us water to drink." Moses said to them, "Why do you quarrel with me? Why do you test the LORD?" But the people thirsted there for water; and the people complained against Moses and said, "Why did you bring us out of Egypt, to kill us and our children and livestock with thirst?"

So Moses cried out to the LORD, "What shall I do with this people? They are almost ready to stone me." The LORD said to Moses, "Go on ahead of the people, and take some of the elders of Israel with you; take in your hand the staff with which you struck the Nile, and go. I will be standing there in front of you on the rock at Horeb. Strike the rock, and water will come out of it, so that the people may drink."

Moses did so, in the sight of the elders of Israel. He called the place Massah and Meribah, because the Israelites quarreled and tested the LORD, saying, "Is the LORD among us or not?"

[Complete reading: Exodus 17:1–7]

READING II — *Romans 5:1–2, 6–8*

Since we are justified by faith, we have peace with God through our Lord Jesus Christ, through whom we have obtained access to this grace in which we stand.

For while we were still weak, at the right time Christ died for the ungodly. Indeed, rarely will anyone die for a righteous person—though perhaps for a good person someone might actually dare to die. But it is proof of God's own love for us in that while we still were sinners Christ died for us.

[Revised Common Lectionary: Romans 5:1–11]

GOSPEL — *John 4:5–10, 14–26, 39, 40–42*

Jesus came to a Samaritan city called Sychar, near the plot of ground that Jacob had given to his son Joseph. Jacob's well was there, and Jesus, tired out by his journey, was sitting by the well. It was about noon.

A Samaritan woman came to draw water, and Jesus said to her, "Give me a drink." (His disciples had gone to the city to buy food.) The Samaritan woman said to him, "How is it that you, a Jewish man, ask a drink of me, a woman of Samaria?" (Jewish people do not share things in common with Samaritans.) Jesus answered her, "If you knew the gift of God, and who it is that is saying to you, 'Give me a drink,' you would have asked him, and he would have given you living water. The water that I will give will become in them a spring of water gushing up to eternal life." The woman said to Jesus, "Sir, give me this water, so that I may never be thirsty or have to keep coming here to draw water."

Jesus said to her, "Go, call your husband, and come back." The woman answered him, "I have no husband." Jesus said to her, "You are right in saying, 'I have no husband'; for you have had five husbands, and the one you have now is not your husband. What you have said is true!" The woman said to Jesus, "Sir, I see that you are a prophet. Our ancestors worshiped on this mountain, but you say that the place where people must worship is in Jerusalem."

Jesus said to her, "Woman, believe me, the hour is coming when you will worship the Father neither on this mountain nor in Jerusalem. You worship what you do not know; we worship what we know, for salvation is from the Jewish people. But the hour is coming, and is now here, when the true worshipers will worship the Father in spirit and truth, for such worshipers the Father seeks. God is spirit, and those who worship God must worship in spirit and truth." The woman said to him, "I know that Messiah is coming" (who is called Christ). "When he comes, he will proclaim all things to us." Jesus said to her, "Here I am, the one who is speaking to you."

Many Samaritans from that city believed in Jesus because of the woman's testimony. They asked him to stay with them; and Jesus stayed there two days. And many more believed because of his word. They said to the woman, "It is no longer because of what you said that we believe, for we have heard for ourselves, and we know that this is truly the Savior of the world."

[Complete reading: John 4:5–42]

R E F L E C T I O N

Even though this is Year B of the three-year cycle of lectionary readings (the year of the Gospel of Mark), many more of the readings proclaimed between now and Pentecost come from the Gospel of John than from the Gospel of Mark. On this Sunday we find the first of the readings from John. One of the reasons that the Gospel of John appears in the days related to Easter is because its understanding of who Jesus was (and who Christ is) is so magnificent, so transcendent, so lofty. The theology of the Gospel of John is far more exalted than that of Matthew, Mark or Luke. Today's narrative of the woman at the well is key in the theology of your parish's preparation for the initiations that will happen at Easter.

The woman at the well — tradition has named her "Photina," a word derived from the Greek word *"phos,"* meaning light — is a model for the candidates for initiation. In the long passage proclaimed in today's liturgy, the woman moves from misunderstanding and confusion to inquiry and gradually into the depths of exploration of the mystery who is Christ. Eventually the woman herself becomes the bearer of the good news.

The beginning of the Gospel of John, in its original Greek, identifies Jesus as the "word": "In the beginning was the word" (1:1). It does so using the Greek word *logos.* When the gospel reading for today ends with the sentence, "Many Samaritans believed because of the woman's testimony," the same term, *logos,* is used for "testimony" as was used to identify Jesus at the gospel's beginning. In effect this makes the woman herself a kind of evangelist. Her *logos* ("testimony") is what brings the *logos* ("word") of the Father to the Samaritans and into the world. She, as a bearer of the word of God to those who had not received it, is also a model for us, the already baptized. By word and by the testimony of our lives, we bring ourselves as words *(logoi)* of God to others.

■ **Like the Samaritan woman, we are called to bring the *logos* of God, Jesus Christ, to others and to the world. How does the celebration of the eucharist strengthen your ability to be a bearer of the word of God?**

IN OUR MIDST. "Is the Lord in our midst or not?" The Israelites in today's passage from Exodus had received so much from God, yet demanded more and were angry with God because they were suffering on their long journey. It is part of our human nature that when all is going well, we take it for granted; it does not always come to mind to thank God for the blessings of good health, employment and success. How easily we run to God in adversity. But like the Israelites, we can become angry with God when our problems seem to stay with us. But God is always here among us, whether we are aware of it or not. Spend some time this week examining your problems and needs. See if you can discern God's presence even in your needs. (RG)

LIVING WATER. Today's gospel reading has been long used by the church during Lent as a way of instructing catechumens on the meaning of faith and baptism. When you hear this story about Jesus' encounter with the Samaritan woman at Jacob's well, their dialogue about water and her growth into discipleship, savor it as you savor good water. But as the Samaritan woman found out, the living water provided by Jesus cannot be contained. It needs to flow freely to others. Share with someone this week the living water you have tasted. (MP)

LIVING DOWNSTREAM. In Sandra Steingraber's book, *Living Downstream,* we learn how years of water runoff from farm fields covered with pesticides and from city lots contaminated with industrial waste are poisoning the waters of the central Illinois River basin. Disturbingly, a sharp increase in many forms of cancer has been found. This frightening reality is not unique to this area, to the Midwest or the United States. It is a worldwide threat. But before we can tackle something globally, we must act locally. The Nature Conservancy is an organization that works diligently to improve water, land and air quality throughout the United States. Call 1-800-628-6860 to find the local group nearest you. Get involved! "Whatever befalls the earth, befalls the sons and daughters of the earth. We did not weave the web of life; we are merely a strand in it. Whatever we do to the web, we do to ourselves."— Chief Seattle

WEEKDAY READINGS (Mo) 2 Kings 5:1 – 15; (Tu) Daniel 3:25, 34 – 43; (We) Deuteronomy 4:1, 5 – 9; (Th) Jeremiah 7:23 – 28; (Fr) Hosea 14:2 – 10; (Sa) 6:1 – 6

READING I *2 Chronicles 36:14–16, 19–23*

All the leading priests and the people also were exceedingly unfaithful, following all the abominations of the nations; and they polluted the house of the LORD that had been consecrated in Jerusalem. The LORD, the God of their ancestors, persistently sent messengers to them, because the LORD had compassion on the chosen people and on the sacred house; but they kept mocking the messengers of God, despising God's words, and scoffing at the prophets, until the wrath of the LORD against the chosen people became so great that there was no remedy.

They burned the house of God, broke down the wall of Jerusalem, burned all its palaces with fire, and destroyed all its precious vessels. The king took into exile in Babylon those who had escaped from the sword, and they became servants to him and to his sons until the establishment of the kingdom of Persia, to fulfill the word of the LORD by the mouth of Jeremiah, until the land had made up for its sabbaths. All the days that it lay desolate it kept sabbath, to fulfill seventy years. In the first year of King Cyrus of Persia, in fulfillment of the word of the LORD spoken by Jeremiah, the LORD stirred up the spirit of King Cyrus of Persia so that he sent a herald throughout all his kingdom and also declared in a written edict: "Thus says King Cyrus of Persia: The LORD, the God of heaven, has given me all the kingdoms of the earth, and has charged me to build a house for God at Jerusalem, which is in Judah. Those among you who are of God's people, may the LORD their God be with them! Let them go up."

[Revised Common Lectionary: Numbers 21:4–9]

READING II *Ephesians 2:1–10*

You were dead through the trespasses and sins in which you once lived, following the course of this world, following the ruler of the power of the air, the spirit that is now at work among those who are disobedient. All of us once lived among them in the passions of our flesh, following the desires of flesh and senses, and we were by nature children of wrath, like everyone else. But God, who is rich in mercy, out of the great love with which God loved us even when we were dead through our trespasses, made us alive together with Christ—by grace you have been saved. With Christ God raised us up and enthroned us in the heavenly places in Christ Jesus, so that in the ages to come might be shown the immeasurable riches of God's grace in kindness toward us in Christ Jesus. For by grace you have been saved through faith, and this is not your own doing; it is the gift of God—not the result of works, so that no one may boast. For we are what God has made us, created in Christ Jesus for good works, which God prepared beforehand to be our way of life.

GOSPEL *John 3:14–21*

Jesus said: "Just as Moses lifted up the serpent in the wilderness, so must the Son-of-Man be lifted up, that whoever believes in him may have eternal life. For God loved the world in this way, that God gave the Son, the only begotten one, so that everyone who believes in him may not perish but may have eternal life.

"Indeed, God did not send the Son into the world to condemn the world, but in order that the world might be saved through him. Those who believe in him are not condemned; but those who do not believe are condemned already, because they have not believed in the name of the only Son of God. And this is the judgment, that the light has come into the world, and people loved darkness rather than light because their deeds were evil. For all who do evil hate the light and do not come to the light, so that their deeds may not be exposed. But those who do what is true come to the light, so that it may be clearly seen that their deeds have been done in God."

R E F L E C T I O N

I remember walking down the hall on the third floor of a hospital a few years ago and seeing Room 316. Someone had taken a piece of chalk, crossed out "Room" and written "John"; they had also inserted a colon between the 3 and the 1, thereby making the door read "John 3:16," among the most popular and well-known verses of the Bible: "For God so loved the world that he gave his only Son, that whosoever believes in him should not perish but have eternal life" (King James Version).

The symbol at the heart of today's gospel reading is the serpent raised up by Moses in the wilderness. Perhaps you have seen this symbol on Medic-Alert jewelry, which people with chronic illnesses wear on their wrists or around their necks. It comes originally from the Hebrew scriptures, from Numbers 21:4–9, in which the Israelites are being bitten by poisonous snakes and dying as a result. The Lord instructs Moses to set a snake up on a pole, so that "everyone who is bitten shall look at it and live" (21:8).

The author of the Gospel of John takes the same image and applies it to Jesus, who on the cross is like the snake on the pole. All who look at Christ on the cross, according to this Johannine theology, shall live, shall have eternal life.

During this season of Lent the catechumens are our example of faith; they too seek the new life that is gained in the cross. In turn, the support and encouragement of the community, of the parish, is important in their formation, so that the candidates not lose heart in the face of the rigors of preparation and of ordinary life in the Christian faith.

■ **We, the already baptized, have experienced the presence of Christ: We have seen the serpent that, raised up on the cross for all to see, brings new life. Why do you think the church proclaims this image of Christ as the serpent on the pole during Lent? How does it work for our imaginations at this time?**

PRACTICE OF FAITH

BE GENEROUS. God will not be outdone in generosity. This is a truth we understand more and more as we grow in faith and move closer to God, whose generosity surrounds us even in our distress. We suffer with our families and friends through death, illness and the heartbreak of someone dear to us choosing a path of self-destruction. We question where God's generosity is when we need it. The fact that we survive these crises is a blessing. That we survive them, grow through the experience and gain a deeper understanding of God's love for us, is generous blessing. Parents teach their children to be generous first with family members, then neighbors, friends, classmates, co-workers and the world at large. Ask your child who he or she thinks is the most generous person they know and why. Does this person give time, money, talent, emotional or physical support without thought of reward? If we can be generous to each other, try to imagine the scope of God's generosity to us. (RG)

PRACTICE OF HOPE

DARKNESS TO LIGHT. Nicodemus made quite an effort to ask questions of Jesus, coming by night either because of fear or because his only free time was after dark. How many inquiry classes and scripture study meetings are held in the dark of the evening! Our parish sometimes has students from the nearby university inquire about the faith. One year, a student from China joined the RCIA. She had an evening class at the university, and would then rush to the parish, often arriving late. We would listen for her knock at the door. After coming so often in darkness, she was baptized in the glorious light of Easter. (MP)

PRACTICE OF CHARITY

LOOK BEYOND. World Health Day, celebrated on April 7, is an opportunity for us to look beyond the health problems of our local and national communities to those that face others around the globe. Heart disease, cancer and diabetes plague millions, but AIDS is wiping out entire communities. It is estimated that two American teens become infected with HIV every hour. Around the world, 8,500 new infections occur each day. These staggering statistics are projected to spiral upward. From whence shall come our help and hope? From you! Get involved in your own community's HIV/AIDS education efforts.

WEEKDAY READINGS (Mo) Isaiah 65:17–21; (Tu) Ezekiel 47:1–9, 12; (We) Isaiah 49:8–15; (Th) Exodus 32:7–14; (Fr) Wisdom 2:1, 12–22; (Sa) Jeremiah 11:18–20

READING I *1 Samuel 16:1, 5–7, 10–13*

The LORD said to Samuel, "I will send you to Jesse the Bethlehemite, for I have provided for myself a king among his sons." And Samuel sanctified Jesse and his sons and invited them to the sacrifice.

When they came, Samuel looked on Eliab and thought, "Surely the LORD's anointed is now before the LORD." But the LORD said to Samuel, "Do not look on his appearance or on the height of his stature, because I have rejected him; for the LORD does not see as mortals see; they look on the outward appearance, but the LORD looks on the heart." Jesse made seven of his sons pass before Samuel, and Samuel said to Jesse, "The LORD has not chosen any of these."

Samuel said to Jesse, "Are all your sons here?" And he said, "There remains yet the youngest, but he is keeping the sheep." And Samuel said to Jesse, "Send and bring him; for we will not sit down until he comes here." Jesse sent and brought him in. Now he was ruddy, and had beautiful eyes, and was handsome. The LORD said, "Rise and anoint him; for this is the one." Then Samuel took the horn of oil, and anointed him in the presence of his brothers; and the spirit of the LORD came mightily upon David from that day forward. Samuel then set out and went to Ramah.

[Revised Common Lectionary: 1 Samuel 16:1–13]

READING II *Ephesians 5:8–14*

Once you were darkness, but now in the Lord you are light. Live as children of light—for the fruit of the light is found in all that is good and right and true. Try to find out what is pleasing to the Lord. Take no part in the unfruitful works of darkness, but instead expose them. For it is shameful even to mention what such people do secretly; but everything exposed by the light becomes visible, for everything that becomes visible is light.

Therefore it says, "Sleeper, awake! Rise from the dead, and Christ will shine on you."

GOSPEL *John 9:1, 6–17, 34–38*

As Jesus walked along, he saw a man blind from birth. Jesus spat on the ground and made mud with the saliva and spread the mud on the man's eyes, saying to him, "Go, wash in the pool of Siloam" (which means Sent). Then he went and washed and came back able to see.

The neighbors and those who had seen him before as a beggar began to ask, "Is this not the man who used to sit and beg?" Some were saying, "It is he." Others were saying, "No, but it is someone like him." He kept saying, "I am the man." But they kept asking him, "Then how were your eyes opened?" He answered, "The man called Jesus made mud, spread it on my eyes, and said to me, 'Go to Siloam and wash.' Then I went and washed and received my sight." They said to him, "Where is he?" He said, "I do not know."

They brought to the Pharisees the man who had formerly been blind. Now it was a sabbath day when Jesus made the mud and opened his eyes. Then the Pharisees also began to ask him how he had received his sight. He said to them, "He put mud on my eyes. Then I washed, and now I see." Some of the Pharisees said, "This man is not from God, for he does not observe the sabbath." But others said, "How can a man who is a sinner perform such signs?" And they were divided. So they said again to the blind man, "What do you say about him? It was your eyes he opened." He said, "He is a prophet."

They answered him, "You were born entirely in sins, and are you trying to teach us?" And they drove him out.

Jesus heard that they had driven him out, and when he found him, he said, "Do you believe in the Son-of-Man?" He answered, "And who is he, sir? Tell me, so that I may believe in him." Jesus said to him, "You have seen him, and he is the one speaking with you." He said, "Lord, I believe." And he worshiped Jesus.

[Complete reading: John 9:1–41]

R E F L E C T I O N

Like much of John's gospel, the story of the man born blind is a long, detailed and nuanced narrative of a journey of faith. Here both the blind man and the disciples are changed, for the disciples ask Jesus, "Who sinned, this man or his parents, that he was born blind?" (9:2).

Jesus' answer reveals clearly that the man's disability is not a result of his or his parents' sin (see 9:3), but many Christians still attribute illness or misfortune to personal morality. While faith and incorporation into the church do indeed change the life of a believer, they are not assurances of health, good fortune or long life. Like Jesus himself, Christians suffer and die. The example of the life of Jesus makes it clear to us that sinlessness and righteousness do not exempt one from this life's inevitable difficulties or end.

These stories from John have also made their way into the liturgies of the Sundays of Lent because of water's baptismal associations. Those preparing for initiation should be encouraged by the simplicity of the witness of the formerly blind man. Asked, "How were your eyes opened?" he responds, "I went and washed and received my sight" (9:11); later, "I washed, and now I see" (9:15); finally, "One thing I do know, that though I was blind, now I see" (9:25). We, the already baptized, can also learn from his witness that the best answers to others' inquiries about our Christian faith are the most honest and the simplest. People become Christian not because of carefully worded doctrine or even beautiful churches, but rather from the witness of other peoples' lives of faith.

■ **If catechumens were to ask you, "Why did you become a Christian?" what would you say? If they asked, "And why do you continue to practice the faith?" What would you say? Why is your faith important to you? How does it animate your life and your vocation?**

■ **What do you make of the connection some people draw between illness or misfortune and personal morality? What was Jesus' response to such a way of thinking?**

PRACTICE OF FAITH

LIGHT AND DARKNESS. If you were to ask a child the difference between light and darkness they might reply: You can see when it's light; when it's dark you can't. God's meanings of light and darkness are as simple as a child's and as straightforward as the lesson Jesus was teaching. Jesus wanted his hearers to learn that while they may be subject to physical darkness, they can still know the light of faith. And that someone can see the physical world does not mean they are in the light.

The learned people of Jesus' day did not quite understand. They failed to see the light and the sight Jesus offered. What light do you walk by? Where might you be blind even when you think you see? (RG)

PRACTICE OF HOPE

STRENGTH IN ANOINTING. The reading from Samuel and the gospel reading from John contain a similar reference: There is an anointing in each one. David was anointed king to lead his people in justice, and the blind man was anointed by Jesus with mud so that he might see. In a similar spirit, our newly baptized are anointed with the perfumed oil known as chrism, sealing their status as disciples of Christ. Think of these and other religious anointings you know of — for example, the anointing of the sick. What can you say about the meaning of our anointings to someone who asks? How would you tell another about the strengthening that anointing gives? (MP)

PRACTICE OF CHARITY

LIGHT, NOT DARKNESS. Father Roy Bourgeois is exposing the "unfruitful works of darkness." His opposition to the U.S. Army School of the Americas in Fort Benning, Georgia, has landed him behind prison bars for three years. Research conducted by Roy and others has led to allegations that many of the atrocities against civilians in Latin America have been planned and conducted by graduates of the school. Some of the most infamous cases include the assassination of Oscar Romero, the rape and murder of four churchwomen in El Salvador in 1980 and the disappearances of political activists in Honduras and Guatemala. As a Maryknoll missionary who served in South and Central America, Roy knows firsthand the suffering created by economic and political oppression. Legislation to cut school funding has repeatedly failed. Contact your members of Congress and urge them to close the School of the Americas.

WEEKDAY READINGS (Mo) Isaiah 65:17 – 21; (Tu) Ezekiel 47:1 – 9, 12; (We) Isaiah 49:8 – 15; (Th) Exodus 32:7 – 14; (Fr) Wisdom 2:1, 12 – 22; (Sa) Jeremiah 11:18 – 20

READING I *Jeremiah 31:31–34*

The days are surely coming, says the LORD, when I will make a new covenant with the house of Israel and the house of Judah. It will not be like the covenant that I made with their ancestors when I took them by the hand to bring them out of the land of Egypt—a covenant that they broke, though I was married to them, says the LORD.

But this is the covenant that I will make with the house of Israel after those days, says the LORD: I will put my law within them, and I will write it on their hearts; and I will be their God, and they shall be my people. No longer shall they teach one another, or say to each other, "Know the LORD," for they shall all know me, from the least of them to the greatest, says the LORD; for I will forgive their iniquity, and remember their sin no more.

READING II *Hebrews 5:5–10*

Christ did not glorify himself in becoming a high priest, but was appointed by the one who said to him, "You are my Son, today I have begotten you"; as God says also in another place, "You are a priest forever, according to the order of Melchizedek." In the days of his flesh, Jesus offered up prayers and supplications, with loud cries and tears, to the one who was able to save him from death, and he was heard because of his reverent submission. Although he was a Son, he learned obedience through what he suffered; and having been made perfect, he became the source of eternal salvation for all who obey him, having been designated by God a high priest according to the order of Melchizedek.

GOSPEL *John 12:20–33*

Now among those who went up to worship at the festival were some Greeks. They came to Philip, who was from Bethsaida in Galilee, and said to him, "Sir, we wish to see Jesus." Philip went and told Andrew; then Andrew and Philip went and told Jesus. Jesus answered them, "The hour has come for the Son-of-Man to be glorified. Very truly, I tell you, unless a grain of wheat falls into the earth and dies, it remains just a single grain; but if it dies, it bears much fruit. Those who love their life lose it, and those who hate their life in this world will keep it for eternal life. Whoever serves me must follow me, and where I am, there will my servant be also. Whoever serves me, the Father will honor.

"Now my soul is troubled. And what should I say—'Father, save me from this hour'? No, it is for this reason that I have come to this hour. Father, glorify your name." Then a voice came from heaven, "I have glorified it, and I will glorify it again." The crowd standing there heard it and said that it was thunder. Others said, "An angel has spoken to him." Jesus answered, "This voice has come for your sake, not for mine. Now is the judgment of this world; now the ruler of this world will be driven out. And I, when I am lifted up from the earth, will draw all people to myself." Jesus said this to indicate the kind of death he was to die.

REFLECTION

The prophet Jeremiah, so unique in his message to the Hebrew people in the seventh century before the birth of Jesus and to us at the start of this millennium, speaks in the first reading of the "new covenant." The vocation of Jeremiah was to bring the people to a new and deeper awareness of the presence of God. As we know from the stories of the Hebrew Bible, the historical disasters and misfortunes of the nation Israel led to moments of insecurity, griping, pleading and seeking direction.

The prophets were those who, like Jeremiah, were able to discern the presence and will of God through the shifting tides of the nation's life. The prophet gave the people hope: "I will make a new covenant with the house of Israel and the house of Judah." And he was as realistic in describing the providence of the Lord, "I took them by the hand to bring them out of the land of Egypt," as he was sober in highlighting the wrong ways of the people, "for they broke the covenant."

We who observe God's law in a new age, at the dawn of the millennium, are called to be like both Jeremiah — a prophet attentive to God's presence and courageous in proclaiming it to others — and like the people, able to withstand an indictment of our wrong ways, to take steps to hear again the word of God and make a new covenant in the context of our worshiping community. For, says the Lord, more than 2500 years ago and to us today, "I will be their God and they will be my people." In the gospel Jesus similarly encourages us, "And I, when I am lifted up, will draw all people to myself."

■ **The call of God for you might be to become more involved, if even in just a small way, in your parish community. Consider assisting with the preparation of the catechumens in your parish. See if a new widow or widower in your neighborhood might want to ride to church with you or spend some time with you during the week.**

PRACTICE OF FAITH

APOLOGY ACCEPTED. The Sunday readings during Lent point out the many times the Israelites raged against the Lord and broke the covenant. Each time God was not only willing, but eager, to restore the relationship. Like a parent whose child throws a tantrum and stamps out of the house in a rage, God is anxious for us to return.

Doing penance voluntarily can be very satisfying. One of our children, on seeing a sibling start a fight with a younger sister, admonished, "Oh! Now you've made God cry. Hurry and say you're sorry and don't do that again." To grow in awareness of our faults, offer apologies when needed and learn not to make the same mistakes over and over — this is the opportunity Lent provides us. (RG)

PRACTICE OF HOPE

DEATH AND HOPE. In today's gospel, the Greeks wanting to see Jesus were like a signal to Jesus that his mission would flourish throughout the world, but that he would first need to die. The forces against Jesus were growing stronger and he here predicts his passion and death for the third time.

It is unlikely that any of us will pretend to the dimensions of the passion and death that Jesus endured. But we are his followers and we should spend time discerning the meaning of our own death, as difficult as it may be to think about. Like Jesus, we must prepare ourselves and develop an obedient attitude, trusting in God that we will be glorified. How can the story of the grain of wheat nourish your hope? (MP)

PRACTICE OF CHARITY

GET INVOLVED. Speaking out when confronted with obvious injustice can be dangerous business. Looking the other way and not wanting to get involved are responses we can all relate to. It can be convenient to come up with a good excuse or convince ourselves that our rationalizations have merit. "That's a problem, but not my problem!" "Let someone else deal with it!" "What's this going to cost me?" But there are those who take notice, speak up, call for justice and suffer the consequences for their participation. Learn more about Amnesty International this week: 322 Eighth Ave., New York NY 10001. Consider joining. If you are already a member, write that letter you have been postponing.

WEEKDAY READINGS (Mo) Daniel 13:1 – 9, 15 – 62; (Tu) Numbers 21:4 – 9; (We) Daniel 3:14 – 20, 91 – 92, 95; (Th) Genesis 17:3 – 9; (Fr) Jeremiah 20:10 – 13; (Sa) Ezekiel 37:21 – 28

READING I *Ezekiel 37:12 – 14*

Thus says the Lord GOD: I am going to open your graves, and bring you up from your graves, O my people; and I will bring you back to the land of Israel. And you shall know that I am the LORD, when I open your graves, and bring you up from your graves, O my people. I will put my spirit within you, and you shall live, and I will place you on your own soil; then you shall know that I, the LORD, have spoken and will act, says the LORD.
[*Revised Common Lectionary: Ezekiel 37:1 – 14*]

READING II *Romans 8:6 – 11*

To set the mind on the flesh is death, but to set the mind on the Spirit is life and peace. For this reason the mind that is set on the flesh is hostile to God; it doesn't submit to God's law — indeed it cannot, and those who are in the flesh cannot please God. But you are not in the flesh; you are in the Spirit, since the Spirit of God dwells in you. Anyone who does not have the Spirit of Christ does not belong to Christ. But if Christ is in you, though the body is dead because of sin, the Spirit is life because of righteousness. If the Spirit of the one who raised Jesus from the dead dwells in you, the one who raised Christ from the dead will give life to your mortal bodies also through this Spirit dwelling in you.

GOSPEL *John 11:3 – 7, 17, 20 – 27, 33 – 45*

Mary and Martha sent a message to Jesus, "Lord, he whom you love is ill." But when Jesus heard it, he said, "This illness does not lead to death; rather it is for God's glory, so that the Son of God may be glorified through it." Accordingly, though Jesus loved Martha and her sister and Lazarus, after having heard that Lazarus was ill, he stayed two days longer in the place where he was.

Then after this he said to the disciples, "Let us go to Judea again."

When Jesus arrived, he found that Lazarus had already been in the tomb four days.

When Martha heard that Jesus was coming, she went and met him, while Mary stayed at home. Martha said to Jesus, "Lord, if you had been here, my brother would not have died. But even now I know that whatever you ask from God, God will give you." Jesus said to her, "Your brother will rise again." Martha said to him, "I know that he will rise again in the resurrection on the last day." Jesus said to her, "I am the resurrection and the life. Those who believe in me, even though they die, will live, and everyone who lives and believes in me will never die. Do you believe this?" She said to him, "Yes, Lord, I believe that you are the Messiah, the Son of God, the one coming into the world."

Jesus was greatly disturbed in spirit and deeply moved. He said, "Where have you laid him?" They said to him, "Lord, come and see." Jesus began to weep. So the Judeans said, "See how he loved him!" But some of them said, "Could not the one who opened the eyes of the blind man have kept this man from dying?"

Then Jesus, again greatly disturbed, came to the tomb. It was a cave, and a stone was lying against it. Jesus said, "Take away the stone." Martha, the sister of the dead man, said to him, "Lord, already there is a stench because he has been dead four days." Jesus said to her, "Did I not tell you that if you believed, you would see the glory of God?"

So they took away the stone. And Jesus looked upward and said, "Father, I thank you for having heard me. I knew that you always hear me, but I have said this for the sake of the crowd standing here, so that they may believe that you sent me." When Jesus had said this, he cried with a loud voice, "Lazarus, come out!" The dead man came out, his hands and feet bound with strips of cloth, and his face wrapped in a cloth. Jesus said to them, "Unbind him, and let him go."

Many of the Judeans therefore, who had come with Mary and had seen what Jesus did, believed in him.
[*Complete reading: John 11:1 – 45*]

R E F L E C T I O N

When I was just out of college, I lived in an apartment in Philadelphia one floor below the apartment of a man younger than I, who worked as an auto mechanic. One day he wired a rifle to the radiator and shot himself to death. No one heard the shot and he did not have a phone. After some time, with his apartment thermostat set at 80° for weeks, the smell was so horrible that I broke into his place and found his darkened, decomposing corpse on the living room floor. Whenever I hear Martha's words in this Lenten gospel narrative proclaimed two Sundays before the Triduum — "Lord, already there is a stench because he has been dead four days" — I remember the mechanic and am shaken by the tangibility of this long scene of the Gospel of John.

The raising of Lazarus is truly an incredible story. The details provided by the evangelist, and the closeknit family at the heart of the narrative — the two sisters and their brother, all loved deeply by Jesus — draw us in, making us imagine that we ourselves are there, watching this unbelievable event take place.

Of the many stories of healing and raising from the dead in the ministry of Jesus and his disciples, none is simultaneously so grim and so hope-filled. Perhaps that is why, since the days of the early church, this reading has been part of the lectionary's sequence of readings for those to be baptized.

■ **How does your experience of faith and of the church's pastoral care at the time of death help you accept the inevitability of your own death? What reasons could there be that this story of the raising of Lazarus has, for centuries and centuries, been part of the liturgy for those to be baptized?**

PRACTICE OF FAITH

LIFE, NOT DEATH. We experience death in many ways. Physical death is the way of which we are most aware. The event is often abrupt and has an immediate effect on our relationship with the deceased. Other deaths are slower and more subtle, such as the death of a spirit that leads a believer to reject God, the death of a mind that leads to despair, the death of love that leads to the destruction of personal relationships. Yet God tells us that if we believe, we shall live. Death will have no ultimate power over us. Even when we sin, God's life is in us and we live as long as our faith is alive. It is when sin becomes our life that death takes hold of us. Where in your life does it feel as if something is missing? What part of your life needs the spirit of Christ to bring it out of the darkness of death and into life? (RG)

PRACTICE OF HOPE

HOPE IN TIME OF NEED. Several years ago, one of our children studied in France. She visited Paris and went to the church of Saint Severin on the fifth Sunday of Lent, later sending us a translation of the homily.

"O, my people, I will bring you out of your graves!" the homilist began. There was a workers' strike at the time and the pastor told the people that Ezekiel's prophecy was also for them: The Lord would open their graves, and the spirit of the Lord would be within them. He urged the parishioners to help each other during the work stoppage despite their own deprivations.

This homily, across countries, touched us deeply. It reminded us how God speaks to us in all places and times in the scriptures. When has God's word of hope called you out of the grave? (MP)

PRACTICE OF CHARITY

GOING HOME. Only four people attended Ray Ater's burial. Ray, a homeless man who suffered from emphysema and alcholism, had died horribly. While he was huddled in an alley asleep, two teens toppled a trash dumpster onto him, crushing him to death. When arrested, they claimed they were only trying to trap "the old drunk" under the open dumpster — it was a prank, a joke. As a veteran of World War II, Ray was buried in a nearby national cemetery. The retired priest, two mortuary workers and I had no trouble carrying Ray's body from the hearse to the grave. As the priest read the passage about the raising of Lazarus, I found comfort in the phrase: "Everyone who lives and believes in me will never die." Ray had finally found his home.

WEEKDAY READINGS (Mo) Daniel 13:1 – 9, 15 – 62; (Tu) Numbers 21:4 – 9; (We) Daniel 3:14 – 20, 91 – 92, 95; (Th) Genesis 17:3 – 9; (Fr) Jeremiah 20:10 – 13; (Sa) Ezekiel 37:21 – 28

READING I *Isaiah 50:4–9*

The Lord GOD has given me the tongue of a teacher,
    that I may know how to sustain the weary
    with a word.
Morning by morning the Lord GOD wakens—
    wakens my ear to listen as those who are taught.
The Lord GOD has opened my ear,
    and I was not rebellious,
    I did not turn backward.
I gave my back to those who struck me,
    and my cheeks to those who pulled out the beard;
I did not hide my face from insult and spitting.

The Lord GOD helps me;
    therefore I have not been disgraced;
therefore I have set my face like flint,
    and I know that I shall not be put to shame;
    the one who vindicates me is near.
Who will contend with me?
    Let us stand up together.
Who are my adversaries?
    Let them confront me.
It is the Lord GOD who helps me;
    who will declare me guilty?

READING II *Philippians 2:5–11*

Let the same mind be in you that was in Christ
Jesus, who, although being in the form of God, did
not regard equality with God as something to be
exploited, but relinquished it all, taking the form of a
slave, being born in human likeness. And being
found in human form, he humbled himself and
became obedient to the point of death—even death
on a cross.

Therefore God also highly exalted him and gave
him the name that is above every name, so that at
the name of Jesus every knee should bend, in
heaven and on earth and under the earth, and every
tongue should confess that Jesus Christ is Lord, to
the glory of God, the Father.

GOSPEL *Mark 14:1—15:39*

It was two days before the Passover and the festival
of Unleavened Bread. The chief priests and the
scribes were looking for a way to arrest Jesus by
stealth and kill him; for they said, "Not during the
festival, or there may be a riot among the people."

While Jesus was at Bethany in the house of
Simon the leper, as he sat at the table, a woman
came with an alabaster jar of very costly ointment of
nard, and she broke open the jar and poured the
ointment on his head. But some were there who said
to one another in anger, "Why was the ointment
wasted in this way? For this ointment could have
been sold for more than three hundred denarii, and
the money given to the poor." And they scolded her.
But Jesus said, "Let her alone; why do you trouble
her? She has performed a good service for me. For
you always have the poor with you, and you can
show kindness to them whenever you wish; but you
will not always have me. She has done what she
could; she has anointed my body beforehand for its
burial. Truly I tell you, wherever the good news is
proclaimed in the whole world, what she has done
will be told in remembrance of her."

Then Judas Iscariot, who was one of the twelve,
went to the chief priests in order to betray Jesus to
them. When they heard it, they were greatly
pleased, and promised to give Judas money. So he
began to look for an opportunity to betray Jesus.

On the first day of Unleavened Bread, when the
Passover lamb is sacrificed, his disciples said to him,
"Where do you want us to go and make the preparations for you to eat the Passover?" So Jesus sent
two of his disciples, saying to them, "Go into the
city, and a man carrying a jar of water will meet you;
follow him, and wherever he enters, say to the
owner of the house, 'The Teacher asks, Where is my
guest room where I may eat the Passover with my
disciples?' The owner will show you a large room
upstairs, furnished and ready. Make preparations
for us there." So the disciples set out and went to the
city, and found everything as Jesus had told them;
and they prepared the Passover meal.

When it was evening, Jesus came with the twelve. And when they had taken their places and were eating, Jesus said, "Truly I tell you, one of you will betray me, one who is eating with me." They began to be distressed and to say to him one after another, "Surely, not I?" He said to them, "It is one of the twelve, one who is dipping bread into the bowl with me. For the Son-of-Man goes as it is written of him, but woe to that one by whom the Son-of-Man is betrayed! It would have been better for that one not to have been born."

While they were eating, Jesus took a loaf of bread, and after blessing it he broke it, gave it to them, and said, "Take; this is my body." Then he took a cup, and after giving thanks he gave it to them, and all of them drank from it. He said to them, "This is my blood of the covenant, which is poured out for many. Truly I tell you, I will never again drink of the fruit of the vine until that day when I drink it new in the dominion of God."

When they had sung the hymn, they went out to the Mount of Olives. And Jesus said to them, "You will all become deserters; for it is written,

'I will strike the shepherd,

and the sheep will be scattered.'

But after I am raised up, I will go before you to Galilee." Peter said to him, "Even though all become deserters, I will not." Jesus said to him, "Truly I tell you, this day, this very night, before the cock crows twice, you will deny me three times." But Peter said vehemently, "Even though I must die with you, I will not deny you." And all of them said the same.

They went to a place called Gethsemane; and Jesus said to his disciples, "Sit here while I pray." He took with him Peter and James and John, and began to be distressed and agitated. And he said to them, "I am deeply grieved, even to death; remain here, and keep awake." And going a little farther, Jesus threw himself on the ground and prayed that, if it were possible, the hour might pass from him. He said, "Abba, Father, for you all things are possible; remove this cup from me; yet, not what I want, but what you want." Jesus came and found them sleeping; and he said to Peter, "Simon, are you asleep?

Could you not keep awake one hour? Keep awake and pray that you may not come into the time of trial; the spirit indeed is willing, but the flesh is weak." And again Jesus went away and prayed, saying the same words. And once more he came and found them sleeping, for their eyes were very heavy; and they did not know what to say to him. He came a third time and said to them, "Are you still sleeping and taking your rest? Enough! The hour has come; the Son-of-Man is betrayed into the hands of sinners. Get up, let us be going. See, my betrayer is at hand."

Immediately, while Jesus was still speaking, Judas, one of the twelve, arrived; and with him there was a crowd with swords and clubs, from the chief priests, the scribes, and the elders. Now the betrayer had given them a sign, saying, "The one I will kiss is the man; arrest him and lead him away under guard." So when Judas came, he went up to Jesus at once and said, "Rabbi!" and kissed him. Then they laid hands on Jesus and arrested him. But one of those who stood near drew his sword and struck the slave of the high priest, cutting off his ear. Then Jesus said to them, "Have you come out with swords and clubs to arrest me as though I were a bandit? Day after day I was with you in the temple teaching, and you did not arrest me. But let the scriptures be fulfilled." All of them deserted him and fled.

A certain youth was following him, wearing nothing but a linen cloth. They caught hold of him, but he left the linen cloth and ran off naked.

They took Jesus to the high priest; and all the chief priests, the elders, and the scribes were assembled. Peter had followed him at a distance, right into the courtyard of the high priest; and he was sitting with the guards, warming himself at the fire. Now the chief priests and the whole council were looking for testimony against Jesus to put him to death; but they found none. For many gave false testimony against Jesus, and their testimony did not agree. Some stood up and gave false testimony against him, saying, "We heard him say, 'I will destroy this temple that is made with hands, and in three days I will build another, not made with hands.'" But even on this point their testimony did not agree.

Then the high priest stood up before them and asked Jesus, "Have you no answer? What is it that they testify against you?" But Jesus was silent and did not answer. Again the high priest asked him, "Are you the Messiah, the Son of the Blessed One?" Jesus said, "I am; and

> 'you will see the Son-of-Man
> seated at the right hand of the Power,'
> and 'coming with the clouds of heaven.'"

Then the high priest tore his clothes and said, "Why do we still need witnesses? You have heard his blasphemy! What is your decision?" All of them condemned him as deserving death. Some began to spit on him, to blindfold him, and to strike him, saying to him, "Prophesy!" The guards also took him over and beat him.

While Peter was below in the courtyard, one of the servants of the high priest came by. When she saw Peter warming himself, she stared at him and said, "You also were with Jesus, the man from Nazareth." But he denied it, saying, "I do not know or understand what you are talking about." And he went out into the forecourt. Then the cock crowed. And the servant, on seeing him, began again to say to the bystanders, "This man is one of them." But again he denied it. Then after a little while the bystanders again said to Peter, "Certainly you are one of them; for you are a Galilean." But he began to curse, and he swore an oath, "I do not know this man you are talking about." At that moment the cock crowed for the second time. Then Peter remembered that Jesus had said to him, "Before the cock crows twice, you will deny me three times." And he broke down and wept. As soon as it was morning, the chief priests held a consultation with the elders and scribes and the whole council. They bound Jesus, led him away, and handed him over to Pilate. Pilate asked him, "Are you the King of the Jews?" Jesus answered him, "You say so." Then the chief priests accused him of many things. Pilate asked him again, "Have you no answer? See how many charges they bring against you." But Jesus made no further reply, so that Pilate was amazed.

Now at the festival Pilate used to release a prisoner for them, anyone for whom they asked. Now a man called Barabbas was in prison with the rebels who had committed murder during the insurrection. So the crowd came and began to ask Pilate to do for them according to his custom. Then he answered them, "Do you want me to release for you the King of the Jews?" For he realized that it was out of jealousy that the chief priests had handed him over. But the chief priests stirred up the crowd to have Pilate release Barabbas for them instead. Pilate spoke to them again, "Then what do you wish me to do with the man you call the King of the Jews?" They shouted back, "Crucify him!" Pilate asked them, "Why, what evil has he done?" But they shouted all the more, "Crucify him!" So Pilate, wishing to satisfy the crowd, released Barabbas for them; and after flogging Jesus, he handed him over to be crucified.

Then the soldiers led Jesus into the courtyard of the palace (that is, the governor's headquarters); and they called together the whole cohort. And they clothed him in a purple cloak; and after twisting some thorns into a crown, they put it on him. And they began saluting him, "Hail, King of the Jews!" They struck his head with a reed, spat upon him, and knelt down in homage to him. After mocking him, they stripped him of the purple cloak and put his own clothes on him. Then they led him out to crucify him.

They compelled a passer-by, who was coming in from the country, to carry his cross; it was Simon of Cyrene, the father of Alexander and Rufus. Then they brought Jesus to the place called Golgotha (which means the place of a skull). And they offered him wine mixed with myrrh; but he did not take it. And they crucified him, and divided his clothes among them, casting lots to decide what each should take.

It was nine o'clock in the morning when they crucified him. The inscription of the charge against him read, "The King of the Jews." And with him they crucified two bandits, one on his right and one on his left. Those who passed by derided Jesus, shaking their heads and saying, "Aha! You who would destroy the temple and build it in three days, save yourself, and come down from the cross!" In the same way the chief priests, along with the scribes, were also mocking him among themselves and saying, "He saved others; he cannot save himself. Let the Messiah, the King of Israel, come down from the cross now, so that we may see and believe." Those who were crucified with him also taunted him.

When it was noon, darkness came over the whole land until three in the afternoon. At three o'clock Jesus cried out with a loud voice, "Eloi, Eloi, lema sabachthani?" which means, "My God, my God, why have you forsaken me?" When some of the bystanders heard it, they said, "Listen, he is calling for Elijah." And someone ran, filled a sponge with sour wine, put it on a stick, and gave it to him to drink, saying, "Wait, let us see whether Elijah will come to take him down." Then Jesus gave a loud cry and breathed his last. And the curtain of the temple was torn in two, from top to bottom. Now when the centurion, who stood facing him, saw that in this way Jesus breathed his last, he said, "Truly this man was God's Son!"

[Complete reading: Mark 14:1 – 15:47]

R E F L E C T I O N

In the past month we have heard the gospels for the Third, Fourth and Fifth Sundays of Lent drawing us into the approaching narrative of Jesus' passion. As members of the body of Christ eagerly and gratefully looking forward to celebrating the initiation of new members, we might wrinkle our brows and wonder why the church is so intent on proclaiming these stories of human misery and death into the ears of those who are preparing to join the community of faith. Wouldn't anyone hearing death, death and more death say, "No thanks"?

Well, in its liturgy and mission, the church provides a keen indictment of our culture's practice of keeping the sick and dying out of sight. Although it is most likely beneficial that the progress of medical science has resulted in longer life spans for many, the technical side of medical practice means that we rarely witness the inevitability and omnipresence of death. But the fact of the matter is that each of us, like Jesus of Nazareth in the long proclamation of the passion this Sunday, will die, and new members are often attracted to the church after the death of someone they've loved when they recognize the underlying deception of the culture and the stark truth proclaimed by the church in its liturgy and preaching.

This intimate juxtaposition of death and resurrection in the gospels is at the heart of Christian life, not just at the end of our lives but day by day. The passion of Jesus, which we will hear again from the Gospel of John on Good Friday, is itself at the heart of this mystery in which we live every day of our lives and into which the catechumens are about to cast themselves.

■ **How closely has death come to your own life? To your family? To your friends and loved ones? How has the nearness of death changed your appreciation of the church's mission in everyday life?**

WEEKDAY READINGS (Mo) Isaiah 42:1 – 7; (Tu) 49:1 – 6; (We) 50:4 – 9; Holy Thursday; Good Friday; Holy Saturday

PASCHAL TRIDUUM

Holy is God! Holy and Strong!
Holy, immortal One, have mercy on us!

All you sheltered by the Most High,
who live in Almighty God's shadow,
say to the Lord, "My refuge, my fortress,
my God in whom I trust!"

God will free you from the hunters' snares,
will save you from deadly plague,
will cover you like a nesting bird.
God's wings will shelter you.

No nighttime terror shall you fear,
no arrows shot by day,
no plague that prowls the dark,
no wasting scourge at noon.

You have only to open your eyes
to see how the wicked are repaid.
You have the Lord as refuge,
have made the Most High your stronghold.

No evil shall ever touch you,
no harm come near your home.
God instructs angels
to guard you wherever you go.

"I deliver all who cling to me,
raise the ones who know my name,
answer those who call me,
stand with those in trouble.
These I rescue and honor,
satisfy with long life,
and show my power to save."

—Psalm 91:1 – 6, 8 – 11, 14 – 16

Holy God,
praise be yours for this tree of Paradise,
this tree that made Noah's saving Ark,
this tree whose branches embraced Jesus
and so shade and shelter us all.
Here may all the weary rest
these holy days,
hungry and thirsty for your word,
eating and drinking only your word
until, in the darkness between
Saturday and Sunday,
Heaven and earth shall here be wed.
Then drowning waters shall be
waters of life
and the Savior's blood a banquet.
Holy God, praise be yours.

— Prayer of the Triduum

THE THREE DAYS

Holy Thursday brings the end to the Forty Days of Lent, which make up the season of anticipation of the great Three Days. Composed of prayer, almsgiving, fasting and the preparation of the catechumens for baptism, the season of Lent is now brought to a close and the Three Days begin as we approach the liturgy of Holy Thursday evening. As those to be initiated into the church have prepared themselves for their entrance into the fullness of life, so have we been awakening in our hearts, minds and bodies our own entrances into the life of Christ, experienced in the life of the church.

The Three Days, this Easter *Triduum* (Latin for "three days"), is the center, the core, of the entire year for Christians. These days mark the mystery around which our entire lives are played out. Adults in the community are invited to plan ahead so that the whole time from Thursday night until Easter Sunday is free of social engagements, free of entertainment and free of meals except for the simplest nourishment. We measure these days — indeed, our very salvation in the life of God — in step with the catechumens themselves; our own rebirths are revitalized as we participate in their initiation rites and as we have supported them along the way.

We are asked to fast on Good Friday and to continue fasting, if possible, all through Holy Saturday as strictly as we can so that we come to the Easter Vigil hungry and full of excitement, parched and longing to feel the sacred water of the font on our skin. Good Friday and Holy Saturday are days of paring down distractions so that we may be free for prayer and anticipation, for reflection, preparation and silence. The church is getting ready for the Great Night of the Easter Vigil.

As one who has been initiated into the church, as one whose life has been wedded to this community gathered at the table, you should anticipate the Triduum with concentration and vigor. With you, the whole church knows that our presence for the liturgies of the Triduum is not just an invitation.

Everyone is needed. We "pull out all the stops" for these days. As human persons, wedded to humanity by the joys and travails of life and grafted onto the body of the church by the sanctifying waters of baptism, we lead the new members into new life in this community of faith.

To this end, the Three Days are seen not as three liturgies distinct from one another but as one movement. These days have been connected intimately and liturgically from the early days of the Christian church. As a member of this community, you should be personally committed to preparing for and anticipating the Triduum and its culmination in the Vigil of the Great Night, Holy Saturday.

The church proclaims the direction of the Triduum by the opening antiphon of Holy Thursday, which comes from Paul's Letter to the Galatians (6:14). With this verse the church sets a spiritual environment into which we as committed Christians enter the Triduum:

We should glory in the cross of our Lord Jesus Christ, for he is our salvation, our life and resurrection; through him we are saved and made free.

HOLY THURSDAY

On Thursday evening we enter into this Triduum together. Whether presider, baker, lector, preacher, wine maker, greeter, altar server, minister of the eucharist, decorator or person in the remote corner in the last pew of the church, we begin, as always, by hearkening to the word of God. These are the scriptures for the liturgy of Holy Thursday:

Exodus 12:1 – 8, 11 – 14
Ancient instructions for the meal of the Passover

1 Corinthians 11:23 – 26
Eat the bread and drink the cup until the return of the Lord

John 13:1 – 15
Jesus washes the feet of the disciples

Then we, like Jesus, do something strange: We wash feet. Jesus gave us this image of what the church is supposed to look like, feel like, act like. Our position — whether as washer or washed, servant or served — is a difficult one for us to take. Yet we learn from the discomfort, from the awkwardness.

Then we celebrate the eucharist. Because it is connected to the other liturgies of the Triduum on Good Friday and Holy Saturday night, the evening liturgy of Holy Thursday has no ending. Whether we stay to pray awhile or leave, we are now in the quiet, peace and glory of the Triduum.

GOOD FRIDAY

We gather quietly in community on Friday and again listen to the Word of God:

Isaiah 52:13 — 53:12
The servant of the Lord was crushed for our sins

Hebrews 4:14 – 16; 5:7 – 9
The Son of God learned obedience through his suffering

John 18:1 — 19:42
The passion of Jesus Christ

After the sermon, we pray at length for all the world's needs: for the church; for the pope, the clergy and all the baptized; for those preparing for initiation; for the unity of Christians; for Jews; for non – Christians; for atheists; for all in public office; and for those in special need.

Then there is another once-a-year event: The holy cross is held up in our midst and we come forward one by one to do reverence with a kiss, bow or genuflection. This communal reverence of an instrument of torture recalls the painful price, in the past and today, of salvation, the way in which our redemption is wrought, the stripes and humiliation of Jesus Christ that bring direction and life back to a humanity that is lost and dead. During the veneration of the cross, we sing not only of the sorrow but of the glory of the cross by which we have been saved.

Again, we bring to mind the words of Paul: "The cross of Jesus Christ . . . our salvation, our life and resurrection; through him we are saved and made free."

We continue in fasting and prayer and vigil, in rest and quiet, through Saturday. This Saturday for us is God's rest at the end of creation. It is Christ's repose in the tomb. It is Christ's visit with the dead.

EASTER VIGIL

Hungry now, pared down to basics, lightheaded from vigilance and full of excitement, we committed members of the church, the already baptized, gather in darkness and light a new fire. From this blaze we light a great candle that will make this night bright for us and will burn throughout the Easter season.

We hearken again to the Word of God with some of the most powerful narratives and proclamations of our tradition:

Genesis 1:1 — 2:2
Creation of the world

Genesis 22:1 – 18
The sacrifice of Isaac

Exodus 14:15 — 15:1
The Red Sea

Isaiah 54:5 – 14
You will not be afraid

Isaiah 55:1-11
Come, come to the water

Baruch 3:9 – 15, 32 — 4:4
The shining light

Ezekiel 36:16 – 28
The Lord says: I will sprinkle water

Romans 6:3 – 11
United with him in death

Mark 16:1 – 8
Jesus has been raised up

After the readings, we pray to all our saints to stand with us as we go to the font and bless the waters. The chosen of all times and all places attend to what is about to take place. The catechumens renounce evil, profess the faith of the church and are baptized and anointed.

All of us renew our baptism. For us these are the moments when death and life meet, when we reject evil and give our promises to God. All of this is in the communion of the church. So together we go to the table and celebrate the Easter eucharist.

EASTERTIME

Christ is risen! Christ is truly risen!

Give thanks, the Lord is good,
God's love is for ever!
Now let Israel say,
"God's love is for ever!"

I was pushed to falling,
but the Lord gave me help.
My strength, my song is the Lord,
who has become my savior.

I shall not die but live
to tell the Lord's great deeds.
The Lord punished me severely,
but did not let me die.

The stone the builders rejected
has become the cornerstone.
This is the work of the Lord,
how wonderful in our eyes.

This is the day the Lord made,
let us rejoice and be glad.
Lord, give us the victory!
Lord, grant us success!

Blest is the one who comes,
who comes in the name of the Lord.
We bless you from the Lord's house.
The Lord God is our light:
adorn the altar with branches.

— Psalm 118:1 – 2, 13 – 14, 17 – 18, 22 – 27

The heavens rumble alleluias,
earth dances to the tune
and the wail of the graves
itself becomes song.
All are singing with you, savior God,
at this wedding feast
for you have turned the world around,
inside out and upside down.
Now the homeless are at home
and the martyred embrace their assassins
and the rulers and bosses wonder
whose world this is after all.
After all, let us stand and sing
with the heavens and earth and the graves
and so proclaim that we live now only
in Christ who is Lord for ever and ever.

— Prayer of the Season

READING I *Acts 10:34 – 43*

Peter began to speak to the people: "I truly understand that God shows no partiality, but in every nation anyone who is God-fearing and does what is right is acceptable to God.

"You know the message God sent to the people of Israel, preaching peace by Jesus Christ — who is Lord of all. That message spread throughout Judea, beginning in Galilee after the baptism that John announced: how God anointed Jesus of Nazareth with the Holy Spirit and with power; how Jesus went about doing good and healing all who were oppressed by the devil, for God was with him. We are witnesses to all that he did both in Judea and in Jerusalem. They put him to death by hanging him on a tree; but God raised him on the third day and allowed him to appear, not to all the people but to us who were chosen by God as witnesses, and who ate and drank with him after he rose from the dead.

"Jesus commanded us to preach to the people and to testify that he is the one ordained by God as judge of the living and the dead. All the prophets testify about him that everyone who believes in him receives forgiveness of sins through his name."
[Revised Common Lectionary alternate reading: Isaiah 25:6 – 9]

READING II *Colossians 3:1 – 4*

If you have been raised with Christ, seek the things that are above, where Christ is, seated at the right hand of God. Set your minds on things that are above, not on things that are on earth, for you have died, and your life is hidden with Christ in God. When Christ who is your life is revealed, then you also will be revealed with him in glory.
[Revised Common Lectionary: 1 Corinthians 15:1 – 11 or Acts 10:34 – 43]

GOSPEL *John 20:1 – 18*

Early on the first day of the week, while it was still dark, Mary Magdalene came to the tomb and saw that the stone had been removed from the tomb. So she ran and went to Simon Peter and the other disciple, the one whom Jesus loved, and said to them, "They have taken the Lord out of the tomb, and we do not know where they have laid him."

Then Peter and the other disciple set out and went toward the tomb. The two were running together, but the other disciple outran Peter and reached the tomb first. He bent down to look in and saw the linen wrappings lying there, but he did not go in. Then Simon Peter came, following him, and went into the tomb. He saw the linen wrappings lying there, and the cloth that had been on Jesus' head, not lying with the linen wrappings but rolled up in a place by itself. Then the other disciple, who reached the tomb first, also went in, and he saw and believed; for as yet they did not understand the scripture, that Jesus must rise from the dead.

But Mary stood weeping outside the tomb. As she wept, she bent over to look into the tomb; and she saw two angels in white, sitting where the body of Jesus had been lying, one at the head and the other at the feet. They said to her, "Woman, why are you weeping?" She said to them, "They have taken away my Lord, and I do not know where they have laid him." When she had said this, she turned around and saw Jesus standing there, but she did not know that it was Jesus. Jesus said to her, "Woman, why are you weeping: Whom are you looking for?" Supposing him to be the gardener, she said to him, "Sir, if you have carried him away, tell me where you have laid him, and I will take him away." Jesus said to her, "Mary!" She turned and said to him in Hebrew, "Rabbouni!" (which means Teacher). Jesus said to her, "Do not hold on to me, because I have not yet ascended to the Father. But go to my borthers and say to them, 'Iam ascending to my Father and your Father, to my God and your God.'"

Mary Magdalene went and announced to the disciples, "I have seen the Lord"; and she told them that Jesus had said these things to her.

R E F L E C T I O N

The second reading from the Letter to the Colossians is a key text, not only for helping us to enter into this great feast of Easter, but for helping us, the baptized of the church, enter into the paschal mystery with Jesus of Nazareth, with him who was raised. The author presumes that if we "seek the things that are above," then we will share in the glory of the resurrection; we will be "raised with Christ." Our sharing in the resurrection with Christ is not dependent, thank God, on our own deserving. It is the gift of God that we received at baptism, the free gift of faith.

Unfortunately, we human beings are more readily inclined to accept our entering into the sufferings of Christ, ignoring the glorification! For who among us cannot identify with the difficulties of life as these are connected to the cross of Christ? Who among us, conscious of the passion of Christ, does not recognize that the injustices and the sadnesses, the anger that can tear human relationships and family apart are somehow tied into that passion of 2000 years ago? Who among us did not, on this very Good Friday, sense the ways life's difficulties — in the world, in the nation, in our cities or towns or communities, in our relationships and even in our bodies — are tied into that agonizing aspect of the paschal mystery? I suspect that this is not the hardest part of celebrating the mysteries of Easter.

The Letter to the Colossians highlights, however, that we cannot stop there. We find it hard to accept our participation in Christ's glorification, this great gift of God in faith. But, whether we accept it or not, it is true: We are indeed co-heirs with Christ in the life of God. By baptism, we share in the resurrection of Jesus Christ. The sacrifice of Jesus Christ on the cross was the price of our freedom, our glorification, our union with him in the life of the saints. That price has been paid; let us rejoice.

■ **What is there in your life that you are reluctant to bring into the light of the resurrection? In what ways have you died in Christ? How is your life "hidden" with Christ? What does that mean? What holds you back from participating fully in Christ's glorification?**

PRACTICE OF FAITH

HE IS RISEN. Resurrection! We see it so clearly as glorious and joyful. The apostles found it frightening, stunning and confusing. Jesus had told the apostles many times that for salvation to be accomplished he would have to die and then rise from the dead. But it was fear, not joy, that gripped the followers of Christ and compelled them to hide. The authorities might accuse them of stealing the body; their first reactions were bewilderment and self-preservation.

Without the resurrection, however, Good Friday is meaningless. Jesus told of the glorious future that would come to those who believed. He spoke of death, but also of the promise of the resurrection. The empty tomb showed that the promise had been kept. Cast fear aside and rejoice. Christ is risen!

PRACTICE OF HOPE

REJOICE AND BE GLAD. Today's gospel passage gives an account of the disciples finding the empty tomb on Easter morning, and the first reading sets before us our understanding of who this risen Christ is and what he has to offer. The reading from Acts provides Peter's testimony about the meaning of Easter, which he gave during his visit to the home of the centurion Cornelius. As a result of Peter's witness, Cornelius and his household were some of the first Gentiles baptized.

In our own time, the church is immediately pulled into the Easter experience by our celebration of baptism. As Jesus was raised, we who have been baptized have also been raised into a hidden life with Christ in God.

PRACTICE OF CHARITY

STEWARDSHIP. The promise of new life reminds us of our responsibility to be good stewards of creation. Wise use, conservation and preservation of our natural resources are the actions of those who understand that we are only passing through this life. It is a wonderful coincidence that in the year 2000, Earth Day and Easter are celebrated one day apart. Earth Day 2000 organizers have set astonishing goals for this year's commemoration of global sustainability: at least 100,000 events world-wide, including 50,000 religious or spiritual ones, with at least of 2 billion participants; 20 million signatures on petitions; and 100,000 people committed to careers that promote global environmental objectives. Learn more at www.earthday.org.

WEEKDAY READINGS (Mo) Acts 2:14, 22 – 33; (Tu) 2:36 – 41; (We) 3:1 – 10; (Th) 3:11 – 16; (Fr) 4:1 – 12; (Sa) 4:13 – 21

READING I *Acts 4:32–35*

Now the whole group of those who believed were of one heart and soul, and no one claimed private ownership of any possessions, but everything they owned was held in common. With great power the apostles gave their testimony to the resurrection of the Lord Jesus, and great grace was upon them all. There was not a needy person among them, for as many as owned lands or houses sold them and brought the proceeds of what was sold. They laid it at the apostles' feet, and it was distributed to each as any had need.

READING II *1 John 5:1–6*

Everyone who believes that Jesus is the Christ has been born of God, and everyone who loves the parent loves the child. By this we know that we love the children of God, when we love God and obey God's commandments. For the love of God is this, that we obey the commandments, which are not burdensome, for whatever is born of God conquers the world. And this is the victory that conquers the world, our faith. Who is it that conquers the world but the one who believes that Jesus is the Son of God?

This is the one who came by water and blood, Jesus Christ, not with the water only but with the water and the blood. And the Spirit is the one that testifies, for the Spirit is the truth.

[Revised Common Lectionary: 1 John 1:1 — 2:2]

GOSPEL *John 20:19–31*

When it was evening on that day, the first day of the week, and the doors of the house where the disciples had met were locked for fear of the Judeans, Jesus came and stood among them and said, "Peace be with you." After he said this, he showed them his hands and his side. Then the disciples rejoiced when they saw the Lord. Jesus said to them again, "Peace be with you. As the Father has sent me, so I send you." When he had said this, he breathed on them and said to them, "Receive the Holy Spirit. If you forgive the sins of any, they are forgiven them; if you retain the sins of any, they are retained."

But Thomas (who was called the Twin), one of the twelve, was not with them when Jesus came. So the other disciples told him, "We have seen the Lord." But he said to them, "Unless I see the mark of the nails in his hands, and put my finger in the mark of the nails and my hand in his side, I will not believe."

A week later his disciples were again in the house, and Thomas was with them. Although the doors were shut, Jesus came and stood among them and said, "Peace be with you." Then he said to Thomas, "Put your finger here and see my hands. Reach out your hand and put it in my side. Do not doubt but believe." Thomas said to Jesus, "My Lord and my God!" Jesus said to him, "Have you believed because you have seen me? Blessed are those who have not seen and yet have come to believe."

Now Jesus did many other signs in the presence of his disciples, which are not written in this book. But these are written so that you may come to believe that Jesus is the Messiah, the Son of God, and that through believing you may have life in his name.

R E F L E C T I O N

In the later part of the first century, when the Gospel of John was written, the community of John's gospel faced some opponents who thought that the importance of faith was merely interior, that it was a secret *knowledge* that Jesus would share with his followers for salvation, and that our bodies did not matter for faith. This is contrary to our faith; our bodies do indeed matter. That is why we hear from the beginning of the First Letter of John: "What we have heard, what we have seen . . . what we have looked at and touched with our hands" (1:1). John's community, as we know it from the gospel and from the three Letters of John, was making a case for the importance of the human body, for human bodies in community with one another, in the life of faith. Today's gospel narrative about Thomas reflects this emphasis on the body.

Though we may regret that in our own lives of faith we seem not to have had the opportunity that Thomas had to see and touch the body of Jesus, we need to remember that in our community we meet the resurrected body of Jesus each week when we come together to celebrate the sacred rites. The church teaches that the body and blood of Christ are present not only on the altar; the body and blood of Christ are also present in the community of the baptized gathered in the assembly, including the ministers. At the end of the Gospel of John the evangelist writes that there are so many manifestations of the resurrected Jesus that "I suppose the world itself could not contain the books that would be written" (21:25). The wonders of the resurrected body of Christ in your own parish are themselves among the wonders not able to be contained. Claim them; proclaim them; rejoice in them.

■ **Are there aspects of Christian faith that can leave us with the impression that our bodies are not worthy of salvation? What are they?**

■ **Our tradition believes that the human body is important for our salvation. How do you view your own body in your personal theology and spirituality?**

PRACTICE OF FAITH

MY GOD. Thomas never imagined that by his refusal to believe that Jesus had visited the disciples in his absence his name would become part of our vocabulary — "doubting Thomas." It wasn't that he did not believe in Jesus, but the events of the past week had unnerved him. He knew Jesus died on the cross and was buried, and he wanted to know for himself that Jesus really was alive. A week later when he did see Jesus alive, his faith came to the forefront: "My Lord (a term the apostles used frequently) and my God." No one had ever used the phrase "my God" in speaking about Jesus; nor did Jesus ever use it himself. Thomas was the first to acknowledge the risen Jesus as God. People of faith since that time accept that Jesus is God. But Thomas had to learn this truth slowly and in stages. "Doubting Thomas," infused with faith, made the leap from Jesus of Nazareth to "my God." (RG)

PRACTICE OF HOPE

TO CONQUER THE WORLD. The First Letter of John reminds us that those born of God will conquer this world of unbelief. Faith is the agent of this victory — but faith may fade if we do not see signs of hope and encouragement in our daily effort to bring the world the love of God. Thomas' unbelief demonstrates this reality. Without the experience of Jesus' presence to give him encouragement, he could not believe in the resurrection. Yet Jesus' appearance overwhelms his doubt and fear, and Thomas proclaims Jesus "Lord and God."

But what of us who "have not seen and yet have come to believe"? We too must experience manifestations of God's love in our lives if we are to have faith. What people give you hope of God's love in the world? Where do you look for signs of the active love of God in the world?

PRACTICE OF CHARITY

TOOLS AND TALENTS. Today's reading from Acts is a challenging one, especially in our society. Just think of the possibilities if more of us took some cues from this reading. Try something as simple as subscribing jointly to your local daily newspaper with your coworkers. The paper is delivered at work, gets passed along, trees are saved and all enjoy it at a fraction of the cost. Church members with talents of "hammers and hands" can assist elderly fellow parishioners in small-scale home repair. A pooling of our tools and talents will call us to live more simply and become better stewards of God's gifts.

WEEKDAY READINGS (Mo) Acts 4:23 – 31; (Tu) 4:32 – 37; (We) 1 Corinthians 15:1 – 8; (Th) Acts 5:27 – 33; (Fr) 5:34 – 42; (Sa) 6:1 – 7

READING I *Acts 3:12–19*

Peter addressed the people, "You Israelites, why do you wonder at this, or why do you stare at us, as though by our own power or piety we had made this man walk? The God of Abraham, Isaac, and Jacob, the God of our ancestors has glorified Jesus, the servant of God, whom you handed over and rejected in the presence of Pilate, though Pilate had decided to release him. But you rejected the Holy and Righteous One and asked to have a murderer given to you, and you killed the Author of life, whom God raised from the dead. To this we are witnesses. And by faith in the name of Jesus, his name itself has made this man strong, whom you see and know; and the faith that is through Jesus has given him this perfect health in the presence of all of you.

"And now, friends, I know that you acted in ignorance, as did also your rulers. In this way God fulfilled what had been foretold through all the prophets, that the Messiah of God would suffer. Repent therefore, and turn to God so that your sins may be wiped out."

READING II *1 John 2:1–5*

My little children, I am writing these things to you so that you may not sin. But if anyone does sin, we have an advocate with the Father, Jesus Christ the righteous, who is the atoning sacrifice for our sins, and not for ours only but also for the sins of the whole world. Now by this we may be sure that we know God, if we obey God's commandments. Whoever says, "I have come to know God," but does not obey God's commandments, is a liar, and in such a person the truth does not exist; but whoever obeys God's word, truly in this person the love of God has reached perfection. By this we may be sure that we are in God.

[Revised Common Lectionary: 1 John 3:1–7]

GOSPEL *Luke 24:36–48*

Jesus himself stood among them and said to them, "Peace be with you." They were startled and terrified, and thought that they were seeing a ghost. He said to them, "Why are you frightened, and why do doubts arise in your hearts? Look at my hands and my feet; see that it is I myself. Touch me and see; for a ghost does not have flesh and bones as you see that I have." And when he had said this, he showed them his hands and his feet. While in their joy they were disbelieving and still wondering, he said to them, "Have you anything here to eat?" They gave him a piece of broiled fish, and he took it and ate in their presence.

Then Jesus said to them, "These are my words that I spoke to you while I was still with you — that everything written about me in the law of Moses, the prophets, and the psalms must be fulfilled." Then he opened their minds to understand the scriptures, and said to them, "Thus it is written, that the Messiah is to suffer and to rise from the dead on the third day, and that repentance and forgiveness of sins is to be proclaimed in his name to all nations, beginning from Jerusalem. You are witnesses of these things."

R E F L E C T I O N

What strikes us most clearly about the passage from the Gospel of Luke is just how much, all these centuries after the writing of the Gospel of Luke in about the year 85 (about 15 years after the Gospel of Mark), the experience of the two disciples on the way to Emmaus resembles our own Christian experience. Like the two disciples of the story, we can be "disbelieving and still wondering" (24:41) about the events of our lives and about the presence of God in this messy and sometimes joyless life. And also like the two disciples, who stood in the presence of the risen Jesus and did not recognize him, we come Sunday after Sunday, Easter after Easter, to our parish assembly and wonder if all the claims of faith and stories about Jesus are true. These disciples even saw the hands and feet of the risen Jesus and still were afraid, still did not believe.

Yet also like the two disciples, we listen to the proclamation of God's word; we come to the table and eat in the presence of the risen Messiah, present in our congregation. And, though we may not see the "hands and feet" (24:40) or the "flesh and bones" (24:39) of the risen Messiah *in the same way* as these two disciples, we do come each Sunday as flesh and bones, we come each Easter with hands that clasp and feet that carry us to those in need. And in this way our life in the Lord of heaven and earth is not far different from the life of those who walked with the Messiah on the road to Emmaus.

As the Messiah said to Cleopas and his companion, "You are the witnesses of these things." Proclaim these events with passion and bring others to the life of faith by your witness.

■ **The passage of time can make us think that we are more and more separated from the experience of the followers of Jesus, but the gift of grace, of God's life in our lives, does not diminish with time. Think about what the main impediments are in your finding God's presence in everyday life.**

PRACTICE OF FAITH

SHARE A MEAL. It's something of a cliché that we live in a "fast-food" society, one that encourages the mass provision of goods for high-turnover consumers uninterested in the source or means of production. Cliché or not, when it comes to our meals it does seem that we invest ourselves less and less in their preparation and in sharing them with others. Take some time this week to share a meal with someone. Don't just eat at the same time; spend time together over a meal, with good talk and active listening. Sharing food, drink and conversation is a very good way to grow in mutual understanding.

PRACTICE OF HOPE

WITNESS. Today's gospel tells of one of Jesus' appearances to the disciples after the resurrection. Jesus tells them: Repentance and forgiveness of sins is to be proclaimed; you are witnesses to the death and rising of the Messiah. In the first reading, Peter is already witnessing to Jesus as he preaches repentance.

In Acts we learn of the actual witnessing to Christ, the Messiah of God, by the early disciples. The words and actions recorded in the scriptures that are proclaimed each Sunday during the Easter season encourage us in faith and call us to witness to Christ by our lives and our words. How do you witness to the risen Christ? How do you live the life of a disciple in your daily life?

PRACTICE OF CHARITY

PEACE BE WITH YOU. Have you ever noticed how often the gospel writers have the risen Christ greet his startled disciples with the phrase, "Peace be with you"? Did they listen? What impact did it have on their lives? In 1983 and again in 1993, the American Catholic bishops addressed the issue of peace in the modern age. *The Challenge of Peace: God's Promise and Our Response* and *The Harvest of Justice Is Sown in Peace* both generated some attention when they were first published, but have been largely ignored ever since. Are issues of war and peace often brought up by your homilists? Have you made your commitment to nonviolence and peace clear to your children, your grandchildren, your neighbors? The next time you turn to another to offer this greeting, make it mean more than "Have a nice day!" Live peace today!

WEEKDAY READINGS (Mo) Acts 6:8 – 15; (Tu) 7:51 — 8:1; (We) 8:1 – 8; (Th) 8:26 – 40; (Fr) 9:1 – 20; (Sa) 9:31 – 42

READING I *Acts 4:5–12*

The next day their rulers, elders, and scribes assembled in Jerusalem, with Annas the high priest, Caiaphas, John, and Alexander, and all who were of the high-priestly family. When they had made the prisoners Peter and John stand in their midst, they inquired, "By what power or by what name did you do this?" Then Peter, filled with the Holy Spirit, said to them, "Rulers of the people and elders, if we are questioned today because of a good deed done to someone who was sick and are asked how this man has been healed, let it be known to all of you, and to all the people of Israel, that this man is standing before you in good health by the name of Jesus Christ of Nazareth, whom you crucified, whom God raised from the dead. This Jesus is

> 'the stone that was rejected by you, the builders;
>   it has become the cornerstone.'

There is salvation in no one else, for there is no other name under heaven given among mortals by which we must be saved."

READING II *1 John 3:1–2*

See what love the Father has given us, that we should be called children of God; and that is what we are. The reason the world does not know us is that it did not know God. Beloved, we are God's children now; what we will be has not yet been revealed. What we do know is this: when it is revealed, we will be like God, for we will see God as God is.

[Revised Common Lectionary: 1 John 3:16–24]

GOSPEL *John 10:11–18*

Jesus said: "I am the good shepherd. The good shepherd lays down his life for the sheep. The hired hand, who is not the shepherd and does not own the sheep, sees the wolf coming and leaves the sheep and runs away — and the wolf snatches them and scatters them. The hired hand runs away because a hired hand does not care for the sheep. I am the good shepherd. I know my own and my own know me, just as the Father knows me and I know the Father. And I lay down my life for the sheep. I have other sheep that do not belong to this fold. I must bring them also, and they will listen to my voice. So there will be one flock, one shepherd. For this reason the Father loves me, because I lay down my life in order to take it up again. No one takes it from me, but I lay it down of my own accord. I have power to lay it down, and I have power to take it up again. I have received this command from my Father."

REFLECTION

One of the temptations when thinking about the resurrection is to consider it merely something that happened in the past, something that does not touch our lives today. The liturgy we celebrate cautions us against this distancing when we as an assembly proclaim during the eucharistic prayer that "Christ has died, Christ *is risen*, Christ will come again." This antiphon reveals that the resurrection is not just something we remember; it is part of the ongoing Easter experience in which we participate both in the celebration of the sacraments and in our daily lives as baptized Christians. The scriptures during the Fifty Days of the Easter season remind us that, as the baptized, we are heirs of the power of the resurrection of Christ.

Today's reading from Acts is the follow-up to the story of the healing of a man who had been "lame from birth" (3:2) but who ends up walking, jumping and leaping (3:8). In today's first reading Peter explains the source of the power by which he performs such works. And in his words we discover that for Peter, the power of the resurrection is not simply a nice memory; he is claiming as his own the powers of healing and salvation wrought in the life, death and resurrection of Jesus Christ of Nazareth.

The second reading from the First Letter of John uses different imagery, but confirms Peter's claim when it calls us "God's children," and, though we do not know now what we will be later, we know that "we will be like him, for we will see him as he is" (3:2).

The gospel reading, again from John during the Easter season, is the familiar reading about Jesus as the good shepherd. As members of the worshiping assembly in our church, we are the flock united in Christ, the one shepherd. As that flock we claim the experience of the resurrection that is our gift from God in the example of Jesus.

■ **Sometimes the family-based imagery found in the liturgy and in sacred scripture — fatherhood, sonship, childhood — can be an impediment to those whose memories of family life are not always good. How does your parish provide a welcome to those whose experience of family life has not been positive?**

PRACTICE OF FAITH

GOOD SHEPHERD SUNDAY. The fourth Sunday of Easter is called Good Shepherd Sunday because in the gospel, Jesus refers to himself by this title, a favorite of the early Christians. Bake a cake today using a lamb mold as an Easter season treat. Memorize Psalm 23. And before you go to bed, say or sing this prayer from the Mass: "Lamb of God, you take away the sin of the world, have mercy on us/grant us peace." (DP)

PRACTICE OF HOPE

THE SHEPHERD. The image of Jesus as the good shepherd is a way of telling us that he cares for us deeply, and will be our faithful and vigilant provider and protector. Even though few of us probably have any first-hand experience with herding sheep, the image of the good shepherd still holds meaning for us.

At a Benedictine monastery that we frequently visit, sheep graze on the rolling hills. There are barns, rock fences, sheep gates and caring shepherds. A sculpture of the Good Shepherd, the most popular early image of Christ, overlooks the cemetery. Just as Christ laid down his life for us, he will shepherd us in life, through death and into future glory. (MP)

PRACTICE OF CHARITY

I KNOW MINE. Deep in the rolling hills of northwest Missouri and down a winding, dusty road lives a shepherd, Ron, a quiet man whose spirituality is lived out daily in the gentle care of his large flock of sheep. Standing guard beside him while the sheep graze the green hills are his companions, the watchful and intelligent sheepdogs. Just over another slight rise the eye catches a field ablaze with black-eyed susans. It's a little piece of heaven and this good shepherd knows the true meaning of sacrifice, hard work and enduring presence. The world needs more farmers and shepherds like him. Through gifts of livestock, trees and beehives, Heifer Project International assists struggling families in more than 110 countries to become self-sufficient. Call 1-800-422-0474 to learn how you or your church can help.

WEEKDAY READINGS (Mo) Acts 11:1 – 18; (Tu) 11:19 – 26; (We) 12:24 – 13:5; (Th) 13:13 – 25; (Fr) 13:26 – 33; (Sa) 13:44 – 52

READING I *Acts 9:26 – 31*

When Saul had come to Jerusalem, he attempted to join the disciples; and they were all afraid of him, for they did not believe that he was a disciple. But Barnabas took him, brought him to the apostles, and described for them how on the road he had seen the Lord, who had spoken to him, and how in Damascus Saul had spoken boldly in the name of Jesus.

So Saul went in and out among them in Jerusalem, speaking boldly in the name of the Lord. He spoke and argued with the Hellenists; but they were attempting to kill him. When the believers learned of it, they brought Saul down to Caesarea and sent him off to Tarsus. Meanwhile the church throughout Judea, Galilee, and Samaria had peace and was built up. Living in the fear of the Lord and in the comfort of the Holy Spirit, it increased in numbers.

[Revised Common Lectionary: Acts 8:26 – 40]

READING II *1 John 3:18 – 24*

Little children, let us love, not in word or speech, but in truth and action. And by this we will know that we are from the truth and will reassure our hearts before God whenever our hearts condemn us; for God is greater than our hearts, and God knows everything. Beloved, if our hearts do not condemn us, we have boldness before God; and we receive from God whatever we ask, because we obey the commandments and do what pleases God.

And this is God's commandment, that we should believe in the name of Jesus Christ, the Son of God, and love one another, just as Jesus has commanded us. All who obey God's commandments abide in God, and God abides in them. And by this we know that God abides in us, by the Spirit that God has given us.

[Revised Common Lectionary: 1 John 4:7 – 12]

GOSPEL *John 15:1 – 8*

Jesus said: "I am the true vine, and my Father is the vinegrower. My Father removes every branch in me that bears no fruit. Every branch that bears fruit my Father prunes to make it bear more fruit. You have already been cleansed by the word that I have spoken to you. Abide in me as I abide in you. Just as the branch cannot bear fruit by itself unless it abides in the vine, neither can you unless you abide in me. I am the vine, you are the branches. Those who abide in me and I in them bear much fruit, because apart from me you can do nothing. Whoever does not abide in me is thrown away like a branch and withers; such branches are gathered, thrown into the fire, and burned.

"If you abide in me, and my words abide in you, ask for whatever you wish, and it will be done for you. My Father is glorified by this, that you bear much fruit and become my disciples."

REFLECTION

For most of the Sundays of the Fifty Days of Easter, we hear passages from the Acts of the Apostles as the first readings and from John as the gospel readings. Last week in Acts we learned of Peter's claim to the power of the resurrection in his healing of the man lame from birth. This week we are introduced to Saul, who will become a major character in the book of Acts. Known later as Paul, he travels throughout the ancient world spreading the good news.

In today's first reading, however, we learn about the fear and hesitation of the disciples because of Saul's reputation as a persecutor of Christians. Barnabas's testimony to the disciples convinced them that this Saul did indeed converse with the Lord and had been speaking out in the name of Jesus. The witness of Paul's conversion, of the disciples' fear and of Barnabas's testimony to the community is important for us to hear now centuries later. For in our own churches today we can be discomforted by the presence of someone new or someone with a "bad reputation." It takes effort and attention to deal with someone new. But the witness of Jesus in the gospels and of the disciples in Acts encourages us to give the new person a hearty welcome and allow their gifts to the community to be exercised and incorporated.

The reading from Acts ends with the assurance that the church "had peace and was built up. . . . [I]n the comfort of the Holy Spirit, it increased in numbers." The reading from the First Letter of John similarly encourages us: "[W]e should believe in the name of Jesus Christ, the Son of God, and love one another, just as Jesus has commanded us."

■ **Does your parish have an active ministry of welcome and hospitality? How are those who come to your parish for the first time assured that they are welcome to return? How are those who make the assembly nervous and uncomfortable assured that they are welcome to return?**

PRACTICE OF FAITH

LISTEN. This week find ways to break down any barriers that may prevent you from listening to others in your life. Begin with friends and family members, and move outward to include acquaintances and co-workers. Try to include even someone with whom you do not necessarily see eye to eye. Express an interest in their lives, ask a question or two, and then listen attentively. Don't interrupt; don't judge; don't plan your next remark. Just listen. It is a first step to peace and to building up a community of the comfort of the Holy Spirit.

PRACTICE OF HOPE

ABIDE IN CHRIST. All along Lake Erie there are acres of vineyards. I used to work with a woman whose father owned a vineyard. She told me what hard work it was to prune the vines correctly. The weather would be snow-cold at pruning time and the vines were thick and woody where they needed to be cut back. Oddly, that information gave me great comfort. Grape branches were not necessarily delicate tendrils that one could break with a mere twist.

It is not easy to separate us from the love of Christ. If the Lord's words abide in us, we will abide in the Lord. What great hope it gives us when we abide in the words of Christ. Invite a friend or two to study scripture with you, to spend some time learning and abiding in the words of Christ. (MP)

PRACTICE OF CHARITY

SOLIDARITY FOREVER. Did you know that the church has long recognized the right of workers to organize? The labor unrest of the 19th century was the catalyst for a revolutionary document published in 1891, *Rerum Novarum,* by Pope Leo XIII. Pope Leo, who was in no way a liberal, understood that humans dignified labor, not that labor dignified humans. The document received harsh criticism from both left and right, but it initiated what has become known as "Catholic social teaching." Over the past century several church documents dealing with social justice have been written, many issued to coincide with the anniversary of *Rerum Novarum.* Pope John Paul II has stressed repeatedly that labor unions are not "necessary evils," but rather are essential tools to guarantee that human rights and human dignity are respected and fostered.

WEEKDAY READINGS (Mo) Acts 14:5 – 18; (Tu) 14:19 – 28; (We) 15:1 – 6; (Th) 15:7 – 21; (Fr) 15:22 – 31; (Sa) 16:1 – 10

READING I *Acts 10:25–26, 34–35, 44–48*

On Peter's arrival Cornelius met him, and falling at his feet, worshiped him. But Peter made him get up, saying, "Stand up; I am only a mortal." Peter began to speak to the people: "I truly understand that God shows no partiality, but in every nation anyone who is God-fearing and does what is right is acceptable to God.

While Peter was still speaking, the Holy Spirit fell upon all who heard the word. The believers from among the Jewish people who had come with Peter were astounded that the gift of the Holy Spirit had been poured out even on the Gentiles, for they heard them speaking in tongues and extolling God. Then Peter said, "Can anyone withhold the water for baptizing these people who have received the Holy Spirit just as we have?" So Peter ordered them to be baptized in the name of Jesus Christ. Then they invited him to stay for several days.

READING II *1 John 4:7–10*

Beloved, let us love one another, because love is from God; everyone who loves is born of God and knows God. Whoever does not love does not know God, for God is love. God's love was revealed among us in this way: God sent into the world God's only Son so that we might live through him. In this is love, not that we loved God but that God loved us and sent the Son to be the atoning sacrifice for our sins.

[Revised Common Lectionary: 1 John 5:1–6]

GOSPEL *John 15:9–17*

Jesus said: "As the Father has loved me, so I have loved you; abide in my love. If you keep my commandments, you will abide in my love, just as I have kept my Father's commandments and abide in my Father's love. I have said these things to you so that my joy may be in you, and that your joy may be complete.

"This is my commandment, that you love one another as I have loved you. No one has greater love than this, to lay down one's life for one's friends. You are my friends if you do what I command you. I do not call you servants any longer, because the servant does not know what the master is doing; but I have called you friends, because I have made known to you everything that I have heard from my Father. You did not choose me but I chose you. And I appointed you to go and bear fruit, fruit that will last, so that the Father will give you whatever you ask in my name. I am giving you these commands so that you may love one another."

Thursday, June 1, 2000

THE ASCENSION OF THE LORD

Acts 1:1–11 *Why stand staring at the skies?*

Ephesians 1:17–23 *The fullness of Christ has filled the universe.*

Mark 16:15–20 *Go into the whole world.*

On this 40th day of Easter, we are told to stop gazing at the clouds and to start spreading the good news. The resurrection of Christ did not stop with the Lord Jesus. All creation is ascending into glory. All the universe is becoming divine.

Note: U.S. dioceses may decide by region to move the celebration of the Ascension of the Lord to Sunday June 4.

R E F L E C T I O N

Surely the greatest crisis of Christianity in its first century after the death of Jesus was the debate about accepting Gentiles (non-Jews) into its fellowship, and following that, if the Gentiles were welcomed, whether the church should require them to follow the ritual practices of Judaism — such as circumcision and the dietary laws of the Hebrew Bible. In the middle of the first century, about two decades after the death of Jesus, the apostles and elders of the church met in Jerusalem to consider the two sides of the matter in a conference. (There are two accounts of the conference in Jerusalem in the New Testament; see Galatians 2:1–21 and Acts 15:1–35.)

At the start Peter sided with those who thought that the Jewish practices should be maintained, and Paul, as the "apostle to the Gentiles," was the advocate for abolishing the disciplines of the Hebrew law so that the Gentiles would not find obstacles in their path to faith. Having had a vision, which is recorded in Acts just before today's reading (see 10:9–16), Peter comes to understand that "God shows no partiality" and that the traditional observances can cease.

The Gospel of John recommends love to us as individual Christians and to our churches as communities of faith. Jesus says, "This is my commandment, that you love one another as I have loved you." The familiarity of this commandment makes it no easier to heed today than in the early church. The decision to admit the Gentiles into the church's communion surely brought new problems to a community just getting on its feet. But the embrace of the church was clearly from God, and as a church we need to be aware of such moments so that our community will grow strong, both in membership and faith.

■ **The example of the Father's love for Jesus and Jesus' love for us can seem to be too perfect for us to be able to follow. But this exemplary love is lived out for us one day at a time. In what small way can you imitate the love of Jesus and the love of God?**

PRACTICE OF FAITH

NOVENA. The Acts of the Apostles tells us that after Jesus ascended into heaven, the disciples prayed nine days for the coming of the Holy Spirit, the Advocate and Comforter that Jesus had promised he would send them. These nine days of prayer made up a novena, and throughout the ages Christians developed other nine-day periods of prayer called novenas. Begin your own novena this Friday; pray for the coming of the Holy Spirit every day from Friday until the feast of Pentecost on June 11. Use these words from Eucharistic Prayer III: "Grant that we, who are nourished by his body and blood, may be filled with his Holy Spirit, and become one body, one spirit in Christ." (DP)

PRACTICE OF HOPE

NO PARTIALITY. It had to have been the work of the Spirit that Cornelius, a Roman centurion, asked Peter for instruction. Cornelius, a Gentile, a Roman and a soldier, was not the usual follower of Jesus! As Peter proclaimed the good news, the Holy Spirit fell upon all present, *even the Gentiles.* No one would be refused baptism!

Recall Jesus' farewell speech in today's gospel: "You did not choose me but I chose you." The story of Cornelius and his household is a story of hope for this millennial year of reconciliation. We must proclaim clearly that God shows no partiality. Let us imitate our God! (MP)

PRACTICE OF CHARITY

HARVEST OF SHAME. Detasseling corn in an Illinois field in mid-July is excruciatingly wearisome work. Local teens know that summer farm work is only a passing experience; they are on their way to better careers in the future. But for the migrant workers who are expected to do twice the work twice as fast, there is no such assurance. Constant travel, mind-numbing repetitive work, pesticide poisoning, back-breaking labor and dismal living conditions are the reality of most migrant agricultural workers in the United States today. Despite the fame of the late Cesar Chavez and the United Farm Workers union he founded, most farm laborers are an invisible part of American agribusiness. Inform yourself this week about the food you eat and those who grow and harvest it.

WEEKDAY READINGS (Mo) Acts 16:11–15; (Tu) 16:22–34; (We) Zephaniah 3:14–18 or Romans 12:9–16; (Th) Ascension, see box; (Fr) Acts 18:9–18; (Sa) 18:23–28

READING I *Acts 1:15 – 17, 20 – 26*

In those days Peter stood up among the believers (together the crowd numbered about one hundred twenty persons) and said, "Friends, the scripture had to be fulfilled, which the Holy Spirit through David foretold concerning Judas, who became a guide for those who arrested Jesus — for he was numbered among us and was allotted his share in this ministry. For it is written in the book of Psalms, 'Let another take his position of overseer.'

"So one of the men who have accompanied us during all the time that the Lord Jesus went in and out among us, beginning from the baptism of John until the day when Jesus was taken up from us — one of these must become a witness with us to his resurrection." So they proposed two, Joseph called Barsabbas, who was also known as Justus, and Matthias. Then they prayed and said, "Lord, you know everyone's heart. Show us which one of these two you have chosen to take the place in this ministry and apostleship from which Judas turned aside to go to his own place." And they cast lots for them, and the lot fell on Matthias; and he was added to the eleven apostles.

READING II *1 John 4:11 – 16*

Beloved, since God loved us so much, we also ought to love one another. No one has ever seen God; if we love one another, God lives in us, and God's love is perfected in us.

By this we know that we abide in God and God in us, because we have been given of God's own Spirit. And we have seen and do testify that the Father has sent the Son as the Savior of the world. God abides in those who confess that Jesus is the Son of God, and they abide in God. So we have known and believe the love that God has for us. God is love, and those who abide in love abide in God, and God abides in them.

[Revised Common Lectionary: 1 John 5:9 – 13]

GOSPEL *John 17:11 – 19*

Jesus prayed: "Holy Father, protect them in your name that you have given me, so that they may be one, as we are one. While I was with them, I protected them in your name that you have given me. I guarded them, and not one of them was lost except the one destined to be lost, so that the scripture might be fulfilled. But now I am coming to you, and I speak these things in the world so that they may have my joy made complete in themselves. I have given them your word, and the world has hated them because they do not belong to the world, just as I do not belong to the world. I am not asking you to take them out of the world, but I ask you to protect them from the evil one. They do not belong to the world, just as I do not belong to the world. Sanctify them in the truth; your word is truth. As you have sent me into the world, so I have sent them into the world. And for their sakes I sanctify myself, so that they also may be sanctified in truth."

[Complete reading: John 17:6 – 19]

**Saturday night through Sunday dawn,
June 10 – 11, 2000**

PENTECOST VIGIL

Genesis 11:1 – 19 *At Babel the Lord confused their speech.*

   or

Exodus 19:3 – 8, 16 – 20 *Fire and wind descended on Sinai.*

   or

Ezekiel 37:1 – 14 *O spirit, breathe on the dead!*

   or

Joel 2:28 – 32 *On the Day of the Lord I will impart my own spirit.*

Romans 8:22 – 27 *We have the Spirit as first fruits.*

John 7:37 – 39 *Let the thirsty come to drink of living waters.*

We end Eastertime the way we began it, with a nighttime vigil, poring over the scriptures. We keep watch on Mount Sinai, where we meet God face to face, where we receive the life-giving Spirit. Our paschal journey, begun so long ago in ashes, is finished in fire.

R E F L E C T I O N

The author of the Gospel of Luke is also the author of the Acts of the Apostles. Just as the gospel reveals the public ministry and mission of Jesus of Nazareth, so does Acts reveal the ministry and mission of the early church. Without the stories of the early church in Acts, there would be many gaps in our understanding of Christianity's origins. The stories at the end of the gospel reach ahead to connect with the temporal sequence of Acts and move us to the gathered community's reception of the Holy Spirit at Pentecost. The reading from Acts today unfolds one part of the community's efforts to build itself up in the time immediately after the advent of the Spirit at Pentecost.

In this passage from Acts we find out about how the eleven apostles went about choosing a successor for Judas, the disciple who had handed Jesus over. Since Judas' departure, the apostles had been merely eleven in number, and now the community discerned that Matthias was to be the twelfth. As Christians we can see a few things in this passage to enlighten our understanding of the church. First, along with its many gifts and charisms, the church, in our own communities and worldwide, is an institution. Maintaining itself is part of its mission, as we hear in Acts, even though it might not appear to be as fulfilling as other actions, like caring for the sick, for example, or feeding the hungry.

Secondly, we note that even this very practical action is accompanied by prayer (1:24 – 25). In this we are reminded of the prayer of Jesus himself before choosing the twelve in the Gospel of Luke (6:12 – 13). This is yet another example of how the mission and ministry of Jesus are being carried on and fulfilled in the community celebrating its liturgies and carrying out its mission in the world today.

■ **How does the institutional church serve as an instrument of God's presence? Are there times it seems like an obstacle? Or does it sometimes seem like both? In what ways?**

PRACTICE OF FAITH

SEEK GOD'S BLESSINGS. Before the Ascension, while the risen Christ continued to walk the earth with his disciples, he prayed for them. He knew these disciples. He knew their strengths, weaknesses, personalities and hearts, and was sending them into the world to preach the good news to all people.

Parents teach their children the things they need to know to function in the world. They teach good nutrition, health practices, faith, morals and values. When the time comes to send your children off to college, or to a new job, or to live on their own, turn to the Father in prayer as Jesus did. Seek God's blessings of strength and protection upon your children whenever they take new steps in their own lives.

PRACTICE OF HOPE

CHRIST OUR HOPE. A once-popular prayer declared that Christ has not abandoned us, but is our hope. Where Christ has gone, we hope to follow. In today's gospel passage we read that Jesus consecrated his disciples to continue his mission. How can we, bearing the title of baptized Christians, carry on Jesus' work in the world? Following Jesus' example of prayer would be one good way. Jesus prayed that we would be one with God and one with each other. Pray today that we too will one day be one with God as Christ now is. (MP)

PRACTICE OF CHARITY

FLING WIDE YOUR DOORS. What image comes to mind when you hear the words "safe and secure"? How about a bed with big fluffy pillows, clean sheets and thick, soft blankets? Most of us reading these words never have to worry about where we will lay our heads after a long, weary day. We crawl into our beds, dream our dreams and wake the next morning to cozy kitchens and cups of hot coffee. Not so for the thousands of families who daily live in their cars or roam the streets seeking shelter, food and work. What can the churches in your community do to alleviate their suffering? Fling wide your doors and become active participants in Interfaith Hospitality Network, which unites churches of all denominations in providing shelter and support for the homeless. Call the Interfaith Hospitality Network today at 908-273-1100 for more information.

WEEKDAY READINGS (Mo) Acts 19:1 – 8; (Tu) 20:17 – 27; (We) 20:28 – 38; (Th) 22:30; 23:6 – 11; (Fr) 25:13 – 20; (Sa) 28:16 – 20, 30 – 31

READING I *Acts 2:1–11*

When the day of Pentecost had come, they were all together in one place. And suddenly from heaven there came a sound like the rush of a violent wind, and it filled the entire house where they were sitting. Divided tongues, as of fire, appeared among them, and a tongue rested on each of them. All of them were filled with the Holy Spirit and began to speak in other languages, as the Spirit gave them ability.

Now there were devout Jews from every nation under heaven living in Jerusalem. And at this sound the crowd gathered and was bewildered, because each one heard them speaking in the native language of each. Amazed and astonished, they asked, "Are not all these who are speaking Galileans? And how is it that we hear, each of us, in our own native language? Parthians, Medes, Elamites, and residents of Mesopotamia, Judea and Cappadocia, Pontus and Asia, Phrygia and Pamphylia, Egypt and the parts of Libya belonging to Cyrene, and visitors from Rome, both Jewish-born and proselytes, Cretans and Arabs — in our own languages we hear them speaking about God's deeds of power."

[Revised Common Lectionary: Acts 2:1–21 or Ezekiel 37:1–14]

READING II *Galatians 5:16–25*

Brothers and sisters: Live by the Spirit, and do not gratify the desires of the flesh. For what the flesh desires is opposed to the Spirit, and what the Spirit desires is opposed to the flesh; for these are opposed to each other, to prevent you from doing what you want. But if you are led by the Spirit, you are not subject to the law. Now the works of the flesh are obvious: fornication, impurity, licentiousness, idolatry, sorcery, enmities, strife, jealousy, anger, quarrels, dissensions, factions, envy, drunkenness, carousing, and things like these. I am warning you, as I warned you before: those who do such things will not inherit the kingdom of God. By contrast, the fruit of the Spirit is love, joy, peace, patience, kindness, generosity, faithfulness, gentleness, and self-control.

There is no law against such things. And those who belong to Christ Jesus have crucified the flesh with its passions and desires. If we live by the Spirit, let us also be guided by the Spirit.

[Revised Common Lectionary: Romans 8:22–27]

GOSPEL *John 15:26–27; 16:4–15*

Jesus spoke to the disciples: "When the Advocate comes, whom I will send to you from the Father, the Spirit of truth who comes from the Father, the Advocate will testify on my behalf. You also are to testify because you have been with me from the beginning.

"I did not say these things to you from the beginning, because I was with you. But now I am going to the one who sent me; yet none of you asks me, 'Where are you going?' But because I have said these things to you, sorrow has filled your hearts. Nevertheless I tell you the truth: it is to your advantage that I go away, for if I do not go away, the Advocate will not come to you; but if I go, I will send the Advocate to you. And having come, the Advocate will prove the world wrong about sin and righteousness and judgment: about sin, because they do not believe in me; about righteousness, because I am going to the Father and you will see me no longer; about judgment, because the ruler of this world has been condemned.

"I still have many things to say to you, but you cannot bear them now. When the Spirit of truth comes, you will be guided into all the truth; for the Spirit will not speak out of the Spirit's own authority, but will speak whatever the Spirit hears, and the Spirit will declare to you the things that are to come. The Spirit will glorify me, taking what is mine and declaring it to you. All that the Father has is mine. For this reason I said that the Spirit will take what is mine and declare it to you."

R E F L E C T I O N

The wonder of the tongues of flame resting on each of the gathered disciples and of the Holy Spirit's gift enabling them to speak in different languages is certainly profound and perplexing. We do not ususaly experience such drama in our communities today. Yet we must not consider it too remote from the daily work of the church in proclaiming the word of God and of ministering to the needy.

Such ministering in the church calls for a commitment to the inculturation of the word of God and of the liturgy, which in itself requires time and attention for learning new languages and adapting to new cultures. While it would be terrific (and certainly speedier) for tongues of flame to bring new languages to us in an instant, we can be consoled by recognizing that learning new languages for service in the church from grammar books and dictionaries, though tedious and time-consuming, is a way of continuing the work of God.

The letter of the apostle Paul to the Galatians lists other gifts brought by the Holy Spirit, more interior than the speaking of new languages. He lists them as "love, joy, peace, patience, kindness, generosity, faithfulness, gentleness, and self-control." The earliest Christian communities needed to be reminded of these gifts of the Spirit. We can romanticize the early church, supposing that there was no tension or bickering while those who had been eyewitnesses to the ministry of Jesus were still alive. Paul's letter to the Galatians, among the earliest pieces of extant Christian literature, reminds us that even back then community life was not easy. Today, as then, we can trust in the message of the Gospel of John for this Sunday: "When the Spirit of truth comes, you will be guided into all the truth; for the Spirit . . . will declare to you the things that are to come."

■ **Have you ever celebrated the eucharist in another city or country and it seemed both familiar and foreign to you? That comes from the church's encouragement to inculturate the liturgy. How does the liturgy in your parish express your local culture?**

PRACTICE OF FAITH

SOUND AND FLAME. "Mom, I don't think I believe the Holy Spirit is real." This from a daughter preparing to be confirmed. Instead of snapping, "How can you say such a thing?" I collected myself and asked her to explain. Her reply? "Well, you can't see the Spirit. We have pictures of God, Jesus, Mary, Joseph, the saints, and even angels, but no pictures of the Spirit. So how do we know the Spirit is real?" The first responses that came to my mind involved theology, philosophy, and complex sentences. Fortunately, the Spirit suggested a simpler approach.

I told her that we can envision the Spirit as the sound of a strong wind, a sound that often makes us take greater notice of our surroundings. Or that we can imagine the Spirit as a flame that enlightens our minds and hearts when we need to make difficult decisions. Whenever we grow in forgiveness, wisdom and sensitivity to others and the world around us, that is the work of the Spirit. That is how we know the Spirit is in fact real. (RG)

PRACTICE OF HOPE

SPIRIT AND TRUTH. Jesus sent the Spirit of truth upon those marked as children of God. That same Spirit leads the church to an ever deeper understanding of the gospel of Jesus Christ and its meaning in our lives. The Spirit keeps the church as a whole close to the truth, and will not allow the community of believers to go astray in the long run. Let us be hopeful always that the Spirit will guide us in the ways of God.

PRACTICE OF CHARITY

GOING HOME. Her frail, emaciated body sat slumped in the wheelchair as she was brought on stage to address the waiting crowd. A vividly colored turban wrapped her head and a matching caftan draped her bones. The cancer was consuming her body but as she slowly rose to the microphone, a miraculous transformation took place. Her dark, deep-set eyes came alive, a smile lit her face and her marvelous throaty voice came to life with the song, "Motherless Child." She was Sister Thea Bowman, a truly remarkable woman! She shared her spirituality, artistic gifts, gospel songs, culture and love for the Lord with everyone she met. This was a modern-day "saint with skin," prophet and evangelist who has gone home to God. But her legacy lives on. Read *Thea Bowman: Handing On Her Legacy* (Sheed & Ward).

WEEKDAY READINGS (Mo) 1 Kings 17:1 – 6; (Tu) 17:7 – 16; (We) 18:20 – 39; (Th) 18:41 – 46; (Fr) 19:9, 11 – 16; (Sa) 19:19 – 21

SUMMER ORDINARY TIME

You crown the year with riches.
All you touch is fertile.

Praise is yours, God in Zion.
Now is the moment
to keep our vow.

You soak the furrows
and level the ridges.
With softening rain
you bless the land with growth.

You crown the year with riches.
All you touch comes alive:
untilled lands yield crops,
hills are dressed in joy,

flocks clothe the pastures,
valleys wrap themselves in grain.
They all shout for joy
and break into song.

—Psalm 65:2, 11 – 14

God who called each day's creation good,
all we have for our food
and shelter and clothing
are the crust and air, the light and water
of this planet.
Give us care like yours for this earth:
to share its bounty
with generations to come
and with all alike in this generation,
to savor its beauty and respect its power,
to heal what greed and war and foolishness
have done to your earth and to us.
Bring us finally to give thanks,
always and everywhere.

— Prayer of the Season

READING I *Deuteronomy 4:32–34, 39–40*

For ask now about former ages, long before your own, ever since the day that God created human beings on the earth; ask from one end of heaven to the other: has anything so great as this ever happened or has its like ever been heard of? Has any people ever heard the voice of a deity speaking out of a fire, as you have heard, and lived? Or has any deity ever attempted to go and claim a nation from the midst of another nation, by trials, by signs and wonders, by war, by a mighty hand and an outstretched arm, and by terrifying displays of power, as the LORD your God did for you in Egypt before your very eyes?

So acknowledge today and take to heart that the LORD is God in heaven above and on the earth beneath; there is no other. Keep the statutes and the commandments of the LORD, which I am commanding you today for your own well-being and that of your descendants after you, so that you may long remain in the land that the LORD your God is giving you for all time.

[Revised Common Lectionary: Isaiah 6:1–8]

READING II *Romans 8:12–17*

Brothers and sisters, we are debtors, not to the flesh, to live according to the flesh — for if you live according to the flesh, you will die; but if by the Spirit you put to death the deeds of the body, you will live. For all who are led by the Spirit of God are children of God. For you did not receive a spirit of slavery to fall back into fear, but you have received a spirit of adoption. When we cry, "Abba! Father!" it is that very Spirit bearing witness with our spirit that we are children of God, and if children, then heirs, heirs of God and joint heirs with Christ — if, in fact, we suffer with Christ so that we may also be glorified with Christ.

GOSPEL *Matthew 28:16–20*

Now the eleven disciples went to Galilee, to the mountain to which Jesus had directed them. When they saw Jesus, they worshiped him; but some doubted.

And Jesus came and said to them, "All authority in heaven and on earth has been given to me. Go therefore and make disciples of all nations, baptizing them in the name of the Father and of the Son and of the Holy Spirit, and teaching them to obey everything that I have commanded you. And remember, I am with you always, to the end of the age."

[Revised Common Lectionary: John 3:1–17]

Saturday, June 24, 2000

BIRTH OF JOHN THE BAPTIST

VIGIL

Jeremiah 1:4–10 *Before I formed you in the womb, I knew you.*

1 Peter 1:8–12 *Rejoice with inexpressible joy.*

Luke 1:5–17 *Many will rejoice at John's birth.*

DAY

Isaiah 49:1–6 *From my mother's womb I am given my name.*

Acts 13:22–26 *John's message is for all children of Abraham.*

Luke 1:57–66, 80 *What will the child be?*

John said, "I must decrease if Christ is to increase." As the hours of daylight now begin to decrease, we celebrate the midsummer nativity. John is born to be the best man of the Bridegroom, the lamp of the Light and the voice of the Word. Rejoice in John's birth!

R E F L E C T I O N

It has been almost two months now since our celebration of the rites of initiation — baptism, confirmation and eucharist — at the Easter Vigil. The Gospel of Matthew reminds us of the invitation we should offer to others to join us on the journey of faith, both by the example of our lives of faith and in specific, spoken invitations. As mere individuals, we cannot expect to make much of a dent in Matthew's counsel to "go therefore and make disciples of all nations," but the body of Christ is built up one inquirer at a time, attracted to the faith and coming to appreciate its impact in our lives by the testimony of one committed Christian.

Now just past the Fifty Days of Easter, this may not seem to be an issue with which we would be concerned, for we are closer to the Vigil just past than to next year's. But the journey of faith for an inquirer, particularly if that person does not know much about the Christian faith and has not had much exposure to it, can be long and complex. The community's invitation to and support for inquirers must be part of its ongoing mission and self-understanding.

The second reading, from Paul's Letter to the Romans, prompts us to appreciate just what it is that we have to offer such inquirers: "We are children of God, and if children, then heirs, heirs of God and joint heirs with Christ." That we members of the church are indeed "heirs of God and joint heirs with Christ" can be a foreboding message. It is easy to think of the life of Jesus and the early church's experience of the risen Christ as far removed from our own lives 20 centuries later, but Paul closes the gap for us with the theology we hear proclaimed on Trinity Sunday.

■ **Does your study of the Bible prompt you to be proud of your faith — proud enough to talk about it with neighbors and even strangers? Think about inviting someone to come to church with you, or with you and your family.**

PRACTICE OF FAITH

MIDSUMMER NATIVITY. Because John the Baptist said that he must decrease in order that Christ may increase, the birthday of the great forerunner is celebrated on June 24, once thought to be the day when the daylight hours began to diminish. (The birth of Christ is celebrated on December 25 as that was once thought to be the day when daylight hours began to lengthen.) The midsummer nativity of John the Baptist has traditionally been a day of fire and water — a day for bonfires at the beach. Even if your bonfire is a barbecue grill, use this prayer to bless God:

Almighty God, unfailing ray and source of all light, sanctify this fire that we have kindled in joy at the birth of John, the herald of your Son and the great forerunner of the Way. Grant that we may remain always in you, who are light eternal. (DP)

PRACTICE OF HOPE

STEADFAST LOVE. Today we joyfully proclaim our faith in the Trinity. We are initiated into a relationship with God. The Father reveals steadfast love in creation, in scripture and in the incarnate Word, Jesus, who in turn reveals God's plan to us. The Holy Spirit of God gives us gifts to help us respond in hope to God's plan. The Trinity is an expression of God's constant love for us; we are never left alone, orphaned, defenseless, without love or left to fend for ourselves. Instead, our God steadfastly accompanies us as Father, Son and Holy Spirit. (MP)

PRACTICE OF CHARITY

REVERENCE FOR LIFE. Albert Schweitzer was a medical missionary, musician, scripture scholar and winner of the 1952 Nobel Peace Prize. In 1913, he founded a hospital in Lambarene, Gabon, where he practiced medicine until his death in 1965 at the age of 90. Recognizable by his bushy mustache, white pith helmet, white clothing and black tie, he was often sought out during his travels to Europe and the United States by those interested in his views. Once he was interrupted during dinner by visitors seeking an explanation of his ethical views. His answer took twenty minutes, and then one asked him for a detailed example of "reverence for life." Schweitzer replied, "Reverence for life means my answering your kind inquiries; it also means your reverence for my dinner hour." He then returned to his meal. Patience is indeed a virtue!

WEEKDAY READINGS (Mo) 1 Kings 21:1 – 16; (Tu) 21:17 – 29; (We) 2 Kings 2:1, 6 – 14; (Th) Sirach 48:1 – 14; (Fr) 2 Kings 11:1 – 4, 9 – 18, 20; (Sa) Birth of John the Baptist, see box

READING I *Exodus 24:3–8*

Moses came and told the people all the words of the LORD and all the ordinances; and all the people answered with one voice, and said, "All the words that the LORD has spoken we will do." And Moses wrote down all the words of the LORD. He rose early in the morning, and built an altar at the foot of the mountain, and set up twelve pillars, corresponding to the twelve tribes of Israel. Moses sent youths of the people of Israel, who offered burnt offerings and sacrificed oxen as offerings of well-being to the LORD. Moses took half of the blood and put it in basins, and half of the blood he dashed against the altar. Then he took the book of the covenant, and read it in the hearing of the people; and they said, "All that the LORD has spoken we will do, and we will be obedient." Moses took the blood and dashed it on the people, and said, "See the blood of the covenant that the LORD has made with you in accordance with all these words."

READING II *Hebrews 9:11–15*

When Christ came as a high priest of the good things that have come, then through the greater and perfect tent (not made with hands, that is, not of this creation), he entered once for all into the Holy Place, not with the blood of goats and calves, but with his own blood, thus obtaining eternal redemption.

For if the blood of goats and bulls, with the sprinkling of the ashes of a heifer, sanctifies those who have been defiled so that their flesh is purified, how much more will the blood of Christ, who through the eternal Spirit offered himself without blemish to God, purify our conscience from dead works to worship the living God!

For this reason Christ is the mediator of a new covenant, so that those who are called may receive the promised eternal inheritance, because a death has occurred that redeems them from the transgressions under the first covenant.

GOSPEL *Mark 14:12–16, 22–26*

On the first day of Unleavened Bread, when the Passover lamb is sacrificed, his disciples said to him, "Where do you want us to go and make the preparations for you to eat the Passover?" So Jesus sent two of his disciples, saying to them, "Go into the city, and a man carrying a jar of water will meet you; follow him, and wherever he enters, say to the owner of the house, 'The Teacher asks, Where is my guest room where I may eat the Passover with my disciples?' The owner will show you a large room upstairs, furnished and ready. Make preparations for us there." So the disciples set out and went to the city, and found everything as Jesus had told them; and they prepared the Passover meal. While they were eating, Jesus took a loaf of bread, and after blessing it he broke it, gave it to them, and said, "Take; this is my body." Then he took a cup, and after giving thanks he gave it to them, and all of them drank from it. He said to them, "This is my blood of the covenant, which is poured out for many. Truly I tell you, I will never again drink of the fruit of the vine until that day when I drink it new in the dominion of God." When they had sung the hymn, they went out to the Mount of Olives.

Thursday, June 29, 2000

PETER AND PAUL, APOSTLES

VIGIL

Acts 3:1–10 *Peter cried: "Look at us!"*

Galatians 1:11–20 *God chose to reveal Christ to me.*

John 21:15–19 *Simon Peter, do you love me?*

DAY

Acts 12:1–11 *The chains dropped from Peter's wrists.*

2 Timothy 4:6–8,17–18 *I have kept the faith.*

Matthew 16:13–19 *I entrust to you the keys of the kingdom.*

Today we keep a festival in honor of the two apostles who began the harvest of God's reign. They preached from Jerusalem to Rome, keeping the Easter commandment to bring the good news to the ends of the earth.

REFLECTION

Throughout two millennia of Christian life and Christian history, from the table of the Last Supper with Jesus and his disciples to the altars of our churches with our gathered communities eating and drinking today, the celebration of the eucharist has been the heartbeat of our faith. Though for centuries the frequent reception of the bread and the wine ebbed as the church lost sight of the importance of the eucharist as part of the celebration of initiation, we have gradually begun to recover this necessary rite of Christian life experienced together. The Gospel of Mark, the central text of this liturgical Year B, is one of our earliest sources for the practice of this age-old tradition of breaking bread and pouring wine when we come together.

It is not an accident that the basic symbolic elements of the eucharist are foods that need human effort to become part of the meal. The eucharist is not apples and water, which could be eaten and drunk just as they are, seconds after being obtained. Rather, grains and grapes take much human preparation to be made into the bread and the wine that become the elements for the celebration of the eucharist. In other words, the bread and wine suggest that our participating human nature is necessary for the eucharist, as prescribed by our churches, to take place. This should be a great consolation to us, who can often find our own fragile human natures to be far from things of God. In the bread and the wine of the eucharist, God is saying, "Now, as in the life of Jesus of Nazareth, human nature is needed for God's presence to be brought into the world." God's gift comes through our human nature and for this we can rejoice.

■ **In its Greek form the word *eucharist* means giving thanks. For what — as an individual or together with a community of faith — do you give thanks to God at this time?**

PRACTICE OF FAITH

AS THEY WERE EATING. Because Christ gave us the eucharist as an everlasting memorial of his dying and rising, every meal we eat with others echoes the eucharist's joy. In our time, with processed foods and tight schedules, we often eat hurriedly, with little enjoyment. Begin to take small steps so that at least one day a week, you share a meal with others at a leisurely pace, with attention to such details as a tablecloth, candles and flowers. If you live alone, invite someone over. Renew the habit of praying before eating. Today, in honor of the feast and as an echo of the eucharist, search out or bake a fresh, whole loaf of bread to share. Make sangria (from the Spanish word *sangre*, meaning blood) by adding sliced oranges, lemons, pineapples and strawberries to red wine. (DP)

PRACTICE OF HOPE

PRESENCE. All feasts celebrate some aspect of the paschal mystery of Jesus Christ. Today's feast began in the Middle Ages from the desire to celebrate the presence of Christ in the elements of the bread and wine of the eucharist.

When I remember meals, I remember my grandmother's meals. In the dining room was a framed, embroidered print of the popular motto: "Jesus, the silent guest at every meal." Also, the Irish custom was to set an extra place at every meal. My grandmother sat, not at one end of the table, but at whatever place was nearest the kitchen, and the extra place was next to her. It was a ritual of our life. We learned presence from absence. Christ was present to us in that house through our meals. (MP)

PRACTICE OF CHARITY

THOSE WHO HUNGER. As we stand at the beginning of a new millenium, the greatest scandal of the passing century is the pitiful progress made toward resolving the scourge of hunger. Famine haunts many parts of Africa and Asia. Hunger and its related diseases kill more people annually than all other causes combined. The eucharist reminds us that all are called to the table, regardless of gender, material wealth, age, nationality or ability. Yet the gulf between the "haves" and the "have-nots," the fed and the hungry, and the developed and developing nations widens daily. To assist the hungry, contact Catholic Relief Services, P.O. Box 17090, Baltimore MD 21298-9664; 410-625-2220.

WEEKDAY READINGS (Mo) 2 Kings 17:5 – 8, 13 – 15, 18; (Tu) 19:9 – 11, 14 – 21, 31 – 36; (We) 22:8 – 13; 23:1 – 3; (Th) Peter and Paul, see box; (Fr) Hosea 11:1 – 9; (Sa) Lamentations 2:2, 10 – 14, 18 – 19

READING I *Job 38:1–11*

The LORD answered Job out of the whirlwind: "Who is this that darkens counsel by words without knowledge? Brace yourself like a warrior: I will question you, and you shall declare to me.

"Where were you when I laid the foundation of the earth? Tell me, if you have understanding. Who determined its measurements—surely you know! Or who stretched the line upon it? On what were its bases sunk, or who laid its cornerstone when the morning stars sang together and all the heavenly beings shouted for joy?

"Who shut in the sea with doors when it burst out from the womb?—when I made the clouds its garment, and thick darkness its swaddling band, and prescribed bounds for it, and set bars and doors, and said, 'Thus far shall you come, and no farther, and here shall your proud waves be stopped'?"

READING II *2 Corinthians 6:1–13*

As we work together with God, we urge you also not to accept the grace of God in vain. For God says, "At an acceptable time I have listened to you, and on a day of salvation I have helped you." See, now is the day of salvation! We are putting no obstacle in anyone's way, so that no fault may be found with our ministry, but as servants of God we have commended ourselves in every way: through great endurance, in afflictions, hardships, calamities, beatings, imprisonments, riots, labors, sleepless nights, hunger; by purity, knowledge, patience, kindness, holiness of spirit, genuine love, truthful speech, and the power of God; with the weapons of righteousness for the right hand and for the left; in honor or dishonor, in ill repute and good repute. We are treated as impostors and yet are true; as unknown, and yet are well known; as dying, and see—we are alive; as punished, and yet not killed; as sorrowful, yet always rejoicing; as poor, yet making many rich; as having nothing, and yet possessing everything.

We have spoken frankly to you Corinthians; our heart is wide open to you. There is no restriction in our affections, but only in yours. In return—I speak to you as to children—open your hearts also.

GOSPEL *Mark 4:35–41*

When evening had come, Jesus said to his disciples, "Let us go across to the other side." And leaving the crowd behind, they took Jesus with them in the boat, just as he was. Other boats were with him. A great windstorm arose, and the waves beat into the boat, so that the boat was already being swamped. But Jesus was in the stern, asleep on the cushion; and they woke him up and said to him, "Teacher, do you not care that we are perishing?" He woke up and rebuked the wind, and said to the sea, "Peace! Be still!" Then the wind ceased, and there was a dead calm. Jesus said to them, "Why are you afraid? Have you still no faith?" And they were filled with great awe and said to one another, "Who then is this, that even the wind and the sea obey him?"

R E F L E C T I O N

Of the four gospels in the New Testament, Mark is the one that portrays the disciples in the least complimentary light. Often we can wonder what the author's intention was in including the details of the disciples' misunderstandings and fears.

The gospel text for this Sunday is one of those stories. This narrative is known commonly as "the calming of the sea." What is especially striking is that Jesus was so soundly asleep in the midst of what the evangelist describes as "a great windstorm," so great that "the boat was already being swamped." The disciples appear quite frantic as the sea is raging around them, but Jesus, in the stern, sleeps right through it. Many of us who sleep uneasily in times of stress might think of the story as "the sleeping of the Savior" instead of the "calming of the sea"!

In ancient literature the sea held great symbolic meaning. Its expansiveness and its ever-present threat of force made the sea an appropriate symbol for all the unknown and threatening possibilities that life holds. It is likely that this gospel story, beyond the event itself, was meant to touch on the looming and mysterious threats and possibilities of human life.

The reading from Second Corinthians reveals that Paul and his early Christian followers found many such threats to their existence; he mentions "afflictions, hardships, calamities, beatings, imprisonments, riots, labors, sleepless nights, [and] hunger" in this passage.

■ **If you were to make a list of the things in your life that contributed to a feeling of being "at sea," what would be on that list?**

■ **Does your belonging to and celebrating with a Christian community Sunday after Sunday make the "sea" less threatening? How does it do this? And how could it do this better?**

PRACTICE OF FAITH

WAKING JESUS. Jesus had to calm his apostles' fears often. They were ordinary people called to an extraordinary mission. A good number of them were fishermen who knew the sea, but as today's gospel reading shows us they could still become very frightened — especially if their leader was sound asleep during a storm that threatened their lives. But even then they had the wisdom to awaken Jesus and seek his help.

As Paul knew, there are many difficulties in life that can challenge Christian faith. Follow the example of the apostles and wake Jesus with the things that trouble you. Bring your concerns to the Lord in prayer and unite them to the Sunday prayer of your church.

PRACTICE OF HOPE

HOPE AND CONTROL. This gospel challenges and purifies our hope. Sometimes in our fear we may think that Jesus is still asleep in the boat. "Who is in control of this boat?" "Doesn't the Lord care?" "Isn't the Lord concerned?"

Last summer, the dinghy that my daughter was rowing started taking on water as we went toward the dock. I did not think that we would reach safety. "Shall I bail?" I asked anxiously. Looking at the dock and gauging the distance and the flow of water, she said, "Don't worry, we'll make it."

Through baptism, we live as a new creation. That new order means professing our hope in Jesus. It also means daring to trust that God, the creator of all things, controls the cosmos, that God will still the chaos of evil for us so we can make it to the shore. (MP)

PRACTICE OF CHARITY

STAND FIRM. Franz Jaegerstaetter faced a political storm — the fascism that swept across his native Austria in the 1930s. After a rebellious youth, Franz embraced Christianity through his marriage to a faithful woman and became a responsible father of three daughters. As his faith matured, he became convinced of the impossibility of loyalty to both Christ and Hitler. As a farmer his compulsory military service was twice deferred, but in 1943 he was ordered to report. His response was a resounding "No!" Imprisoned until his execution on August 9, he steadfastly refused to assist an unjust war. Even his bishop urged him to take the oath for the sake of his family. A few days before his death, he wrote, "I am convinced that it is still best that I speak the truth even if it costs me my life."

WEEKDAY READINGS (Mo) 2 Kings 17:5 – 8, 13 – 15, 18; (Tu) 19:9 -11, 14 – 21, 31 – 36; (We) 22:8 – 13; 23:1 – 3; (Th) Peter and Paul, see box, page 106; (Fr) Hosea 11:1 – 9; (Sa) Lamentations 2:2, 10 – 14, 18 – 19

READING I *Wisdom 1:13–15; 2:23–24*

God did not make death, and he does not delight in the death of the living. For he created all things so that they might exist; the generative forces of the world are wholesome, and there is no destructive poison in them, and the dominion of Hades is not on earth. For righteousness is immortal. For God created us for incorruption, and made us in the image of his own eternity, but through the devil's envy death entered the world, and those who belong to his company experience it.

READING II *2 Corinthians 8:7–15*

Now as you excel in everything—in faith, in speech, in knowledge, in utmost eagerness, and in our love for you—so we want you to excel also in this generous undertaking. For you know the generous act of our Lord Jesus Christ, that though he was rich, yet for your sakes he became poor, so that by his poverty you might become rich. I do not mean that there should be relief for others and pressure on you, but it is a question of a fair balance between your present abundance and their need, so that their abundance may be for your need, in order that there may be a fair balance. As it is written, "The one who had much did not have too much, and the one who had little did not have too little."

GOSPEL *Mark 5:21–43*

When Jesus had crossed in the boat to the other side, a great crowd gathered around him; and he was by the sea. Then one of the synagogue leaders named Jairus came and, when he saw Jesus, fell at his feet and begged him repeatedly, "My little daughter is at the point of death. Come and lay your hands on her, so that she may be made well, and live."

R E F L E C T I O N

As we return to Mark today, we find a literary device of ancient Greek literature called "intercalation." The device is commonly called "sandwiching," for in it an author takes one story and splits in in two, like two slices of bread. Another story is inserted in the middle, and the effect is greater than if the two stories were told separately. The evangelist Mark used this device to highlight two events in the ministry of Jesus of Nazareth.

This particular sandwich is made up of stories of Jesus ministering to two women, one 12 years old and the other older. The slices of bread come from the story of the raising of Jairus' daughter. Jairus is a leader of the synagogue, a man of authority in the area where Jesus is ministering. Before Jesus reaches the girl, who is "at the point of death," she dies. Jesus proceeds to the house and wakes the girl.

The story in the middle is about a woman who had been hemorrhaging for 12 years. She touched Jesus' clothes and was cured. (The number 12, found in both stories, is one of the clues that the stories are meant to be related to one another.)

From now until the end of the liturgical year, the church has also effected an intercalation. Even though from now until the end of this year, we concentrate on the Gospel of Mark, we will find a few weeks from now part of chapter 6 from the Gospel of John. (This is the famous "bread of life" discourse in the fourth gospel.) In this intercalation, the Gospel of Mark plays the role of thick slices of bread, in which we will have a thin layer of John for four weeks in July and August.

■ **The creativity of the evangelists in using literary devices like intercalation lets us know that artistry communicates the presence of God. Are there works of art that you have found inspirational and uplifting? How did the art connect with your faith in a unique way?**

PRACTICE OF FAITH

MOVE MOUNTAINS. I've never heard of anyone whose faith actually did move a mountain, but the saying was not meant to be interpreted literally. Rather it is a device to suggest to us that with faith we can accomplish the seemingly impossible.

Our faith is not a static thing. Just as our minds and bodies change and grow over time, so does our faith. We nurture our bodies with food, our minds with information. We nurture our faith with the eucharist, prayer and good works. I don't see anyone moving Mount Shasta from California to the Florida Everglades, but I do see any one of us helping the homeless find shelter, and the unemployed find work. Nourish your faith by joining with others to bring lasting peace to our families, communities, parishes and workplaces. With a faith that can move mountains, you can bring harmony and peace to our world. (RG)

PRACTICE OF HOPE

JESUS THE HEALER. Nowhere is it recorded that Jesus ever turned anyone away who asked for healing. But still, to come to Jesus and ask? What did the president of the synagogue really know about this itinerant preacher and healer? Probably not much. He hoped in Jesus.

The woman with a hemorrhage waited, pushed through the crowd and simply touched Jesus' cloak. She had no reliable information; she did not know for certain that she would be cured. She only hoped in this person about whom she had heard so much.

God's healing power is for us all. We need only ask. (MP)

PRACTICE OF CHARITY

RISE UP. To have a child who laughs, plays and thrives is a blessing for families. For some, however, clues alert parents that all is not well and after numerous lab tests and examinations, the unthinkable is said: "Your child has cancer." There is help for families living with this ordeal. St. Jude's Children's Hospital in Memphis, Tennessee, is a leader in research, therapy and technology to give sick children the opportunity to lead longer, fuller lives. Affiliate hospitals around the nation assist St. Jude's in carrying out treatment nearer to the patient's home. The amazing thing is the families never pay for the services provided. Dedicated volunteer supporters raise funds in their communities for their local affiliates. Call 1-800-877-5833 today for the location of your nearest affiliate.

WEEKDAY READINGS (Mo) Ephesians 2:19 – 22; (Tu) Amos 3:1 – 8; 4:11 – 12; (We) 5:14 – 15, 21 – 24; (Th) 7:10 – 17; (Fr) 8:4 – 6, 9 – 12; (Sa) 9:11 – 15

READING I *Ezekiel 2:1–5*

A voice said to me: O mortal, stand up on your feet, and I will speak with you. And when the LORD spoke to me, a spirit entered into me and set me on my feet; and I heard the LORD speaking to me, saying, Mortal, I am sending you to the people of Israel, to a nation of rebels who have rebelled against me; they and their ancestors have transgressed against me to this very day. The descendants are impudent and stubborn. I am sending you to them, and you shall say to them, "Thus says the Lord GOD." Whether they hear or refuse to hear (for they are a rebellious house), they shall know that there has been a prophet among them.

READING II *2 Corinthians 12:2–10*

I know a person in Christ who fourteen years ago was caught up to the third heaven — whether in the body or out of the body I do not know; God knows. And I know that such a person—whether in the body or out of the body I do not know; God knows — was caught up into Paradise and heard things that are not to be told, that no mortal is permitted to repeat. On behalf of such a one I will boast, but on my own behalf I will not boast, except of my weaknesses. But if I wish to boast, I will not be a fool, for I will be speaking the truth. But I refrain from it, so that no one may think better of me than what is seen in me or heard from me, even considering the exceptional character of the revelations.

Therefore, to keep me from being too elated, a thorn was given me in the flesh, a messenger of Satan to torment me, to keep me from being too elated. Three times I appealed to the Lord about this, that it would leave me, but the Lord said to me, "My grace is sufficient for you, for power is made perfect in weakness." So, I will boast all the more gladly of my weaknesses, so that the power of Christ may dwell in me. Therefore I am content with weaknesses, insults, hardships, persecutions, and calamities for the sake of Christ; for whenever I am weak, then I am strong.

GOSPEL *Mark 6:1–13*

Jesus came to his hometown, and his disciples followed him. On the sabbath he began to teach in the synagogue, and many who heard him were astounded. They said, "Where did this man get all this? What is this wisdom that has been given to him? What deeds of power are being done by his hands! Is not this the carpenter, the son of Mary and brother of James and Joses and Judas and Simon, and are not his sisters here with us?" And they took offense at him.

Then Jesus said to them, "Prophets are not without honor, except in their hometown, and among their own kin, and in their own house." And Jesus could do no deed of power there, except that he laid his hands on a few sick people and cured them. And he was amazed at their unbelief.

Then Jesus went about among the villages teaching. He called the twelve and began to send them out two by two, and gave them authority over the unclean spirits. He ordered them to take nothing for their journey except a staff; no bread, no bag, no money in their belts; but to wear sandals and not to put on two tunics. Jesus said to them, "Wherever you enter a house, stay there until you leave the place. If any place will not welcome you and they refuse to hear you, as you leave, shake off the dust that is on your feet as a testimony against them." So they went out and proclaimed that all should repent. They cast out many demons, and anointed with oil many who were sick and cured them.

R E F L E C T I O N

There are times when we lament our lives, wishing that things had turned out different, feeling that life could not get any dimmer. Sometimes listening to the readings proclaimed in church when we are in the midst of such times is no consolation, for we might think that Jesus himself or those who lived in the time of Jesus or the people in the churches where Paul ministered were so much better off than we are, because they were so close in time to the "real thing."

We should know that the church has never suggested that as we move through time we move farther away from the "glory days," farther from salvation, farther from God. Two years ago in his apostolic letter, *Dies Domini,* on the significance of Sunday, Pope John Paul II wrote that Sunday "is an invitation to relive in some way the experience of the two disciples of Emmaus" (see Luke 24:13 – 35). Sunday "cuts through human time, the months, the years, the centuries."

The readings of the liturgy for this Sunday are also a testimony to the fact that the disciples' closeness in space and time to Jesus of Nazareth did not exempt them from the difficulties of human life. In the second reading Paul proclaims: "I am content with weaknesses, insults, hardships, persecutions, and calamities for the sake of Christ; for whenever I am weak, then I am strong." The example of Paul's courage in the face of weakness may in itself not be enough to move us out of darkness, but his experience of the resurrection assures us that, with the support of our communities of faith and those who love us, we too have access to that strength.

■ **To whom do you turn when the hardships of life bring you down? Does the example of the followers of Jesus and of the suffering of the saints help see you through?**

PRACTICE OF FAITH

KATERI TEKAKWITHA. On July 14 Catholics in the United States celebrate the memorial of Kateri Tekakwitha. A Native American of the Algonquin tribe, Kateri was born to Christian parents near present-day Auriesville, New York. She was later captured by Iroquois warriors and married to a Mohawk chief. Her Christianity was not accepted by her new people. She endured persecution for her beliefs, and eventually fled. Although she suffered disfigurement and impaired vision due to smallpox, she lived a life caring for others. Kateri died in Canada in 1680.

The National Tekakwitha Conference (PO Box 6759, Great Falls MT 59401) is held each summer to explore the connections between native American heritage and the Catholic tradition. (DP)

PRACTICE OF HOPE

LISTEN. Jesus' neighbors "took offense at him." Other translations say: "They found him too much for them"; "And they would not accept him"; "And they had no confidence in him." Jesus' neighbors thought they knew all there was to know about him. What could he possibly have to say of any importance?

How often do we make that same mistake about someone, or how often is someone mistaken that way about us? We honor others by listening and respecting their truths and their experiences of God, trusting that they have something to teach us. (MP).

PRACTICE OF CHARITY

NONCONFORMITY. Author Henry David Thoreau, whose birthday is remembered this week, believed nonconformity is a virtue. He once wrote: "If a man does not keep pace with his companions, perhaps it is because he hears a different drummer. Let him step to the music he hears, however measured or far away." His own refusal in 1845 to pay a tax meant to finance the war with Mexico landed him in jail overnight. This experience inspired his classic work, "On the Duty of Civil Disobedience." This powerful essay focuses on the authority of conscience and the moral obligation to resist injustice supported by law. This week, challenge yourself to "step to a different drummer" by reading some of Thoreau's work.

WEEKDAY READINGS (Mo) Hosea 2:16 – 22; (Tu) 8:4 – 7, 11 – 13; (We) 10:1 – 3, 7 – 8, 12; (Th) 11:1 – 4, 8 – 9; (Fr) 14:2 – 10; (Sa) Isaiah 6:1 – 8

READING I *Amos 7:7–15*

This is what the Lord GOD showed me: the Lord was standing beside a wall built with a plumb line, holding a plumb line. And the LORD said to me, "Amos, what do you see?" And I said, "A plumb line." Then the Lord said, "See, I am setting a plumb line in the midst of my people Israel; I will never again pass them by; the high places of Isaac shall be made desolate, and the sanctuaries of Israel shall be laid waste, and I will rise against the house of Jeroboam with the sword."

Then Amaziah, the priest of Bethel, sent to King Jeroboam of Israel, saying, "Amos has conspired against you in the very center of the house of Israel; the land is not able to bear all his words. For thus Amos has said, 'Jeroboam shall die by the sword, and Israel must go into exile away from its land.'" And Amaziah said to Amos, "O seer, go, flee away to the land of Judah, earn your bread there, and prophesy there; but never again prophesy at Bethel, for it is the king's sanctuary, and it is a temple of the kingdom."

Then Amos answered Amaziah, "I am no prophet, nor a prophet's son; but I am a shepherd, and a dresser of sycamore trees, and the LORD took me from following the flock, and the LORD said to me, 'Go, prophesy to my people Israel.'"

READING II *Ephesians 1:3–14*

Blessed be the God and Father of our Lord Jesus Christ, who has blessed us in Christ with every spiritual blessing in the heavenly places, just as God chose us in Christ before the foundation of the world that before God we should be holy and blameless in love. God destined us for adoption as children through Jesus Christ; this was God's good pleasure and will, to the praise of God's glorious grace freely bestowed on us in the Beloved.

In Christ we have redemption through his blood, the forgiveness of our trespasses, according to the riches of God's grace lavished on us.

With all wisdom and insight God has made known to us the mystery of the divine will, according to God's good pleasure set forth in Christ, as a plan for the fullness of time, to gather up all things in Christ, things in heaven and things on earth. In Christ we have also obtained an inheritance, having been destined according to the purpose of the one who accomplishes all things according to the divine counsel and will, so that we, who were the first to set our hope on Christ, might live for the praise of God's glory. In Christ you also, when you had heard the word of truth, the gospel of your salvation, and had believed in him, were marked with the seal of the promised Holy Spirit; this is the pledge of our inheritance toward redemption as God's own people, to the praise of God's glory.

GOSPEL *Mark 6:7–13*

He called the twelve and began to send them out two by two, and gave them authority over the unclean spirits. He ordered them to take nothing for their journey except a staff; no bread, no bag, no money in their belts; but to wear sandals and not to put on two tunics. Jesus said to them, "Wherever you enter a house, stay there until you leave the place. If any place will not welcome you and they refuse to hear you, as you leave, shake off the dust that is on your feet as a testimony against them." So they went out and proclaimed that all should repent. They cast out many demons, and anointed with oil many who were sick and cured them.

[Revised Common Lectionary: Mark 6:14–29]

REFLECTION

A popular perception of prophets is that they foretell the future. With this idea about prophecy we would not find much difference between a prophet of the Hebrew Bible and someone today who sets up shop offering to foretell what will happen in people's careers or love lives — except that the latter is hoping for profit. Today's first reading from the prophet Amos quickly dispels any such comparison.

Amos' messages were strong indictments of the townspeoples' way of life and they were not well received. The reading for our liturgy catches Amos being sent away because Amaziah, the priest of Bethel, is tired of Amos' harsh words. Amos' response reveals the results of the mission of true prophets (then and now). To prove to the priest that his prophecies are genuine, Amos tells Amaziah, "I was no prophet, nor did I hang out with a gang of prophets" (7:14, paraphrased). "I was just a shepherd and a dresser of sycamores." (A "dresser of sycamores" is one who tends sycamore trees.) It was only because of the Lord's insistence that Amos left his homeland to deliver the unwelcome messages.

The gospel similarly finds Jesus getting the disciples ready for their mission. It would be no welcome task to travel without food, money or even a change of clothes, but this is what Jesus asked of them. Heeding God's call and God's word is no easy feat!

■ **The drama of many biblical narratives — crossing the Red Sea, walking on water, raising the dead — can lead us to think that without such drama, God is not present in our lives or calling us to act. But our discernment of God's will is necessary to fulfill our baptismal vocation. How might you become more attuned to God's word and call?**

PRACTICE OF FAITH

SENT OUT. Celebrate this Jubilee Year 2000 by making a personal pilgrimage. Pope John Paul II has encouraged each person to make a pilgrimage during the jubilee year. Consider visiting the cathedral of your diocese, or a church in your area that has a special history, such as a mission or shrine. These pilgrimages may be undertaken alone, as a family or with other members of your parish community. Use the pilgrimage as a time to pray together and learn more about the growth of the church in your part of the country.

PRACTICE OF HOPE

SENT ON MISSION. Jesus sent the Twelve out, and in doing so he gave them a share in his mission. They were to proclaim to the people that the time is fulfilled, that the kingdom of God is near, that now is the time to repent and believe the good news. As baptized Christians, we too share in that mission. Every day, Jesus sends us out and we proclaim the good news, expel demons, anoint the sick and bring Christ's healing love to those we meet. We do not need much luggage. We need only be faithful and keep up the good work, confident in Christ's word. (MP)

PRACTICE OF CHARITY

GIVE CARE. Peggy visits Bernadine, an 87-year-old friend living in a modest retirement home. Bernie has a small room which she has furnished with what is left of the treasures of her life. Family photos and pictures of Christ dot the walls. Bernie is no longer able to get around as she once did and so Peggy helps bring the world to her. Weekly visits include stories of family and news from church, fresh fruit and a wheelchair stroll through the garden of Bernie's retirement home. Their relationship as a result of a program called Interfaith Volunteer Caregivers Network. Volunteers provide friendly visits, transportation and minor home repair. Contact the Faith in Action national program office at 914-331-0016 to see about getting your parish involved.

WEEKDAY READINGS (Mo) Isaiah 1:10 – 17; (Tu) 7:1 – 9; (We) 10:5 – 7, 13 – 16; (Th) 26:7 – 9, 12, 16 – 19; (Fr) 38:1 – 6, 21 – 22, 7 – 8; (Sa) Micah 2:1 – 5

READING I *Jeremiah 23:1–6*

Woe to the shepherds who destroy and scatter the sheep of my pasture! says the LORD. Therefore thus says the LORD, the God of Israel, concerning the shepherds who shepherd my people: It is you who have scattered my flock, and have driven them away, and you have not attended to them. So I will attend to you for your evil doings, says the LORD.

Then I myself will gather the remnant of my flock out of all the lands where I have driven them, and I will bring them back to their fold, and they shall be fruitful and multiply. I will raise up shepherds over them who will shepherd them, and they shall not fear any longer, or be dismayed, nor shall any be missing, says the LORD.

The days are surely coming, says the LORD, when I will raise up for David a righteous Branch, who shall reign as king and deal wisely, and shall execute justice and righteousness in the land. In his days Judah will be saved and Israel will live in safety. And this is the name by which he will be called: "The LORD is our righteousness."

READING II *Ephesians 2:13–22*

In Christ Jesus you who once were far off have been brought near by the blood of Christ. For Christ is our peace; in his flesh he has made both groups into one and has broken down the dividing wall, that is, the hostility between us. He has abolished the law with its commandments and ordinances, that he might create in himself one new humanity in place of the two, thus making peace, and might reconcile both groups to God in one body through the cross, thus putting to death that hostility through it. So Christ came and proclaimed peace to you who were far off and peace to those who were near; for through him both of us have access in one Spirit to the Father.

So then you are no longer strangers and aliens, but you are citizens with the saints and also members of the household of God, built upon the foundation of the apostles and prophets, with Christ Jesus himself as the cornerstone. In him the whole structure is joined together and grows into a holy temple in the Lord; in whom you also are built together spiritually into a dwelling place for God. *[Complete reading: Ephesians 2:11–22]*

GOSPEL *Mark 6:30–34, 53–56*

The apostles gathered around Jesus, and told him all that they had done and taught. He said to them, "Come away to a deserted place all by yourselves and rest a while." For many were coming and going, and they had no leisure even to eat. And they went away in the boat to a deserted place by themselves. Now many saw them going and recognized them, and they hurried there on foot from all the towns and arrived ahead of them.

As Jesus went ashore, he saw a great crowd; and he had compassion for them, because they were like sheep without a shepherd; and he began to teach them many things.

When Jesus and the disciples had crossed over, they came to land at Gennesaret and moored the boat. When they got out of the boat, people at once recognized him, and rushed about that whole region and began to bring the sick on mats to wherever they heard he was. And wherever he went, into villages or cities or farms, they laid the sick in the marketplaces, and begged him that they might touch even the fringe of his cloak; and all who touched it were healed.

R E F L E C T I O N

The first reading and the gospel reading in our Sunday liturgy are usually related to one another by a similar event, image or theological point. Here we find a striking connection between the word of the prophet Jeremiah and the ministry of Jesus described in Mark. This message is about leading people to God or driving them away.

The Babylonian captivity came in the sixth century before Christ, when Jerusalem was defeated in war and the Temple destroyed. Most of the Israelite survivors were carried away to live in exile, far, far away from their homeland, in Babylon. This was an inconceivable crisis of faith and hope for the nation, and from it sprang some of the most passionate pieces of literature in the Hebrew Bible. Jeremiah prophesied during this period.

We hear him today passing along a message from the Lord criticizing the corrupt leaders of Israel: "You have scattered my flock, and driven them away." The Lord promises that the people will get a shepherd, a king "who will reign and govern wisely," a message from the Hebrew scriptures that will eventually be adopted by Christians and applied to Jesus of Nazareth.

In the gospel, Jesus is trying to find a deserted place, as he often is in Mark's gospel, but when he sees the vast crowd of people who "like sheep without a shepherd," he is moved to put aside his own need for solitude and teach the people at great length. It is a touching passage that portrays Jesus as immeasurably compassionate.

■ **Often good church leaders must say things that their assemblies do not want to hear. How does the church discern difficult messages from untrue messages? Prophetic leaders from false leaders "who drive the flock away"?**

PRACTICE OF FAITH MARTHA. This Saturday, July 29, is the memorial of St. Martha. In the tradition of some monastic communities, the day is expanded to include the rest of Martha's family and is celebrated in honor of "Martha, Mary and Lazarus — hosts of the Lord." From her portrayal in Luke 10 as busy seeing to the details of a visit from Jesus, Martha has become the patron saint of cooks and hospitality. We too can be hosts of the Lord when we open our homes to others and offer hospitality to those in need. This week, practice Martha's way of meeting the needs of others: Invite someone over for a meal; drop off some canned goods at your local food pantry; consider volunteering for a meals-on-wheels program; pray for those who work to feed our nation's hungry citizens.

PRACTICE OF HOPE JOACHIM AND ANNE. On Wednesday the church remembers the parents of Mary — Joachim and Anne. What little we can say about them comes from folklore. There is no mention of them in scripture, and their names come to us from later believers who felt the need to celebrate the obscure and anonymous grandparents of Jesus. Every time we remember elderly friends and relatives with a phone call or a note, or visit the graves of fellow Christians, we proclaim that membership in the community of faith means that no one goes unremembered by our God.

PRACTICE OF CHARITY ALL WHO TOUCHED WERE HEALED. Jayne could not figure out why she kept losing weight and was tired all the time. But even the knife-like pain in her hip did not deter her from meeting friends and family around town or at church. One day, the usual scans and tests revealed the awful news that cancer had invaded her body. Six weeks later, she died at home, surrounded by family, friends, clergy and the hospice team. Remembered most was her determination of spirit and deep faith in God. Prayers for spiritual healing helped carry her into God's arms.

Hospice is a national organization that helps people to die with dignity and in comfort, and that gives needed help to caregivers. Contact your local hospital to find the hospice nearest you, and consider offering your services.

WEEKDAY READINGS (Mo) Micah 6:1 – 4, 6 – 8; (Tu) 2 Corinthians 4:7 – 15; (We) Jeremiah 1:1, 4 – 10; (Th) 2:1 – 3, 7 – 8, 12 – 13; (Fr) 3:14 – 17; (Sa) 7:1 – 11

READING I *2 Kings 4:42–44*

A man came from Baal-shalishah, bringing food from the first fruits to Elisha, the man of God: twenty loaves of barley and fresh ears of grain in his sack. Elisha said, "Give it to the people and let them eat." But his servant said, "How can I set this before a hundred people?" So he repeated, "Give it to the people and let them eat, for thus says the LORD, 'They shall eat and have some left.'" He set it before them, they ate, and had some left, according to the word of the LORD.

READING II *Ephesians 4:1–6*

I therefore, the prisoner in the Lord, beg you to lead a life worthy of the calling to which you have been called, with all humility and gentleness, with patience, bearing with one another in love, making every effort to maintain the unity of the Spirit in the bond of peace. There is one body and one Spirit, just as you were called to the one hope of your calling, one Lord, one faith, one baptism, one God and Father of all, who is above all and through all and in all.
[Revised Common Lectionary: Ephesians 3:14–21]

GOSPEL *John 6:1–21*

Jesus went to the other side of the Sea of Galilee, also called the Sea of Tiberias. A large crowd kept following him, because they saw the signs that he was doing for the sick. Jesus went up the mountain and sat down there with his disciples. Now the Passover, the festival of the Jewish people, was near. When he looked up and saw a large crowd coming toward him, Jesus said to Philip, "Where are we to buy bread for these people to eat?" Jesus said this to test Philip, for he himself knew what he was going to do. Philip answered him, "Six months' wages would not buy enough bread for each of them to get a little." One of his disciples, Andrew, Simon Peter's brother, said to him, "There is a child here who has five barley loaves and two fish. But what are they among so many people?"

Jesus said, "Make the people sit down." Now there was a great deal of grass in the place; so they sat down, about five thousand in all. Then Jesus took the loaves, and when he had given thanks, he distributed them to those who were seated; so also the fish, as much as they wanted. When they were satisfied, he told his disciples, "Gather up the fragments left over, so that nothing may be lost." So they gathered them up, and from the fragments of the five barley loaves, left by those who had eaten, they filled twelve baskets. When the people saw the sign that Jesus had done, they began to say, "This is indeed the prophet who is to come into the world."

When Jesus realized that they were about to come and take him by force to make him king, he withdrew again to the mountain by himself.

When evening came, his disciples went down to the sea, got into a boat, and started across the sea to Capernaum. It was now dark, and Jesus had not yet come to them. The sea became rough because a strong wind was blowing. When they had rowed about three or four miles, they saw Jesus walking on the sea and coming near the boat, and they were terrified. But Jesus said to them, "Here I am; do not be afraid." Then they wanted to take him into the boat, and immediately the boat reached the land toward which they were going.

R E F L E C T I O N

The first reading from the Second Book of Kings antici- pates the reading from John. In the first reading a servant comes to Elisha, the man of God, with a small amount of barley and grain for feeding a hundred people. The servant does not trust that there will be enough and expresses his doubt, to which Elisha responds simply, "They shall eat and have some left." Elisha believed in the word of the Lord, and the word was indeed fulfilled.

In the gospel passage we find another feeding of a multitude, and here we detect the gospel's eucharistic theology in Jesus' actions. Jesus took the bread, gave thanks, and distributed it to the people — the same actions of a priest presiding at the eucharist even today, two millennia later. This core of the celebration has been a constant from the first century to the beginning of the twenty-first.

The people who witnessed what Jesus had done proclaimed him a prophet, and they started after him in order "to make him king." In John's gospel, just as we have seen time after time in the Gospel of Mark, Jesus recognizes their intention and withdraws to the moun- tain alone.

The second reading, from the Letter to the Ephesians, complements John's eucharistic theology by recom- mending that members of the church live with humility, gentleness and patience, "bearing with one another in love, making every effort to maintain the unity of the Spirit in the bond of peace." The strength of the commu- nity depends on its members making such efforts to bear with one another. This will build up the body of Christ that is knitted together in the weekly celebration of the eucharist.

■ **What does the unbroken tradition of taking bread, giving thanks, and distributing it century after century say to you about the providence of God?**

■ **What connection do you see between today's gospel and your church's dedication to social justice and the feeding of the poor?**

PRACTICE OF FAITH

LOAVES AND FISHES. Today's gospel is a lesson in perception and priorities. While Andrew counted the loaves and fishes as the inadequate offering of a child, Jesus recognized and gave thanks for what they really were, an abundant gift from God.

In that tradition of thankfulness and blessing, the church in western Europe in medieval times celebrated August 1 as Lammas ("Loaf-Mass") Day — the traditional beginning of autumn. The harvest's first wheat was baked into loaves — part of which were consecrated for the eucharist, the bal- ance to be blessed and shared at the Lammas Day feast.

Although today we are less aware of our agrarian heri- tage, it is still important to give God thanks as the harvest begins and to share generously of the bounty.

PRACTICE OF HOPE

A MEAL FOR THE WORLD. Imagine the scene as Jesus crossed the sea and climbed the mountain. John interjects: "Now the Passover, the festival of the Jews, was near." Jesus would have certainly wanted to share a family Passover meal on that holy day. But on this day, the world was coming to Jesus seeking comfort.

We all know the demands of hospitality, the litmus test of goodness. Here, Jesus the host took, blessed and distrib- uted the food. It was a *different* Passover meal. The frag- ments were gathered up and saved; Jesus the host was recognized as the prophet "who is to come into the world." The meal was a sign that God includes everyone. Jesus, by word and deed, revealed God's abundant love for all. (MP)

PRACTICE OF CHARITY

STIR THE POT. St. Joseph's Rectory stands as a fortress in a deteriorating neighborhood. Since 1984, like clock- work at 5:30 every night its oversized steel front door opens and tired, hungry, dirty people are beckoned in and greeted with aromas of food like tuna casserole, green beans, warm cinnamon applesauce and fresh brownies. Prayer gathers those present, and a realiza- tion of relation to one another through Christ is truly felt. Carrying out a commitment to the poor, many dedicated people from several denominations undertake the organiza- tion, planning and preparation of the "feeding of their five thousand." Hunger exists in every part of our country. Don't wait for the government or a charitable agency to take care of it. "Stir the pot" in your church and get cooking!

WEEKDAY READINGS (Mo) Jeremiah 13:1 – 11; (Tu) 14:17 – 22; (We) 15:10, 16 – 21; (Th) 18:1 – 6; (Fr) 26:1 – 9; (Sa) 26:11 – 16, 24

READING I *Daniel 7:9–10, 13–14*

As I watched,
thrones were set in place,
   and an Ancient One sat down on the throne,
whose clothing was white as snow,
   the hair of whose head like pure wool;
whose throne was fiery flames,
   A stream of fire issued
   and flowed out from the presence
   of the Ancient of Days,
whom a thousand thousand served,
   and ten thousand times ten thousand
   stood in attendance.
The court sat in judgment,
   and the books were opened.

As I watched in the night visions,
I saw one like a human being
   coming with the clouds of heaven.
And he came to the Ancient One,
   before whom he was presented.
To him was given dominion
   and glory and kingship,
that all peoples, nations, and languages
   should serve him.
His dominion is an everlasting dominion
   that shall not pass away,
and his reign is one
   that shall never be destroyed.

READING II *2 Peter 1:16–19*

We did not follow cleverly devised myths when we made known to you the power and coming of our Lord Jesus Christ, but we had been eyewitnesses of his majesty. For Jesus received honor and glory from God, the Father, when that voice was conveyed to him by the Majestic Glory, saying, "This is my Son, my Beloved, with whom I am well pleased." We ourselves heard this voice come from heaven, while we were with Jesus on the holy mountain.

So we have the prophetic message more fully confirmed. You will do well to be attentive to this as to a lamp shining in a dark place, until the day dawns and the morning star rises in your hearts.

GOSPEL *Mark 9:2–10*

Six days later, Jesus took with him Peter and James and John, and led them up a high mountain apart, by themselves. And he was transfigured before them, and his clothes became dazzling white, such as no one on earth could bleach them. And there appeared to them Elijah with Moses, who were talking with Jesus. Then Peter said to Jesus, "Rabbi, it is good for us to be here; let us make three dwellings, one for you, one for Moses, and one for Elijah." He did not know what to say, for they were terrified. Then a cloud overshadowed them, and from the cloud there came a voice, "This is my Son, the Beloved; listen to him!" Suddenly when they looked around, they saw no one with them any more, but only Jesus.

As they were coming down the mountain, Jesus ordered them to tell no one about what they had seen, until after the Son-of-Man had risen from the dead.

So they kept the matter to themselves, questioning what the rising from the dead meant.

R E F L E C T I O N

As a general rule, we hear a reading only once every three years in the Sunday liturgy. It is quite rare that the same reading is proclaimed on two different Sundays of the same liturgical year, but it happens this year because the readings for this feast of the Lord, the Transfiguration, displace the readings for the Eighteenth Sunday in Ordinary Time, which would ordinarily have been proclaimed today. This gives us a unique opportunity to consider how the context of a reading contributes to its meaning for the community.

The gospel passage, Mark 9:2–10 was also proclaimed on the Second Sunday of Lent. The first reading then was the story of Abraham's sacrifice of Isaac (Genesis 22:1–18). That pairing gave us the distinct message that the glory of Jesus shown in the transfiguration is connected to the passion he was to suffer when he gave up his life for us.

This time around, the first reading is an apocalyptic passage from the Book of Daniel in which the Son of Man is "given dominion and glory and kingship . . . that shall never be destroyed." Instead of the connection to the passion shown on the Second Sunday of Lent, today's pairing with the reading from Daniel highlights the marvel and splendor of the Son of Man as projected onto Jesus.

Considering the same gospel reading beside two different passages from the Hebrew scriptures reveals to us the genius of the liturgy of the word at Sunday Mass. When we proclaim and reflect on each Sunday's readings, we do not consider each reading in isolation from the others and merely add up their meanings. Instead, we put the readings together and see how their theologies play off one another for our religious instruction and formation in faith.

■ **What contributes most to your personal and to your parish's appreciation of the liturgy of the word at Sunday eucharist? And what detracts most from your appreciation of the scripture readings?**

PRACTICE OF FAITH

TRANSFIGUATION. When Jesus stood with Elijah and Moses and shone brighter than the sun, the apostles Peter, James and John saw him for who he is: Light from Light, true God. Long ago, when iconographers—artists who paint icons, that is, holy pictures — entered into their callings, the first subject each one painted in brilliant gold was the Transfiguration. Gazing at icons is a spiritual practice that opens the heart to see Christ for who he is. This week, make a pilgrimage to an Eastern rite church to pray before an icon of the Transfiguration or some other icon. Take your time. Let the icon help you deepen your prayer. (DP)

PRACTICE OF HOPE

SIGNED WITH GLORY. Just as Jesus went up a mountain and was there transfigured in glory, he went up a mountain and was there executed on the wood of the cross. But the transfiguration was a foretaste of things to come; the crucifixion is not the last word. We live as people who journey through suffering and death to the resurrection. And we do so under the sign of the cross. Each time we trace that sign on our bodies, we mark ourselves as believers in the resurrection. We too are transfigured here and now, as a foretaste of the life to come.

PRACTICE OF CHARITY

TERRIBLE DAWN. Fifty-five years ago over the city of Hiroshima, Japan, the course of history was altered by the use of a terrifying new technology. A few days later, the horror was repeated at Nagasaki. Historians and theologians, politicians and military officers, veterans of WWII and their grandchildren have endlessly argued about the need and the justification for the bombings. All agree that these first and only uses of atomic weapons against people have radically changed how people imagine the present and the future. Now it is possible for humanity to eliminate itself. Now the unthinkable is all too possible. This week read *Hiroshima* by John Hersey.

WEEKDAY READINGS (Mo) Jeremiah 28:1–17; (Tu) 30:1–2, 12–15, 18–22; (We) 31:1–7; (Th) 2 Corinthians 9:6–10; (Fr) Nahum 2:1, 3; 3:1–3, 6–7; (Sa) Hebrews 1:12 — 2:4

READING I *Exodus 16:2–4, 9–15*

The whole congregation of the Israelites complained against Moses and Aaron in the wilderness. The Israelites said to them, "If only we had died by the hand of the LORD in the land of Egypt, when we sat by the fleshpots and ate our fill of bread; for you have brought us out into this wilderness to kill this whole assembly with hunger."

Then the LORD said to Moses, "I am going to rain bread from heaven for you, and each day the people shall go out and gather enough for that day. In that way I will test them, whether they will follow my instruction or not".

Then Moses said to Aaron, "Say to the whole congregation of the Israelites, "Draw near to the LORD, for the LORD has heard your complaining.'" And as Aaron spoke to the whole congregation of the Israelites, they looked toward the wilderness, and the glory of the LORD appeard in the cloud, The LORD spoke to Moses and said, "I have heard the complaining of the Israelites; say to them, 'At twilight you shall eat meat, and in the morning you shall have your fill of bread; then you shall know that I am the LORD your God.'" In the evening quails came up and covered the camp; and in the morning there was a layer of dew around the camp. When the layer of dew lifted, there on the surface of the wilderness was a fine flaky substance, as fine as frost on the ground. When the Israelites saw it, they said to one another, "What is it?" For they did not know what it was. Moses said to them, "It is the bread that the LORD has given you to eat."

READING II *Ephesians 4:1–7, 11–13*

I, the prisoner in the Lord, beg you to lead a life worthy of the calling to which you have been called, with all humility and gentleness, with patience, bearing with one another in love, making every effort to maintain the unity of the Spirit in the bond of peace. There is one body and one Spirit, just as you were called to the one hope of your calling, one Lord, one faith, one baptism, one God and Father of all, who is above all and through all and in all.

But each of us was given grace according to the measure of Christ's gift. The gifts Christ gave were that some would be apostles, some prophets, some evangelists, some pastors and teachers, to equip the saints for the work of ministry, for building up the body of Christ, until all of us come to the unity of the faith and of the knowledge of the Son of God, to the measure of the full stature of Christ.
[Complete reading: Ephesians 4:1–16]

GOSPEL *John 6:24–35*

When the crowd saw that neither Jesus nor his disciples were at the place where Jesus had given the bread, they themselves got into the boats and went to Capernaum looking for Jesus. When they found him on the other side of the sea, they said to him, "Rabbi, when did you come here?" Jesus answered them, "Very truly, I tell you, you are looking for me, not because you saw signs, but because you ate your fill of the loaves. Do not work for the food that perishes, but for the food that endures for eternal life, which the Son of Man will give you. For it is on him that God the Father has set his seal."

Then they said to Jesus, "What must we do to perform the works of God?" Jesus answered them, "This is the work of God, that you believe in him whom he has sent." So they said to him, "What sign are you going to give us then, so that we may see it and believe you? What work are you performing? Our ancestors ate the manna in the wilderness; as it is written, 'He gave them bread from heaven to eat.'" Then Jesus said to them, "Very truly, I tell you, it was not Moses who gave you the bread from heaven, but it is my Father who gives you the true bread from heaven. For the bread of God is that which comes down from heaven and gives life to the world." They said to him, "Sir, give us this bread always."

Jesus said to them, "I am the bread of life. Whoever comes to me will never be hungry, and whoever believes in me will never be thirsty."

R E F L E C T I O N

Roman Catholics read the story of Jesus' transfiguration on this date whether it is a Sunday or a weekday, and other Christian churches continue reading from chapter 6 of the Gospel of John. As last week we found the Old Testament story of the multiplication of the barley and grain at the hands of the prophet Elisha mirrored in the multiplication of the barley loaves and fish at the hands of Jesus, so again today we find an Old Testament "bread" narrative mirrored in the words and actions of Jesus.

In the first reading we find the Israelites, Moses and Aaron in the desert. The people, as so many times in the Book of Exodus, are griping to Moses and Aaron about how good they had it back where they came from. But the Lord sees them through, providing the Israelites with quail and manna.

In the proclamation from John we hear of the people coming to Jesus looking for a "sign" so that "we may see it and believe you." Jesus assures the people that even back in the time of Moses, the Father provided for them. And when the people seek to have the bread that was given to their ancestors, Jesus speaks with perhaps the starkest eucharistic theology of the whole New Testament when he says, "I am the bread of life. Whoever comes to me will never be hungry, and whoever believes in me will never be thirsty." This is the "high theology" of the Gospel of John. While in Matthew, Mark and Luke it is the *actions* of Jesus with the bread and the wine at the supper before his death that constitute the primary eucharistic moment, in the Gospel of John, Jesus explicitly identifies himself as the "bread of life."

■ How many years has it been since you received the eucharist for the first time? Has your understanding about this rite of the church evolved during this span of time? Can you recall some of the earlier thoughts and feelings you had about the eucharist? What caused any change in your appreciation?

PRACTICE OF

FAITH

FASTING. While usually considered a practice of repentance during Lent, fasting can heighten our physical and spiritual senses at many other times. It is a lot to accept Jesus at face value when he says "*I am the bread of life,*" especially without any other proof. It might be one thing to believe when tangible things like manna and quail, fish and loaves are provided, but quite another when only words are offered as evidence.

Just as our senses are sharpened and food often tastes better after a time without anything to eat, fasting can likewise sharpen our spiritual senses. Choose a day this week to enter a fast; begin your day with a light meal and do not eat until evening. Read and meditate on today's gospel throughout the day. Break your fast with a good meal and a prayer of thanksgiving for the nourishment the Lord alone provides.

PRACTICE OF

HOPE

SIGNS. Jesus often had the crowd "in the palm of his hand." The signs he worked drew and fascinated people, and Jesus would seize the occasion as a teachable moment. He would lead his listeners from their desire for something extraordinary to a more meaningful relationship with God and one another. The same thing happens in our own time. People come to our churches at a variety of times, seeking any number of things, and the Lord uses the time as a teachable moment.

PRACTICE OF

CHARITY

TERRIBLE DAWN. Fifty-five years ago, over the city of Hiroshima, Japan, the course of human history was altered by the use of a terrifying new technology. A few days later, the horror was repeated at Nagasaki. Historians and theologians, politicians and military officers, veterans of World War II and their grandchildren have endlessly argued about the need and the justification for the bombings. All agree that these first and only uses of atomic weapons against people have radically changed how people imagine the present and the future. Now it is possible for humanity to eliminate itself. This week read the brief but powerful *Hiroshima* by John Hersey.

WEEKDAY READINGS (Mo) Jeremiah 28:1 – 17; (Tu) 30:1 – 2, 12 – 15, 18 – 22; (We) 31:1 – 7; (Th) 2 Corinthians 9:6 – 10; (Fr) Nahum 2:1, 3; 3:1 – 3, 6 – 7; (Sa) Hebrews 1:12 — 2:4

READING I *1 Kings 19:4–8*

Elijah went a day's journey into the wilderness, and came and sat down under a solitary broom tree. He asked that he might die: "It is enough; now, O LORD, take away my life, for I am no better than my ancestors."

Then he lay down under the broom tree and fell asleep. Suddenly an angel touched him and said to him, "Get up and eat." Elijah looked, and there at his head was a cake baked on hot stones, and a jar of water. He ate and drank, and lay down again.

The angel of the LORD came a second time, touched him, and said, "Get up and eat, otherwise the journey will be too much for you." Elijah got up, and ate and drank; then he went in the strength of that food forty days and forty nights to Horeb the mount of God.

READING II *Ephesians 4:25 — 5:2*

So then, putting away falsehood, let all of us speak the truth to our neighbors, for we are parts of one another. Be angry but do not sin; do not let the sun go down on your anger, and do not make room for the devil. Thieves must give up stealing; rather let them labor and work honestly with their own hands, so as to have something to share with the needy. Let no evil talk come out of your mouths, but only what is useful for building up, as there is need, so that your words may give grace to those who hear. And do not grieve the Holy Spirit of God, with which you were marked with a seal for the day of redemption. Put away from you all bitterness and wrath and anger and wrangling and slander, together with all malice, and be kind to one another, tenderhearted, forgiving one another, as God in Christ has forgiven you.

Therefore be imitators of God, as beloved children, and live in love, as Christ loved us and gave himself up for us, a fragrant offering and sacrifice to God.

GOSPEL *John 6:41–51*

The Judeans began to complain about [Jesus] because he said, "I am the bread that came down from heaven." They were saying, "Is not this Jesus, the son of Joseph, whose father and mother we know? How can he now say, 'I have come down from heaven'?" Jesus answered them, "Do not complain among yourselves. No one can come to me unless drawn by the Father who sent me; and I will raise that person up on the last day. It is written in the prophets, 'And they shall all be taught by God.' Everyone who has heard and learned from the Father comes to me. Not that anyone has seen the Father except the one who is from God; this one has seen the Father.

"Very truly, I tell you, whoever believes has eternal life. I am the bread of life. Your ancestors ate the manna in the wilderness, and they died. This is the bread that comes down from heaven, so that one may eat of it and not die. I am the living bread that came down from heaven. Whoever eats of this bread will live forever; and the bread that I will give for the life of the world is my flesh."

[Complete reading: John 6:35, 41–51]

Tuesday, August 15, 2000

THE ASSUMPTION OF MARY INTO HEAVEN

VIGIL

1 Chronicles 15:3–4, 15–16; 16:1–2 *David before the ark.*

1 Corinthians 15:54–57 *God gave us victory over death.*

Luke 11:27–28 *Blessed is the womb that bore you!*

DAY

Revelation 11:19; 12:1–6, 10 *A woman clothed in the sun.*

1 Corinthians 15:20–27 *Christ is the first fruits of the dead.*

Luke 1:39–56 *He has raised the lowly to the heights.*

Now we keep the festival of Mary's passover. In time, each one of us will be gathered into the reign of God, shining like the sun with the moon at our feet.

R E F L E C T I O N

We do not often hear proclamations from the historical books—Joshua, Judges, 1 and 2 Samuel, 1 and 2 Kings—even though they make up a substantial portion of the Hebrew Bible. Today's first reading, from 1 Kings, is seen by Christians as a foreshadowing of the life-sustaining spiritual nourishment of the eucharist. Elijah is fleeing from Queen Jezebel and he is weary to the point of praying for death. Asleep under a tree, he is touched by an angel and ordered to eat the cake and drink the water that he finds by his head. After taking the nourishment he is able to walk for 40 days and 40 nights to Mount Horeb, where God dwells.

The church brings together this narrative about Elijah's flight from Jezebel with an excerpt from the sixth chapter of the Gospel of John. At this point in the lectionary we are hearing the long and theologically potent eucharistic theology of the Gospel of John. (This is the middle part of the lectionary's intercalation in Year B. See the explanation of "intercalation" on page 111.) This chapter 6 of John is known by New Testament scholars as the "bread of life" discourse, and today's proclamation contains the verse that has lent itself to that title: "I am the bread of life."

Although—unlike the Gospels of Matthew, Mark and Luke—the Gospel of John does not have a Last Supper scene at which Jesus institutes the eucharist, it does have a powerful eucharistic teaching. This is appended to a scene in which a few loaves of bread increases to enough to feed 5000. In many ways—in the order of events and in theology—the Gospel of John is unique among the four gospels. This teaching, where Jesus says that "this bread is my flesh," is part of the uniqueness of John's contribution.

■ **If you have members of your Bible study group or friends or neighbors who are members of other churches, initiate a conversation about their personal understanding and their church's teaching about the celebration of the eucharist. Consider some of the issues where you and your churches agree and disagree.**

PRACTICE OF FAITH

ASSUMPTION JOY. Celebrating Mary's assumption into heaven strengthens our belief that the human body is sacred and destined for glory. Just as Christ was raised from the dead in bodily form—nail prints and all—so we rejoice that when she fell asleep in death, Mary's body was raised to heaven, too. And we celebrate this when the earth is ripe with fruits and flowers and life is abundant everywhere.

Cut flowers from your garden or window box and take them to church to leave at Mary's shrine Tuesday. Do something nice for your own body: Go swimming, take a long walk, enjoy a bath or a massage. Use this prayer, the *Regina Caeli,* before going to bed:

Queen of heaven, rejoice, alleluia!

The son whom you merited to bear, alleluia!

Has risen as he said, alleluia!

Rejoice and be glad, O Virgin Mary, alleluia!

For the Lord has truly risen, alleluia. (DP)

PRACTICE OF HOPE

VIATICUM. Jesus teaches that he is the "living bread that came down from heaven," and that "whoever eats of this bread will live forever." Viaticum is the name given to communion given to the dying Christian. Viaticum is our celebration of communion as the food for the passage through death to eternal life. It is our celebration of Jesus' words that whoever eats of the living bread will live forever. Our ritual of viaticum calls the celebration of communion by someone close to death "the completion and crown of Christian life on this earth, signifying that the Christian follows the Lord to eternal glory and the banquet of the heavenly kingdom."

PRACTICE OF CHARITY

BREAD FOR ALL. At least in Western countries, bread is one of the most common foods. It is found in a variety of cultures in a variety of forms—tortilla, matzo, pita, sliced whole wheat, to name a few. Bread requires the touch of human hands to knead, form, bless and break it. Anyone who has ever engaged in the art of bread-making knows its sacramental nature. Bake a loaf of bread this week, and then gather joyfully with friends and family to bless and break bread together while remembering that Jesus is bread for all.

WEEKDAY READINGS (Mo) Ezekiel 1:2 – 5, 24 – 28; (Tu) Assumption, see box; (We) Ezekiel 9:1 – 7, 10:18 – 22; (Th) 12:1 – 12; (Fr) 16:1 – 15, 60, 63; (Sa) 18:1 – 10, 13, 30 – 32

READING I *Proverbs 9:1–6*

Wisdom has built her house,
   she has hewn her seven pillars.
She has slaughtered her animals, she has mixed
    her wine,
   she has also set her table.
She has sent out her young serving women,
   she calls from the highest places in the town,
"You that are simple, turn in here!"
   To those without sense she says,
"Come, eat of my bread
   and drink of the wine I have mixed.
Lay aside immaturity, and live,
   and walk in the way of insight."

READING II *Ephesians 5:15–20*

Be careful then how you live, not as unwise people but as wise, making the most of the time, because the days are evil. So do not be foolish, but understand what the will of the Lord is. Do not get drunk with wine, for that is debauchery; but be filled with the Spirit, as you sing psalms and hymns and spiritual songs among yourselves, singing and making melody to the Lord in your hearts, giving thanks to God, the Father, at all times and for everything in the name of our Lord Jesus Christ.

GOSPEL *John 6:51–58*

Jesus said, "I am the living bread that came down from heaven. Whoever eats of this bread will live forever; and the bread that I will give for the life of the world is my flesh."

The Judeans then disputed among themselves, saying, "How can this man give us his flesh to eat?" So Jesus said to them, "Very truly, I tell you, unless you eat the flesh of the Son-of-Man and drink his blood, you have no life in you. Those who eat my flesh and drink my blood have eternal life, and I will raise them up on the last day; for my flesh is true food and my blood is true drink. Those who eat my flesh and drink my blood abide in me, and I in them. Just as the living Father sent me, and I live because of the Father, so whoever eats me will live because of me. This is the bread that came down from heaven, not like that which your ancestors ate, and they died. But the one who eats this bread will live forever."

R E F L E C T I O N

During these weeks when we hear the bread-of-life discourse from the sixth chapter of the Gospel of John, the first readings bring us passages from the Hebrew Bible that highlight the importance of feasting, eating and drinking in good times and in bad. The first reading today is from the Book of Proverbs, a collection of sayings written over the course of centuries that praise wisdom in its many divine manifestations.

Personified in the Book of Proverbs as a woman, Wisdom has prepared a table, and she calls out her invitation through the entire city: "Come, eat of my food, and drink of the wine I have mixed!"

While the first reading and the gospel bring out the importance of wine in the tradition — at Wisdom's table and in Jesus' words to the crowd — the second reading, from the Letter to the Ephesians, explicitly warns against drinking wine in excess "for that is debauchery." Scripture occasionally recommends abstinence from wine, but in today's liturgy, Proverbs and John are encouraging consumption — presumably in moderation, and certainly for a far better purpose than debauchery!

The beautiful passage from the Gospel of John is a continuation of the eucharistic theology we have been hearing for a few weeks. The gospel's concentration on the "flesh and blood" of Jesus in the bread and wine is, according to biblical scholars, a kind of sacramental realism. Outside of its religious context, this very specific encouragement to "eat flesh" and "drink blood" would sound strange indeed.

■ **In both bread and wine, the presence of a living organism, yeast, is necessary for the ingredients to become what they are meant to be. The yeast flourishes and then dies as the dough becomes bread, the juice becomes wine. Bread and wine become the body and blood of Christ in the eucharistic feast; bread and wine are often part of our own domestic feasts with family and friends. What does this suggest about the goodness of food and drink?**

PRACTICE OF FAITH

SEEK WISDOM. The Book of Proverbs portrays Wisdom as a woman preparing food and drink to nourish those who come to her. Paul cautions the Ephesians to think about their daily lives: They should behave moderately, and make the best use of their time and abilities. In order to live as Paul encourages, we need wisdom, a gift of the Spirit, to teach us God's ways. We also need to know our own gifts along with our lacks. Make a list of your strengths and weaknesses and use it in your prayer this week. Ask God to nourish you with the wisdom to put your gifts at the service of others and to meet your needs in ways that lead to real life.

PRACTICE OF HOPE

SING PSALMS AND HYMNS. Through song we can express the whole range of human emotions. Singing can involve us in the text in ways that mere speech simply cannot. Our whole being is involved when a song springs from our lips. And more often than not, our singing transcends the limits of our lives and hints at something greater, something beyond our reach. Whenever we sing we are expressing hope. So heed Paul's advice and "sing and make melody to the Lord in your heart."

PRACTICE OF CHARITY

ACTIVE RETIREMENT. Some people look forward to a retirement that is purposely devoid of meaningful activity. This was not true of Sister Mary Miguela Hines, BVM. After fifty years of teaching in Catholic schools, the prospect of returning to the motherhouse was more than she could bear. Invited by Father Bob Reynolds to join him in starting a Catholic Worker House, she jumped at the opportunity. Whether she was scolding Melvin for his drunken arrival at the door or interrogating Orville about job prospects, Miguela was having the time of her life. She laughed more every day at the CWH than she had in years at school. Miguela kept a daily journal that listed guest names but also contained little anecdotes and vignettes that any novelist would have died for. When she died at age 96, she had truly "walked in the way of insight."

WEEKDAY READINGS (Mo) Ezekiel 24:15 – 24; (Tu) 28:1 – 10; (We) 34:1 – 11; (Th) Revelation 21:9 – 14; (Fr) Ezekiel 37:1 – 14; (Sa) 43:1 – 7

READING I *Joshua 24:1–2a, 14–18*

Joshua gathered all the tribes of Israel to Shechem, and summoned the elders, the heads, the judges, and the officers of Israel; and they presented themselves before God. And Joshua said to all the people, "Now therefore revere the LORD, and serve the LORD in sincerity and in faithfulness; put away the deities that your ancestors served beyond the River and in Egypt, and serve the LORD. Now if you are unwilling to serve the LORD, choose this day whom you will serve, whether the gods your ancestors served in the region beyond the River or the gods of the Amorites in whose land you are living; but as for me and my household, we will serve the LORD."

Then the people answered, "Far be it from us that we should forsake the LORD to serve other gods; for it is the LORD our God who brought us and our ancestors up from the land of Egypt, out of the house of slavery, and who did those great signs in our sight. The LORD protected us along all the way that we went, and among all the peoples through whom we passed; and the LORD drove out before us all the peoples, the Amorites who lived in the land. Therefore we also will serve the LORD, for the LORD is our God."

READING II *Ephesians 5:21–32*

Be subject to one another out of reverence for Christ. Wives, be subject to your husbands as you are to the Lord. For the husband is the head of the wife just as Christ is the head of the church, the body of which he is the Savior. Just as the church is subject to Christ, so also wives ought to be, in everything, to their husbands. Husbands, love your wives, just as Christ loved the church and gave himself up for it, in order to make it holy by cleansing it with the washing of water by the word, so as to present the church to himself in splendor, without a spot or wrinkle or anything of the kind — yes, so that it may be holy and without blemish. In the same way, husbands should love their wives as they do their own bodies. He who loves his wife loves himself. For no one ever hates his own body, but he nourishes and tenderly cares for it, just as Christ does for the church, because we are parts of his body. "For this reason a man will leave his father and mother and be joined to his wife, and the two will become one flesh." This is a great mystery, and I am applying it to Christ and the church.

[Revised Common Lectionary: Ephesians 6:10–20]

GOSPEL *John 6:56–69*

Jesus said, "Those who eat my flesh and drink my blood abide in me and I in them. Just as the living Father sent me, and I live because of the Father, so whoever eats me will live because of me. This is the bread that came down from heaven, not like that which your ancestors ate, and they died. But the one who eats this bread will live forever." He said these things while he was teaching in the synagogue in Capernaum.

When many of his disciples heard it, they said, "This teaching is difficult; who can accept it?" But Jesus, being aware that his disciples were complaining about it, said to them, "Does this offend you? Then what if you were to see the Son-of-Man ascending to where he was before? It is the spirit that gives life; the flesh is useless. The words that I have spoken to you are spirit and life. But among you there are some who do not believe." For Jesus knew from the first who were the ones that did not believe, and who was the one that would betray him. And he said, "For this reason I have told you that no one can come to me unless it is granted by the Father."

Because of this many of his disciples turned back and no longer went about with him. So Jesus asked the twelve, "Do you also wish to go away?" Simon Peter answered him, "Lord, to whom can we go? You have the words of eternal life. We have come to believe and know that you are the Holy One of God."

R E F L E C T I O N

The gospel reading brings us to the end of the Gospel of John's bread-of-life discourse, which has come after the feeding of a crowd with what had been only five barley loaves and two fish. The theology of the eucharist presented in the bread-of-life discourse is familiar to our ears, as Jesus teaches his followers that his flesh is "real food" and his blood "real drink."

Today's account anticipates just how resistant people would be to Jesus' teaching about the eucharist as his flesh and blood. The disciples complained, "This teaching is difficult; who can accept it?" Indeed, the claims of Christian faith about the presence of God in worship are not easily received, even today. Though we no longer have adversaries (as did the earliest Christians) who think of Christians as cannibals for "eating flesh" and "drinking blood," we live in a culture in which the claims of faith can sound naïve, simple and irrelevant. In a society that seldom encourages its members to look for meaning in anything beyond things, what possible reason would there be to believe that the Son of God became one of us and that in our Sunday gathering Christ is present again in the assembly and in the bread and wine we share? As the disciples asked Jesus in this gospel, "Who can accept it?"

The only answer that we can give comes from the witness of our lives. They'll know we are Christians by our love, said a simple song after Vatican II. Our participation in the liturgy, a gift of grace, will make a difference in our lives, in the love we share with family and friends and in our commitment to the world around us.

■ **The celebration of the eucharist bears fruit in works of peace and justice. What are some activities of church members in your area that are the fruits of their faith? Are there some activities of Christians and their churches that embarrass you as a Christian? What are they? Why?**

PRACTICE OF FAITH

MONICA AND AUGUSTINE. Tomorrow we celebrate the memorial of Augustine. Today is the feast day of his mother Monica, but we do not celebrate it this year because it falls on the Lord's Day. These two Africans are firm foundations of the early church. Augustine's understanding of faith, preserved in his writings, continues to shape our theology today. We have nothing of Monica's writings, but we know that Augustine would never have come to Christ if not for her faith, her gentle persuasion and her love. (He tells us so!)

Begin reading Augustine's *Confessions* this week. It is widely available. As you read the story of this saint's conversion — and his mother's role — begin to keep a journal. Jot down the events and people in your life that have led or are leading you to the Lord. (DP)

PRACTICE OF HOPE

TO WHOM SHALL WE GO? According to the National Law Center on Homelessness and Poverty, as many as two to three million people are homeless in the United States each year. In late 1997, the first law to allow the use of surplus federal property for permanent housing for homeless persons was enacted. During the ten years prior to this law, nonprofit organizations had been able to use such property for transitional housing, job training, child care, food distribution and other services for the homeless, but no permanent housing was allowed. The new law has changed that: Surplus federal property may now be acquired and used for permanent housing for low-income persons. This law as an important step forward in the fight against homelessness.

PRACTICE OF CHARITY

LOVE AND HONOR. Today's second reading calls us all to love, respect and honor each other in body, mind and spirit. However, the immediate prayer and need of a woman who suffers from domestic violence is for an end to the physical, verbal and emotional abuse, and for sufficient resources to feed and clothe her children. Domestic violence makes no distinctions of social class, age, ethnicity or race. It affects neighbors, church members, co-workers and families everywhere. Larger cities provide telephone help lines and shelters. Call this week and share your gifts.

WEEKDAY READINGS (Mo) 2 Thessalonians 1:1 – 5, 11 – 12; (Tu) 2:1 – 3, 14 – 17; (We) 3:6 – 10, 16 – 18; (Th) 1 Corinthians 1:1 – 9; (Fr) 1:17 – 25; (Sa) 1:26 – 31

READING I — *Deuteronomy 4:1–2, 6–8*

So now, Israel, give heed to the statutes and ordinances that I am teaching you to observe, so that you may live to enter and occupy the land that the LORD, the God of your ancestors, is giving you. You must neither add anything to what I command you nor take away anything from it, but keep the commandments of the LORD your God with which I am charging you. You must observe them diligently, for this will show your wisdom and discernment to the peoples, who, when they hear all these statutes, will say, "Surely this great nation is a wise and discerning people!" For what other great nation has a deity so near to it as the LORD our God is whenever we cry out? And what other great nation has statutes and ordinances as just as this entire law that I am setting before you today?

[Complete reading: Deuteronomy 4:1–2, 6–9]

READING II — *James 1:19–27*

You must understand this, my beloved: let everyone be quick to listen, slow to speak, slow to anger; for your anger does not produce God's righteousness. Therefore rid yourselves of all sordidness and rank growth of wickedness, and welcome with meekness the implanted word that has the power to save your souls.

But be doers of the word, and not merely hearers who deceive themselves. For if any are hearers of the word and not doers, they are like those who look at themselves in a mirror; for they look at themselves and, on going away, immediately forget what they were like. But those who look into the perfect law, the law of liberty, and persevere, being not hearers who forget but doers who act — they will be blessed in their doing.

If any think they are religious, and do not bridle their tongues but deceive their hearts, their religion is worthless. Religion that is pure and undefiled before God, the Father, is this: to care for orphans and widows in their distress, and to keep oneself unstained by the world.

[Complete reading: James 1:17–27]

GOSPEL — *Mark 7:1–3, 5–8, 14–15, 21–23*

Now when the Pharisees and some of the scribes who had come from Jerusalem gathered around Jesus, they noticed that some of his disciples were eating with defiled hands, that is, without washing them. (For the Pharisees, and all the Jewish people, do not eat unless they thoroughly wash their hands, thus observing the tradition of the elders.) So the Pharisees and the scribes asked Jesus, "Why do your disciples not live according to the tradition of the elders, but eat with defiled hands?" He said to them, "Isaiah prophesied rightly about you hypocrites, as it is written,

'This people honors me with their lips,
    but their hearts are far from me;
in vain do they worship me,
    teaching human precepts as doctrines.'

You abandon the commandment of God and hold to human tradition."

Then Jesus called the crowd again and said to them, "Listen to me, all of you, and understand: there is nothing outside a person that by going in can defile, but the things that come out are what defile. For it is from within, from the human heart, that evil intentions come: fornication, theft, murder, adultery, avarice, wickedness, deceit, licentiousness, envy, slander, pride, folly. All these evil things come from within, and they defile a person."

[Complete reading: Mark 7:1–8, 14–15, 21–23]

Friday, September 8, 2000

BIRTH OF THE VIRGIN MARY

Micah 5:1–4 *She who is to give birth is born!*

Romans 8:28–30 *We share the image of Christ.*

Matthew 1:1–16, 18–23 *Of her Jesus was born.*

The words mother — *mater* — and material things — *matter* — are one and the same. In September, Mother Earth gives forth in fruitful abundance our material sustenance. Mother Mary is born, who in her own fruitful body knit together earth and heaven.

REFLECTION

Today's second reading comes from the Letter of James, one of the seven New Testament letters to which tradition has accorded the name "catholic" epistles. The word "catholic" is not meant to signify "Roman Catholic," but "universal." These seven letters — James; 1 and 2 Peter; 1, 2 and 3 John; Jude — are universal in their address because they are not addressed to a specific church, like the letters to the Galatians, Ephesians, Philippians and so on; their message was to all baptized Christians. This universal designation is especially appropriate to today's passage from James, since its message is not merely terrestrial but uniquely astronomical. In no other place in the New Testament do we find God named as "the Father of lights" (verse 17).

The message that James bears is one that we Christians can never hear often enough: All good gifts come from God. Our culture prompts us to think, however, that all good gifts come from money, from hard work, from our own efforts. The Letter of James reveals this to be false. Though we may try our best to live according to the witness of the scriptures and the holy people who have gone before us, it is in the end not our human effort but God's generosity that brings about good things.

The Letter of James also reminds us that faith does not simply result in a change of our interior disposition. Faith changes not only what we think or believe; it changes how we live day by day. As the author says, "If all you do is listen [to the word], you are deceiving yourselves." The practical recommendation following this is to "care for orphans and widows." Whatever situation needs human support in your parish or city, the Letter of James encourages you to do more than simply pray for it or wish the disadvantaged well. It is clear that we must act.

■ **Prayer changes things. How does this happen? How has this happened in your own prayer life?**

PRACTICE OF FAITH

RITUALS. We need rituals in which to engage ourselves daily. Whether they are personal, social, civic or religious, rituals provide meaning and direction by celebrating and consecrating the relationships we live in, and by inviting our complete involvement — heart, mind and spirit — in their structure and movement. There are times, however, when even the best rituals fail, either by celebrating relationships that are not authentic or by forms and content that are not relevant.

As you go through your week, pay attention to the rituals that you engage in. Include "everyday" rituals as well as religious ones. Make a list of the ritual activities and note whether they hold meaning for you. If so, write down that meaning; if a ritual seems to be empty, try to discover its original purpose. Develop your sensitivity to the rituals that surround you, and learn more about their value or need for change.

PRACTICE OF HOPE

A GREAT NATION AS JUST AS THIS. Co-op America is a national nonprofit organization founded in 1982 to provide economic strategies for social and environmental problems. It offers information on socially responsible businesses and investments, and rallies members to protest economic injustice. Co-op America has a growing membership of more than 50,000 individuals and 2,000 businesses. For more information contact them at 800-58-GREEN, or www.coopamerica.org.

PRACTICE OF CHARITY

ECONOMIC REALITIES. As the nation observes Labor Day, issues of social justice and the economy are far from the minds of most people. When times are good, inflation and unemployment low, and the word "recession" almost forgotten, it is easy to let such weighty matters go. But in 1986, the American Catholic bishops reminded us all that "every perspective on economic life that is human, moral, and Christian must be shaped by three questions: What does the economy do *for* people? What does it do to people? And how do people *participate* in it?" Explore the economic realities of your community this week. Who does not share in the prosperity? Who holds social, political and economic power? Is the common good the first priority, or self-interest?

WEEKDAY READINGS (Mo) 1 Corinthians 2:1–5; (Tu) 2:10–16; (We) 3:1–9; (Th) 3:18–23; (Fr) Birth of the Virgin Mary, see box; (Sa) 1 Corinthians 4:6–15

READING I *Isaiah 35:4–7a*

Say to those who are of a fearful heart,
  "Be strong, do not fear!
Here is your God.
  Your God will come with vengeance,
with terrible recompense.
  God will come and save you."
Then the eyes of the blind shall be opened,
  and the ears of the deaf unstopped;
then the lame shall leap like a deer,
  and the tongue of the speechless sing for joy.
For waters shall break forth in the wilderness,
  and streams in the desert;
the burning sand shall become a pool,
  and the thirsty ground springs of water.

READING II *James 2:1–5*

My brothers and sisters, do you with your acts of favoritism really believe in our glorious Lord Jesus Christ? For if a person with gold rings and in fine clothes comes into your assembly, and if a poor person in dirty clothes also comes in, and if you take notice of the one wearing the fine clothes and say, "Have a seat here, please," while to the one who is poor you say, "Stand there," or, "Sit at my feet," have you not made distinctions among yourselves, and become judges with evil thoughts? Listen, my beloved brothers and sisters. Has not God chosen the poor in the world to be rich in faith and to be heirs of the dominion promised to those who love God?
[Complete reading: James 2:1–17]

GOSPEL *Mark 7:24–37*

Jesus set out and went away to the region of Tyre. He entered a house and did not want anyone to know he was there. Yet he could not escape notice, but a woman whose little daughter had an unclean spirit immediately heard about him, and she came and bowed down at his feet. Now the woman was a Gentile, of Syrophoenician origin. She begged him to cast the demon out of her daughter. Jesus said to her, "Let the children be fed first, for it is not fair to take the children's food and throw it to the dogs." But she answered him, "Sir, even the dogs under the table eat the children's crumbs." Then he said to her, "For saying that, you may go—the demon has left your daughter." So she went home, found the child lying on the bed, and the demon gone.

Then Jesus returned from the region of Tyre, and went by way of Sidon towards the Sea of Galilee, in the region of the Decapolis. They brought to him a deaf man who had an impediment in his speech; and they begged him to lay his hand on him. Jesus took him aside in private, away from the crowd, and put his fingers into his ears, and he spat and touched his tongue. Then looking up to heaven, Jesus sighed and said to him, "Ephphatha," that is, "Be opened." And immediately his ears were opened, his tongue was released, and he spoke plainly. Then Jesus ordered them to tell no one; but the more he ordered them, the more zealously they proclaimed it. They were astounded beyond measure, saying, "He has done everything well; he even makes the deaf to hear and the mute to speak."

Thursday, September 14, 2000

THE EXALTATION OF THE HOLY CROSS

Numbers 21:4–9 *Whoever gazed on the serpent received life.*

Philippians 2:6–11 *He accepted death on a cross.*

John 3:13–17 *God so loved the world . . .*

As the darkness of another autumn lowers around us, we lift high the shining cross. The means of the execution of a criminal has become the means of entering into eternal life. The wood of the cross is the ark that rescues us and the tree that feeds us.

REFLECTION

The main event of the reading from the Gospel of Mark is the healing of the deaf man with a speech impediment, but the passage also has an odd verse that reveals something important about the close study of scripture. The evangelist Mark writes that Jesus "returned from the region of Tyre, and went by way of Sidon towards the Sea of Galilee." Turn to a map of Israel, ancient or contemporary, or the map in your Bible, and find these places — Tyre, Sidon (both along the Mediterranean coast), and the Sea of Galilee (slightly southeast). You will see that if Jesus was going from Tyre to the Sea of Galilee, he would not go "by way of Sidon," for that would be many miles out of his way and in the opposite direction. It would also be impractical if he was traveling by foot.

Close study of the Bible can uncover such small, and sometimes larger, discrepancies and thereby pose a challenge to the notion of biblical inerrancy. But as believers we need not find our faith threatened by flaws like this, for we can stop to ask ourselves what the primary purpose of the Bible is. Is its primary purpose to reveal the truth about the geography of ancient world? Or about the chronology of the history of Israel or of the life of Jesus? No, the primary purpose of scripture is to lead persons of faith to discover the nature of God and of the revelation given to us in the coming of the Son of God.

■ **The occasional fallibility of the authors of the many books of the Bible can, in an odd way, be a consolation to us. As people who also make mistakes, with various degrees of consequence, we can trust that in spite of our limitations God loves us and uses us to incarnate gifts to others. Can you think of mistakes of your own that have had surprisingly beneficial consequences?**

PRACTICE OF FAITH

THE HOLY CROSS. This autumn holy day on September 14 was once kept as a solemn fast, a "Good Friday" in the fall. In your home, perhaps in your prayer corner, clear a space to set up a cross for private veneration. If you do not have a household crucifix, think a bit. Do you have the cross from a relative's burial, a cross on a chain, an art book or holy card with an image of a cross? Of course, your holy cross can be as simple as two crossed pieces of wood, even two branches. Surround the cross with fresh herbs and flowers, to remind you that the cross of Christ is also a tree of life. Burn candles in front of your cross. Thoughtfully and deliberately make the sign of the cross on yourself before going to sleep.

PRACTICE OF HOPE

HEALING ACTION. Jesus' healing actions are the same human actions that we employ in our celebration of the sacrament of the anointing of the sick. We come together with those who are sick, we anoint them, lay hands on them and say a word of healing. Whether it is in a hospital room, a bedroom or the assembly space in our churches, whenever we gather to pray for healing we are participating in the mission of Christ. Even everyday acts like a handshake of support, a touch of inclusion, and active and undivided listening can bring healing to others. Following the example of Jesus, our celebrations of healing are signs that God is in our midst, that the Kingdom is at hand and that its fullness will one day make itself known. (MP)

PRACTICE OF CHARITY

EPHPHATHA. What an utterly human Jesus in his interaction with the deaf man! He speaks, he touches, he spits, he prays, he sighs. That encounter with a person in need is both a cure and a revelation. So it is with many high school students who may reluctantly undertake community service as a part of their school experience. Serving the needy is messy business. Leaving the comfort zone of friends and family, students are challenged to meet the "least of their brothers and sisters." They find that the poor are not just statistics or nameless faces on television. Empathy grows, faith becomes action, and the student, like the deaf man, hears Jesus' voice saying, "Be opened!" Is service to the community a required element in your school's curriculum?

WEEKDAY READINGS (Mo) 1 Corinthians 5:1 – 8; (Tu) 6:1 – 11; (We) 7:25 – 31; (Th) Holy Cross, see box; (Fr) 1 Corinthians 9:16 – 19, 22 – 27; (Sa) 10:14 – 22

READING I *Isaiah 50:4–9*

The Lord GOD has given me
  the tongue of a teacher,
that I may know how to sustain
  the weary with a word.
Morning by morning the Lord GOD wakens —
  wakens my ear
  to listen as those who are taught.
The Lord GOD has opened my ear,
  and I was not rebellious,
  I did not turn backward.
I gave my back to those who struck me,
  and my cheeks to those who pulled out the beard;
I did not hide my face
  from insult and spitting.
The Lord GOD helps me;
  therefore I have not been disgraced;
I have set my face like flint,
  and I know that I shall not be put to shame;
  he who vindicates me is near.
Who will contend with me?
  Let us stand up together.
Who are my adversaries?
  Let them confront me.
It is the Lord GOD who helps me;
  who will declare me guilty?

READING II *James 2:14–18*

What good is it, my brothers and sisters, if you say
you have faith but do not have works? Can faith
save you? If brothers or sisters are without clothing
and lack daily food, and one of you says to them,
"Go in peace; keep warm and eat your fill," and yet
you do not supply their bodily needs, what is the
good of that? So faith by itself, if it has no works, is
dead. But someone will say, "You have faith and I
have works." Show me your faith apart from your
works, and I by my works will show you my faith.
[Revised Common Lectionary: James 3:1–12]

GOSPEL *Mark 8:27–35*

Jesus went on with his disciples to the villages of
Caesarea Philippi; and on the way he asked his disciples, "Who do people say that I am?" And they
answered him, "John the Baptist; and others, Elijah;
and still others, one of the prophets." Jesus asked
them, "But who do you say that I am?" Peter
answered him, "You are the Messiah." And he
sternly ordered them not to tell anyone about him.

Then he began to teach them that the Son-of-
Man must undergo great suffering, and be rejected
by the elders, the chief priests, and the scribes, and
be killed, and after three days rise again. He said all
this quite openly. And Peter took him aside and
began to rebuke him. But turning and looking at his
disciples, Jesus rebuked Peter and said, "Get behind
me, Satan! For you are setting your mind not on
divine things but on human things."

Jesus called the crowd with his disciples, and
said to them, "If any want to become my followers,
let them deny themselves and take up their cross
and follow me. For those who want to save their life
will lose it, and those who lose their life for my sake,
and for the sake of the gospel, will save it. Indeed,
what can they give in return for their life? Those
who are ashamed of me and of my words in this
adulterous and sinful generation, of them the Son-
of-Man will be ashamed when he comes in the glory
of his Father with the holy angels."

REFLECTION

This week the Letter of James contains an important and somewhat tart clip: "If a brother or sister is naked and lacks daily food, and one of you says to them, 'Go in peace; keep warm and eat your fill,' and yet you do not supply their bodily needs, what is the good of that?" The Letter of James is a strong witness to the fact that faith does not change only our minds. It also calls us to change our hearts and our behavior. Belief must be accompanied by deeds.

If we could stand back and take a look at the structure of the Gospel of Mark from a distance, we could see how close to its beginning predictions of Jesus' passion appear and how great a portion of the gospel is taken up with the detailed account of Jesus being betrayed, abandoned by the disciples and crucified. For this reason some have suggested that this gospel is "a passion narrative with a long introduction." (See The Liturgical Year and the Gospel of Mark, pages 8–11.) Today's passage, approximately halfway through Mark's 16 chapters, initiates the Gospel of Mark's turn toward the cross.

Just after Peter's confession, "You are the Messiah," Jesus begins to teach the disciples about his impending suffering, rejection and death. As Christians we know that membership in the body of Christ by baptism does not exempt us from pain, rejection or death, and thus the words of Jesus echo consonant with our own life experience. Though Son of God, Jesus was not exempt from abandonment, torture at the hands of his captors and death. In our own vocations, we do not seek out pain and sorrow simply to experience what happened to Jesus, but neither are we to avoid life's difficulties.

■ **How do your thoughts about the church and about your faith "take flesh" in action? How does faith make us better persons?**

PRACTICE OF FAITH

SAINTS OF KOREA. This Wednesday, September 20, the church honors Andrew Kim Taegon, Paul Chong Hasang, and more than 100 of their companions, all of whom were martyred for the faith in Korea in the mid-1800s. Begin the day with this prayer from the Mass in their honor:

O God, you have created all nations and are their salvation. In the land of Korea your call to Catholic faith formed a people of adoption, whose growth you nurtured by the blood of Andrew, Paul, and their companions. Through their martyrdom and their intercession grant us strength that we too may remain faithful to your commandments even until death.

PRACTICE OF HOPE

BODILY NEEDS. According to UNICEF, in the year 2010 anywhere between 83,000 and 357,000 infants will die of AIDS in just nineteen of the most high-risk countries (mainly in Africa)! But these forecasts are based on reports from nations where HIV/AIDS currently rages. The epidemic is only beginning to grow in Asia, and in 10 years likely will have an even greater impact on countries with the largest percentage of the world's children, namely China and India.

Beyond meeting the medical needs of infants with HIV/AIDS, there is the additional reality of meeting the bodily needs of children who are left orphans when their parents die of AIDS. Often these young children must drop out of school to care for younger siblings, go to work, and fight off disease, malnutrition and exploitation. With the global scale of its deadly influence, HIV/AIDS truly challenges our profession to be catholic (universal) and our adherence to the teachings found in the Letter of James.

PRACTICE OF CHARITY

FOLLOW ME. If you are interested in finding some of the best ways to spend your time and talents and get more back than you imagined, consider volunteer work. In addition to providing a chance to help others, volunteer work can also nourish your own interests and develop your abilities. Many nonprofit and charitable organizations rely on the work of volunteers to reach those in need, and will likely welcome your contribution. Consider taking up your cross and following Jesus by becoming a volunteer.

WEEKDAY READINGS (Mo) 1 Corinthians 11:17–26, 33; (Tu) 12:12–14, 27–31; (We) 12:31—13:13; (Th) Ephesians 4:1–7, 1–13; (Fr) 1 Corinthians 15:12–20; (Sa) 15:35–37, 42–49

AUTUMN ORDINARY TIME

Behold! The harvest!

The Lord brings us back to Zion,
we are like dreamers,
laughing, dancing,
with songs on our lips.

Other nations say,
"A new world of wonders!
The Lord is with them."
Yes, God works wonders.
Rejoice! Be glad!

Lord, bring us back
as water to thirsty land.
Those sowing in tears
reap, singing and laughing.

They left weeping, weeping,
casting the seed.
They come back singing, singing,
holding high the harvest.

—Psalm 126

What tears you cry,
sower God, over us all.
But how you laugh in amazement
and what songs you sing
when there is some harvest.
Your saints from Adam and Eve,
from Moses and Miriam,
from Mary and Joseph,
until our own grandparents and parents,
and we too,
need your tears
and long to hear your laughter.
Harvest us home to sing your praise
forever and ever.

—Prayer of the Season

READING I *Wisdom 2:12, 17–20*

[The ungodly say:] Let us lie in
    wait for the righteous man,
because he is inconvenient to us
    and opposes our actions;
he reproaches us for sins against the law,
    and accuses us of sins against our training.
Let us see if his words are true,
    and let us test what will happen
      at the end of his life;
for if the righteous man is God's child,
    God will help him,
and will deliver him
      from the hand of his adversaries.
Let us test him with insult and torture,
    so that we may find out how gentle he is,
    and make trial of his forbearance.
Let us condemn him to a shameful death,
    for, according to what he says, he will be protected.
*[Revised Common Lectionary: Wisdom 1:16 — 2:1,
12 – 22 or Jeremiah 11:18 – 20]*

READING II *James 3:13 — 4:3, 7 – 8a*

Who is wise and understanding among you? Show by your good life that your works are done with gentleness born of wisdom. But if you have bitter envy and selfish ambition in your hearts, do not be boastful and false to the truth. Such wisdom does not come down from above, but is earthly, unspiritual, devilish. For where there is envy and selfish ambition, there will also be disorder and wickedness of every kind. But the wisdom from above is first pure, then peaceable, gentle, willing to yield, full of mercy and good fruits, without a trace of partiality or hypocrisy. And a harvest of righteousness is sown in peace for those who make peace.

Those conflicts and disputes among you, where do they come from? Do they not come from your cravings that are at war within you? You want something and do not have it; so you commit murder. And you covet something and cannot obtain it; so you engage in disputes and conflicts. You do not have, because you do not ask. You ask and do not receive, because you ask wrongly, in order to spend what you get on your pleasures.

Submit yourselves therefore to God. Resist the devil, and the devil will flee from you. Draw near to God, and God will draw near to you.

GOSPEL *Mark 9:30 – 37*

Jesus and the disciples went on and passed through Galilee. He did not want anyone to know it; for he was teaching his disciples, saying to them, "The Son-of-Man is to be betrayed into human hands, and they will kill him, and three days after being killed, he will rise again." But they did not understand what he was saying and were afraid to ask him.

Then they came to Capernaum; and when Jesus was in the house he asked them, "What were you arguing about on the way?" But they were silent, for on the way they had argued with one another who was the greatest. He sat down, called the twelve, and said to them, "Whoever wants to be first must be last of all and servant of all." Then he took a little child and put it among them; and taking it in his arms, he said to them, "Whoever welcomes one such child in my name welcomes me, and whoever welcomes me welcomes not me but the one who sent me."

Friday, September 29, 2000

ARCHANGELS MICHAEL, GABRIEL AND RAPHAEL

Daniel 7:9 – 10, 13 – 14 *A thousand thousand wait upon God.*

Revelation 12:7 – 12 *The warrior Michael defeated the dragon.*

John 1:47 – 51 *You will see heaven open and angels descend.*

The passage from summer to autumn represents the battle of sin and death against the kingdom of heaven. Jesus himself uses this mythological language to describe the reality of his battle against evil. And Christ conquers: Michael defeats the dragon, Gabriel announces the kingdom, and Raphael heals the wounded.

R E F L E C T I O N

We have earlier noted that the Gospel of Mark is sometimes seen as a "passion account with a long introduction" because of its theology of suffering. Virtually the entire second half of this gospel, from chapter 8 on, consists of either Jesus' predictions of his own passion or with the long passion narrative itself. The passage proclaimed for this Sunday starts with one of the three predictions of the passion.

The passion prediction here is bracketed by two characteristically Markan observations: one revealing once again the messianic secret of the gospel ("He did not want anyone to know it," at verse 30) and the other revealing the disciples' confusion and fear ("But they did not understand what he was saying and were afraid to ask him," at verse 32).

The first reading, from the Book of Wisdom, speaks about the suffering of the just. It is very aptly juxtaposed to the gospel's passion prediction, and has been used by many theologians throughout Christian history as they have grappled with the meaning of Jesus' suffering. The uniqueness of the passage is in the voice of its speaker. Unlike other passages in the Bible that testify to such suffering, it is not in the voice of the one suffering, nor in that of an onlooker witnessing the suffering of a just person. Rather, here we find the persecutors, the ones causing the suffering, wondering about how their taunting might have an effect: "Let us find out what will happen," they muse, "let us see whether his words be true."

Juxtaposed to Jesus' prediction of his passion in the gospel and to the torture of the speakers in the first reading, the second reading — advocating peace in the midst of envy and selfish ambition, disorder and wickedness, partiality and hypocrisy — is a tough one for our ears, even baptized as they may be! But James is clear in his message: "A harvest of righteousness is sown in peace for those who make peace."

■ **The Letter of James is tough and good news at the same time. Are you familiar with this book of the New Testament? It is not very long and is quite inspiring. Consider reading it from start to finish before bed some night.**

PRACTICE OF FAITH

BE HUMBLE. "You like Jim better than you like me." "He's allowed to stay up late but I have to go to bed." "You let him do lots of things you won't let me do because you like him better." Lines like these are familiar ones to parents. We each have a need to feel important, and we do not like it when we feel we are being slighted. This is especially true when we find ourselves in positions of authority; we want people to give us the respect due our position.

Jesus teaches that if we want to be important, we are to humble ourselves and become servants to one another. The most beautiful example of this in recent history is Mother Teresa. In humility and simplicity she served the poor and sick, and is an example for us all to follow.

PRACTICE OF HOPE

WELCOME THE CHILDREN. Jesus counsels us to welcome children in his name, and that in doing so we welcome God into our lives. The ways we welcome children can support and nourish us in our discipleship. Think of the children you know — your own as well as those of others – and use this prayer adapted from *Catholic Household Blessings and Prayers* to ask God to bless them:

Loving God, you created all the people of the world,
and you know each of us by name.
Thank you for these children [name(s)].
Bless them with your love and friendship
that they may grow in wisdom, knowledge, and grace.
May they love their families always
and be ever faithful to their friends.
Grant this through Christ our Lord.

PRACTICE OF CHARITY

SEE, THINK AND DO. Retired Bishop Edward O'Rourke of Peoria does not just write about human dignity, he works to see it respected. Although he is now in his 80s, he works daily with Renaissance Stand, a not-for-profit agency he founded to provide the unemployed with job skills. The stroke that caused his retirement has slowed him down, but it has not quenched the fire in his eyes when he speaks about giving the poor and powerless "a hand-up rather than a hand-out." As a former executive secretary of the National Catholic Rural Life Conference and author of numerous books on development through self-help projects, he has observed, reflected and acted. Bishop O'Rourke stands in contrast to those who say much, but do little.

WEEKDAY READINGS (Mo) Proverbs 3:27 – 34; (Tu) 21:1 – 6, 10 – 13; (We) 30:5 – 9; (Th) Ecclesiastes 1:2 – 11; (Fr) The Archangels, see box; (Sa) Ecclesiastes 11:9 — 12:8

READING I *Numbers 11:25–29*

The LORD came down in the cloud and spoke to Moses, and took some of the spirit that was on him and put it on the seventy elders; and when the spirit rested upon them, they prophesied. But they did not do so again.

Two men remained in the camp, one named Eldad, and the other named Medad, and the spirit rested on them; they were among those registered, but they had not gone out to the tent, and so they prophesied in the camp. And a youth ran and told Moses, "Eldad and Medad are prophesying in the camp." And Joshua son of Nun, the assistant of Moses, one of his chosen ones, said, "My lord Moses, stop them!" But Moses said to him, "Are you jealous for my sake? Would that all the LORD's people were prophets, and that the LORD's spirit be given to them all!"

[Revised Common Lectionary: Numbers 11:4–6, 10–16, 24–29]

READING II *James 5:1–6*

Come now, you rich people, weep and wail for the miseries that are coming to you. Your riches have rotted, and your clothes are moth-eaten. Your gold and silver have rusted, and their rust will be evidence against you, and it will eat your flesh like fire. You have laid up treasure for the last days. Listen! The wages of the laborers who mowed your fields, which you kept back by fraud, cry out, and the cries of the harvesters have reached the ears of the Lord of hosts. You have lived on the earth in luxury and in pleasure; you have fattened your hearts in a day of slaughter. You have condemned and murdered the righteous one, who does not resist you.

[Revised Common Lectionary: James 5:13–20]

GOSPEL *Mark 9:38–43, 45, 47–48*

John said to Jesus, "Teacher, we saw some man casting out demons in your name, and we tried to stop him, because he was not following us." But Jesus said, "Do not stop him; for no one who does a deed of power in my name will be able soon afterward to speak evil of me. Whoever is not against us is for us. For truly I tell you, whoever gives you a cup of water to drink because you bear the name of Christ will by no means lose the reward.

"If any of you put a stumbling block before one of these little ones who believe in me, it would be better for you if a great millstone were hung around your neck and you were thrown into the sea. If your hand causes you to stumble, cut it off; it is better for you to enter life maimed than to have two hands and to go to hell, to the unquenchable fire. And if your foot causes you to stumble, cut it off; it is better for you to enter life lame than to have two feet and to be thrown into hell. And if your eye causes you to stumble, tear it out; it is better for you to enter the dominion of God with one eye than to have two eyes and to be thrown into hell, where their worm never dies, and the fire is never quenched.

"For everyone will be salted with fire. Salt is good; but if salt has lost its saltiness, how can you season it? Have salt in yourselves, and be at peace with one another."

REFLECTION

As often happens in the readings for Sunday, there is a similar situation in the first reading and in the gospel. In the first reading from the Book of Numbers, the Lord bestows some of the spirit that was granted to Moses on the 70 elders, and they begin to prophesy. The Israelites expected that *only* the 70 elders who had gone out to the tent with Moses would be prophesying. Eldad and Medad, who had stayed behind, also begin to prophesy and some of the people are alarmed. But Moses' response is not alarm but encouragement: "Would that all the Lord's people were prophets!"

In the gospel, it is not that outsiders are prophesying but that they are expelling demons that worries the followers of Jesus. Throughout Christian history, the church has found itself in similar situations, when "outsiders" start participating in the church's ministry and the "insiders" are alarmed. The two situations — Eldad and Medad among the Israelites and the man expelling demons in Jesus' name in the gospel — are instructive for us in this new age.

Only late in the last century did Christianity spread to all continents of the globe. As the word of God and the traditions of the church are taught in new lands, in new languages and to new peoples, there is always some concern that this might affect the church adversely. But we can expect tensions to emerge as the church and its rites are brought to other cultures and — on the more local scene — as people unlike ourselves are initiated into our assemblies. Change, even divinely-inspired change, is difficult. Today's readings call us to be open to change.

■ **What do the responses of Moses and Jesus teach us about how to respond in the face of change?**

■ **Do you think that the gifts of God are restricted to certain places or people? Why or why not?**

PRACTICE OF FAITH

ALL CREATURES GREAT AND SMALL. This Wednesday the church celebrates the memorial of Francis of Assisi, who abandoned his family wealth to wed "Lady Poverty" for Christ. The words of a familiar hymn, "All creatures of our God and king," are attributed to Francis and certainly are infused with his spirit. Francis is the special patron of animals, and many parishes bless them on this feast. You can do the same in your own household using this simple prayer by Albert Schweitzer:

O Heavenly Father, protect and bless all things that have breath. Guard them from all evil and let them sleep in peace. Amen.

PRACTICE OF HOPE

INSTRUCTION. I am reminded of the letters I wrote to our children while they were away at college. My husband compared my notes to Paul's epistles, since I included instructions, exhortations, admonitions and assurances.

In today's gospel Jesus instructed, exhorted and comforted the disciples. His words gave them hope and confidence as they do for us as well. (MP)

PRACTICE OF CHARITY

CREATION'S GLORY. Francis of Assisi is known for his life of simplicity, peace, radical reliance on God's grace and embrace of creation's majesty. This week celebrate autumn's beauty! Contemplate Francis' Canticle to Creation: "Be praised, my Lord, for Brother Sun, who brings the day and gives us light. He is fair and radiant with a shining face and draws his meaning from on high. Be praised for Sister Moon and the stars, you have made them clear and precious and lovely. Be praised, for our Sister Water, who is helpful and humble, precious and pure. Be praised for our Mother Earth, for she sustains and keeps us, and brings forth all kinds of fruits together with grasses and bright flowers. Be praised for all your creatures. We give you thanks for in each frontier of life we rediscover you, our living God."

WEEKDAY READINGS (Mo) Job 1:6 – 22; (Tu) 3:1 – 3, 11 – 17, 20 – 23; (We) 9:1 – 12, 14 – 16; (Th) 19:21 – 27; (Fr) 38:1, 12 – 21; 40:3 – 5; (Sa) 42:1 – 3, 5 – 6, 12 – 17

READING I *Genesis 2:18–24*

The LORD God said, "It is not good that the man should be alone; I will make him a helper as his partner." So out of the ground the LORD God formed every animal of the field and every bird of the air, and brought them to the man to see what he would call them; and whatever the man called every living creature, that was its name. The man gave names to all cattle, and to the birds of the air, and to every animal of the field; but for the man there was not found a helper as his partner.

So the LORD God caused a deep sleep to fall upon the man, and while he slept, took one of his ribs and closed up its place with flesh. And the rib that the LORD God had taken from the man the LORD God made into a woman and brought her to the man.

Then the man said,
"This at last is bone of my bones
  and flesh of my flesh;
this one shall be called Woman,
  for out of Man this one was taken."

Therefore a man leaves his father and his mother and clings to his wife, and they become one flesh.

READING II *Hebrews 2:5–12*

Now God did not subject the coming world, about which we are speaking, to angels. But someone has testified somewhere, "What are human beings that you are mindful of them, or mortals, that you care for them? You have made them for a little while lower than the angels; you have crowned them with glory and honor, subjecting all things under their feet." Now in subjecting all things to them, God left nothing outside their control. As it is, we do not yet see everything in subjection to them, but we do see Jesus, who for a little while was made lower than the angels, now crowned with glory and honor because of the suffering of death, so that by the grace of God he might taste death for everyone.

It was fitting that God, for whom and through whom all things exist, in bringing many children to glory, should make the pioneer of their salvation perfect through sufferings. For the one who sanctifies and those who are sanctified all have one origin. For this reason Jesus is not ashamed to call them brothers and sisters, saying, "I will proclaim your name to my brothers and sisters, in the midst of the congregation I will praise you."

[*Revised Common Lectionary: Hebrews 1:1–4; 2:5–12*]

GOSPEL *Mark 10:2–16*

Some Pharisees came, and to test Jesus they asked, "Is it lawful for a husband to divorce his wife?" Jesus answered them, "What did Moses command you?" They said, "Moses allowed a husband to write a certificate of dismissal and to divorce her." But Jesus said to them, "Because of your hardness of heart Moses wrote this commandment for you. But from the beginning of creation, 'God made them male and female.' 'For this reason a man shall leave his father and mother and be joined to his wife, and the two shall become one flesh.' So they are no longer two, but one flesh. Therefore what God has joined together, let no one separate." Then in the house the disciples asked Jesus again about this matter. He said to them, "Whatever man divorces his wife and marries another commits adultery against her; and if she divorces her husband and marries another, she commits adultery."

People were bringing little children to Jesus in order that he might touch them; and the disciples spoke sternly to them. But when Jesus saw this, he was indignant and said to them, "Let the little children come to me; do not stop them; for it is to such as these that the dominion of God belongs. Truly I tell you, whoever does not receive the dominion of God as a little child will never enter it." And Jesus took them up in his arms, laid his hands on them, and blessed them.

R E F L E C T I O N

Some Bible stories are told more than once, and in different versions, in the various books of the Bible. Perhaps the presence of *four* gospels, rather than just one, is the most obvious example. The two separate creation stories in the Book of Genesis are another example of different versions of the same story. Often each version of a story will have a different emphasis or a portrait of God or Jesus.

In the first creation account (Genesis 1:1 — 2:4a, the seven days of creation), the creator is called "God" (the English rendering of the Hebrew *Elohim*), man and woman are created at the same time, after the rest of the living creatures. (See especially 1:26 – 27.) In the second creation account (2:4b — 3:24, the story of Adam and Eve), the creator is called "Lord" (English for the Hebrew *Yahweh*), the man is created before all the other living creatures, even plants, and the woman is made from the man's rib.

The two different versions, with their different portraits of God and different social values in the different orders of creating men and women, can lead us to wonder how the two came to be accepted as one seamless account. The gospel for this Sunday gives a clue. Jesus alternately refers to each of the creation accounts in this teaching on marriage and divorce, to the first account (Genesis 1:27) in Mark 10:6 and to the second account (Genesis 2:24) in Mark 10:7 – 8. Because the church has found all of Genesis to be the word of God and divinely inspired, both creation accounts are included in the Bible and in Jesus' teaching about marriage. Yet a close reading of Genesis opens up the complexities of the presence of two very different creation accounts in the first pages of the Bible.

■ **Knowing that there are sometimes different versions of the same story in the Bible can help us understand why Christians sometimes stand on opposite sides of issues in the church and in society. Can you think of such an issue? Can you think of Bible passages that could be employed by either side of the debate?**

PRACTICE OF FAITH

NIGHT PRAYER. Night prayers, important as they are, cannot always be a family ritual. But we can tailor the bedtime routine to the needs and ability of the people who pray together. A father can talk with his child as he helps put toys away. A mother can rub her ten-year-old's back as the child tells her the events of the day. Together parent and child can form this evening talk into prayer. Children need to be brought back to a state of peace at the end of a busy day. Many parents discover that bedtime rituals are the most intimate, precious minutes they spend with their children. The problems and feelings heard and blessed bring families closer to each other and to the Lord.

PRACTICE OF HOPE

ONE FLESH. It has become popular for dioceses to arrange an annual celebration for married couples who have celebrated significant anniversaries. Cathedrals fill with couples celebrating three, four, five and more decades of life together. These gatherings of couples, family members and friends are an annual highlight in the life of the local church. And equally good for the life of the church is that in recent years more than 280,000 couples per year have celebrated the sacrament of marriage in their parishes.

PRACTICE OF CHARITY

HEALING OUR MOTHER. What comes to mind when you hear the word "habitat"? It means more than just house or apartment. Our habitat goes beyond the walls that give us shelter to include the land, trees, water and air around us. October 6 was World Habitat Day, a day to consider how well we are caring for our planet. It is essential to care for our natural environment. We cannot stand by while rainforests are harvested and plowed under, the earth is poisoned and air and water are polluted. Save the Rainforests, Greenpeace, the Wilderness Society and Sierra Club are just a few of the organizations committed to our habitat — planet Earth. Find out more about these groups and learn what part you can play to improve our world.

WEEKDAY READINGS (Mo) Galatians 1:6 – 12; (Tu) 1:13 – 24; (We) 2:1 – 2, 7 – 14; (Th) 3:1 – 5; (Fr) 3:7 – 14; (Sa) 3:22 – 29

READING I   *Wisdom 7:7–11*

Therefore I prayed, and understanding
   was given me;
I called on God, and the spirit of wisdom
   came to me.
I preferred her to scepters and thrones,
and I accounted wealth as nothing in comparison
   with her.
Neither did I liken to her any priceless gem,
because all gold is but a little sand in her sight,
and silver will be accounted as clay before her.
I loved her more than health and beauty,
and I chose to have her rather than light,
because her radiance never ceases.
All good things came to me along with her,
and in her hands uncounted wealth.

[Revised Common Lectionary: Amos 5:6–7, 10–15]

READING II   *Hebrews 4:12–16*

Indeed, the word of God is living and active,
sharper than any two-edged sword, piercing until it
divides soul from spirit, joints from marrow; it is
able to judge the thoughts and intentions of the
heart. And before God no creature is hidden, but all
are naked and laid bare to the eyes of the one to
whom we must render an account.

Since, then, we have a great high priest who has
passed through the heavens, Jesus, the Son of God,
let us hold fast to our confession. For we do not have
a high priest who is unable to sympathize with our
weaknesses, but we have one who in every respect
has been tested as we are, yet without sin. Let us
therefore approach the throne of grace with boldness, so that we may receive mercy and find grace
to help in time of need.

GOSPEL   *Mark 10:17–31*

As Jesus was setting out on a journey, a man ran up
and knelt before him, and asked him, "Good
Teacher, what must I do to inherit eternal life?" Jesus
said to him, "Why do you call me good? No one is
good but God alone. You know the commandments:
'You shall not murder; You shall not commit adultery; You shall not steal; You shall not bear false witness; You shall not defraud; Honor your father and
mother.'" The man said to Jesus, "Teacher, I have
kept all these since my youth." Jesus, looking at him,
loved him and said, "You lack one thing; go, sell
what you own, and give the money to the poor, and
you will have treasure in heaven; then come, follow
me." When the man heard this, he was shocked and
went away grieving, for he had many possessions.

Then Jesus looked around and said to his disciples, "How hard it will be for those who have
wealth to enter the dominion of God!" And the disciples were perplexed at these words. But Jesus said
to them again, "Children, how hard it is to enter the
dominion of God! It is easier for a camel to go
through the eye of a needle than for someone who
is rich to enter the dominion of God." They were
greatly astounded and said to one another, "Then
who can be saved?" Jesus looked at them and said,
"For mortals it is impossible, but not for God; for
God all things are possible."

Peter began to say to Jesus, "Look, we have left
everything and followed you." Jesus said, "Truly I
tell you, there is no one who has left house or brothers or sisters or mother or father or children or
fields, for my sake and for the sake of the good
news, who will not receive a hundredfold now in
this age—houses, brothers and sisters, mothers and
children, and fields, with persecutions—and in the
age to come eternal life. But many who are first will
be last, and the last will be first."

R E F L E C T I O N

This passage from the Gospel of Mark has undoubtedly over the centuries been difficult for conscientious Christians who are wealthy or even merely comfortable. There is no way to get around Jesus' instruction: "Go, sell what you own, and give the money to the poor." But, as with many other issues in the New Testament — such as recommended places in the church for women and men, slaves and free, Gentiles and Jews — there are more perspectives than just this one.

The passage from the Gospel of Mark is unequivocal: "Sell what you own," Jesus says. But consider this passage from elsewhere in the New Testament: The wealthy "are to be rich in good works, generous, and ready to share, thus storing up for themselves the treasure of a good foundation for the future" (1 Timothy 6:18 – 19). A loving recommendation to be generous and ready to share is certainly not the same as the stark command to sell everything and give all the money to the poor.

The New Testament also contains passages that say, on the one hand, that there should be no difference between men and women in the church and on the other, that women must be silent and obedient to men. There is a letter telling a slave owner to treat his slave Onesimus as an equal, and there are passages telling slaves to obey their masters, "not only those who are kind and gentle but also those who are harsh" (1 Peter 2:18). In a way, this variety of perspectives contributes to Christianity's inclusiveness. And it is so not only on issues of society and church, but even in its four gospels, whose portraits of Jesus do not always agree in details or theology.

■ **Can you recall a conversation with someone familiar with the Bible whose point of view on a topic was quite different from your own? Do you find the variety of biblical perspectives on some issues a blessing or a source of frustration? Or perhaps both?**

PRACTICE OF FAITH

FOLLOW ME. My father used to say, "The road to hell is paved with good intentions." We all have good intentions, the desire to be helpful and caring, and we tend to succeed a good deal of the time. Our successes are frequently in small matters; it is the big ones we have trouble with. People living in the so-called Third World need help with education, nutrition, farming and health care. Are we willing to learn a new language and travel across the world to spend a year or two helping? Would we spend a vacation working with Habitat for Humanity or serving in a hospice during the holidays? These are only temporary ways to be of service. Jesus wants us to be ready to forsake everything and make permanent commitments. We are all called to help our fellow humans in need. Finding a way to do so that is right for you is an expression of faith in the Lord of all. (RG)

PRACTICE OF HOPE

INVITATIONS. The rich man who asked Jesus about everlasting life probably did not expect the response he got. Wealth, in his culture, was deemed a sign of blessing by God. Jesus' command to sell all he had was simply inconceivable. The man walked away shocked.

We, too, may be shocked at times by invitations that come into our lives, whether from friends, fellow parishioners or the Lord. Invitations to take new directions, enter a new ministry, begin a new way of life — these can be at least disconcerting. What is needed is trust in Christ that we will have the courage and foresight to discern and accept opportunities that will bring us closer to the Lord. (MP)

PRACTICE OF CHARITY

MAKING A WORLD OF DIFFERENCE. Today's gospel can serve to commemorate the inception of the Peace Corps on October 14, 1960. Peace Corps volunteers have left behind the comforts of their lives for a while to serve others by fighting hunger, disease, illiteracy and poverty. While the Corps maintains its traditional programs in agriculture, health, education and skilled trades, it has evolved to meet changing needs. Today, more than 6,500 volunteers serve in 84 countries, offering help in business, environmental and urban planning, youth development and English-language skills for commerce and technology. The Peace Corps describes itself as "The Toughest Job You'll Ever Love." Call 800-424-8580 to learn more.

WEEKDAY READINGS (Mo) Galatians 4:22 – 24, 26 – 27, 31 — 5:1; (Tu) 5:1 – 6; (We) 2 Timothy 4:10 – 17; (Th) Ephesians 1:1 – 10; (Fr) 1:11 – 14; (Sa) 1:15 – 23

READING I *Isaiah 53:4–12*

Surely he has borne our infirmities
    and carried our diseases;
yet we accounted him stricken,
    struck down by God, and afflicted.
But he was wounded for our transgressions,
    crushed for our iniquities;
upon him was the punishment that made us whole,
    and by his bruises we are healed.
All we like sheep have gone astray;
    we have all turned to our own way,
and the LORD has laid on him
    the iniquity of us all.
He was oppressed, and was afflicted,
    yet did not open his mouth;
like a lamb that is led to the slaughter,
    and like a ewe that is silent before the shearers,
    so he did not open his mouth.
By a perversion of justice he was taken away.
    Who could have imagined his future?
For he was cut off from the land of the living,
    stricken for the transgression of my people.
They made his grave with the wicked
    and his tomb with the rich,
although he had done no violence,
    and there was no deceit in his mouth.
Yet it was the will of the LORD
    to crush him with pain.
When you make his life an offering for sin,
    he shall see his offspring,
        and shall prolong his days;
through him the will of the LORD shall prosper.
    Out of his anguish he shall see light;
he shall find satisfaction through his knowledge.
    The righteous one, my servant,
        shall make many righteous,
    and shall bear their iniquities.
Therefore I will allot him a portion with the great,
    and he shall divide the spoil with the strong;
because he poured out himself to death,
    and was numbered with the transgressors;
yet he bore the sin of many,
    and made intercession for the transgressors.

READING II *Hebrews 4:14–16*

Since, then, we have a great high priest who has passed through the heavens, Jesus, the Son of God, let us hold fast to our confession. For we do not have a high priest who is unable to sympathize with our weaknesses, but we have one who in every respect has been tested as we are, yet without sin. Let us therefore approach the throne of grace with boldness, so that we may receive mercy and find grace to help in time of need.

[Revised Common Lectionary: Hebrews 5:1–10]

GOSPEL *Mark 10:35–45*

James and John, the sons of Zebedee, came forward to Jesus and said to him, "Teacher, we want you to do for us whatever we ask of you." And Jesus said to them, "What is it you want me to do for you?" And they said to him, "Grant us to sit, one at your right hand and one at your left, in your glory." But Jesus said to them, "You do not know what you are asking. Are you able to drink the cup that I drink, or be baptized with the baptism that I am baptized with?" They replied, "We are able." Then Jesus said to them, "The cup that I drink you will drink; and with the baptism with which I am baptized, you will be baptized; but to sit at my right hand or at my left is not mine to grant, but it is for those for whom it has been prepared."

When the ten heard this, they began to be angry with James and John. So Jesus called them and said to them, "You know that among the Gentiles those whom they recognize as their rulers are domineering, and their great ones are tyrants over them. But it is not so among you; but whoever wishes to become great among you must be your servant, and whoever wishes to be first among you must be slave of all. For the Son-of-Man came not to be served but to serve, and to give his life a ransom for many."

R E F L E C T I O N

This Sunday's readings can seem frightening. Each one, in its own way, wakes us up to the inevitable condition and end of our human lives: Like Jesus Christ, we will suffer and die. Though the Messiah has indeed "borne our infirmities and carried our diseases," as the prophet Isaiah proclaimed, this does not exempt us from infirmity and disease. That we were redeemed by the suffering death of Christ does not spare us from suffering and death.

In spite of the fear such proclamations may inspire, there does come a consolation in this awareness. We hear in the second reading, from the Letter to the Hebrews: "We have [a high priest, Jesus, the Son of God] who has been tested as we are, yet without sin." Jesus shared our human condition that we might thereafter recognize the path he trod in our own places and times. Though our lives at the turn of the millennium are quite different from the life of Jesus in first-century Palestine, we have from him a way of life and community of faith in the church in which and with which we might discern our vocation. In so doing we can indeed "approach the throne of grace with boldness," confident that we will "receive mercy and find grace."

The Gospel of Mark forewarns us, however, that drinking from the "cup" that Jesus drank from and being baptized as he was baptized will not make our life any easier or any less painful than his was. But living as he lived and by accepting our baptismal vocation as Jesus accepted his call will prompt us to seek out and to know the presence of God. In this way will we find our purpose and our reason for being. Our particular vocation will be discerned in the community of faith as we gather with it to celebrate the eucharist Sunday after Sunday. And this eucharist will strengthen us long the way so that we will be united with the "great high priest" Jesus Christ, who passed through the heavens before us to show us the way.

■ **Each baptized Christian shares in Christ's identity and work as priest, prophet and king. In what ways do you express this baptismal dignity of yours? How do you fulfill your vocation as one who shares in the priesthood, prophetic activity and kingship of Christ?**

PRACTICE OF FAITH

SAINTS ARE COMING. We live in a cosmos populated by saints in all stages. This added dimension gives us advocates and mentors. All around us we have their example as they challenge and encourage us.

In less than two weeks we will celebrate All Saints' Day, the feast that anticipates the glory of the new and heavenly Jerusalem by celebrating the memory of those who have lived our faith to its fullest. Take some time to pursue some "spiritual networking." Seek out the counsel and insight of the saints. They are present to us especially in the stories of their lives. Begin a tradition of reading about the lives of our saints. Go to the bookstore or parish library and seek out material on the saints. Perhaps you can begin with the story of the saint whose name you share, or who practiced your profession or shared your hardships. The wisdom of the saints is there for our benefit.

PRACTICE OF HOPE

LEADERS. When the sons of Zebedee asked Jesus to exalt them, Jesus responded by teaching the disciples that true greatness lies not in status but in service. The disciple of the Lord must first and foremost imitate the Lord, who was servant of all. Look around you and take hope from those you see who give freely to those in need. There are many such people: caregivers, soup kitchen workers, drivers for people with disabilities, pastoral visitors, attorneys who work *pro bono*, advocates for human rights. It is good to know there are those among us who lead by serving.

PRACTICE OF CHARITY

FORGIVING THE PAST. For more than two years, the people of South Africa watched and listened as more than 21,000 witnesses told their terrible stories to the Truth and Reconciliation Commission. The commission, chaired by Nobel laureate Archbishop Desmond Tutu, documented years of kidnappings, tortures and murders during the apartheid era. Supporters of apartheid, officials of the previous white-only government, black guerrilla fighters, and thousands of victims told their stories. At times, Archbishop Tutu lay his head on the table and wept. The history of a country's tragic and terrifying past now lies open for all to see. Will it lead to reconciliation? Former adversaries in a bloody battle for human rights now hold that possibility in their hands.

WEEKDAY READINGS (Mo) Ephesians 2:1 – 10; (Tu) 2:12 – 22; (We) 3:2 – 12; (Th) 3:14 – 21; (Fr) 4:1 – 6; (Sa) 2:19 – 22

READING I *Jeremiah 31:7–9*

Thus says the LORD:
Sing aloud with gladness for Jacob,
    and raise shouts for the chief of the nations;
proclaim, give praise, and say,
    "Save, O LORD, your people,
    the remnant of Israel."
See, I am going to bring them from the land
        of the north,
    and gather them from the farthest parts
        of the earth,
among them the blind and the lame,
    those with child and those in labor, together;
    a great company, they shall return here.
With weeping they shall come,
    and with consolations I will lead them back,
I will let them walk by brooks of water,
    in a straight path in which they shall not stumble;
for I have become as a father to Israel,
    and Ephraim is my firstborn.

READING II *Hebrews 5:1–6*

Every high priest chosen from among mortals is put in charge of things pertaining to God on their behalf, to offer gifts and sacrifices for sins. The high priest is able to deal gently with the ignorant and wayward, since he himself is subject to weakness; and because of this he must offer sacrifice for his own sins as well as for those of the people. And one does not presume to take this honor, but takes it only when called by God, just as Aaron was.

So also Christ did not glorify himself in becoming a high priest, but was appointed by the one who said to him, "You are my Son, today I have begotten you"; as God says also in another place, "You are a priest forever, according to the order of Melchizedek."

[Revised Common Lectionary: Hebrews 7:23–28]

GOSPEL *Mark 10:46–52*

As Jesus and his disciples and a large crowd were leaving Jericho, Bartimaeus son of Timaeus, a blind beggar, was sitting by the roadside. When he heard that it was Jesus of Nazareth, he began to shout out and say, "Jesus, Son of David, have mercy on me!" Many sternly ordered him to be quiet, but he cried out even more loudly, "Son of David, have mercy on me!" Jesus stood still and said, "Call him here." And they called the blind man, saying to him, "Take heart; get up, he is calling you." So throwing off his cloak, he sprang up and came to Jesus. Then Jesus said to him, "What do you want me to do for you?" The blind man said to him, "My teacher, let me see again." Jesus said to him, "Go; your faith has made you well." Immediately he regained his sight and followed Jesus on the way.

Wednesday, November 1, and Thursday, November 2, 2000

ALL SAINTS

Revelation 7:2–4, 9–14 *The crowd stood before the Lamb.*

1 John 3:1–3 *We shall see God.*

Matthew 5:1–12 *How blest are the poor in spirit.*

We welcome the winter with a harvest homecoming. All God's people are gathered into the new Jerusalem to begin the supper of the Lamb. The poor, the mourning, the meek and the lowly remove their masks and see themselves as they truly are: the beloved children of God, the saints of heaven.

ALL SOULS

Daniel 12:1–3 *The dead will rise to shine like stars.*

Romans 6:3–9 *Like Christ, we will live a new life.*

John 6:37–40 *I will never reject one who comes.*

In the northern hemisphere, nature shows forth the awesome beauty of the harvest. Yesterday we rejoiced in the harvest of the saints. Today we reflect on what made this harvest possible: self-sacrifice, completed labors and death.

R E F L E C T I O N

The exodus of the nation Israel from Egypt was already centuries in the past when Jeremiah proclaimed the prophecy in today's first reading. The prophet drew on that earlier event in Israel's history to offer strength and consolation to the nation now in different dire straits. At the time of Jeremiah's prophecy, Israel has been conquered and the survivors carried away into exile. Jeremiah prophesies their return — particularly the northern tribes, which were conquered first (the reading mentions Ephraim as "my firstborn").

Jeremiah calls this returning people the "remnant" of Israel, a word we do not hear much in everyday conversation. Remnants are the scraps left behind after most of the fabric on the bolt has been sold. Remnants are too small to be considered useful, and are perhaps frayed or faded, so the merchant sells them at a reduced price or throws them away.

Jeremiah sees the remnant of Israel as the chosen people whom the Lord delivers from captivity, those God will gather "from the farthest parts of the earth." In the super-hero culture in which we live, we might expect this "remnant" to be made up of the strong and powerful, the cunning and the scheming, the fittest and the smartest. But Isaiah reveals that the survivors will be those we would least expect: the blind and the lame, those with child and those in labor. This will be the "great company" of this surviving remnant. The most vulnerable people we can imagine were those whom Isaiah saw making up the community of the God's chosen.

The mission and ministering of Jesus, as we know it in the New Testament, were shaped by the vision of the prophet Isaiah. Though many of those surrounding Jesus in the story of today's gospel sought to silence the blind man Bartimaeus, Jesus called him over and healed him. We the baptized, like Bartimaeus and like the remnant of Israel, are God's chosen ones. We, though weighed down and broken, are those on whom God's favor rests.

■ **Do the realities of day-to-day life sometimes make you feel like a remnant, a mere scrap to be thrown away? Our biblical tradition has much to say to you if you do. Be consoled. There is a special place in God's heart for remnants.**

PRACTICE OF FAITH

THE JESUS PRAYER. Bartimaeus' prayer, "Jesus, Son of David, have mercy on me!" had been used for centuries by Christians. Another version is: "Jesus Christ, Son of the living God, have mercy on me, a sinner." Repeating either of these phrases over and over again can lead you into a deep prayer.

Go someplace quiet. Sit comfortably. Pace the words with your breathing. Breathe in with "Jesus, Son of David," or "Jesus Christ, Son of the living God," and hold your breath gently. Slowly breathe out with "have mercy on me," or "have mercy on me, a sinner." (DP)

PRACTICE OF HOPE

HEALING HOPE. How attuned blind Bartimaeus was to the happenings of the world, even with the noisy crowd around him! He had heard of Jesus of Nazareth, perhaps even that he was the Messiah, the Son of David. How resolute Bartimaeus was! He shouted out, over the noise of the crowd and the protests of those around him. And Jesus stopped on his journey to Jerusalem to wait on Bartimaeus.

Bartimaeus called and Jesus responded. Bartimaeus believed in Jesus, he hoped in Jesus and when he was healed and saw Jesus, he followed Jesus. How is this story of Bartimaeus similar to our story as Christians? Do you agree that hope and trust were involved in his healing? How can hope itself be a source of healing? (MP)

PRACTICE OF CHARITY

BLINDNESS. The young American tourists nervously circled the brightly painted well. They watched as bearded Russian Orthodox monks turned the cranks that brought the bucket full of "holy water" to the surface. A monk had explained that the well at the center of the Monastery of the Caves contained miraculous water that when drunk would nourish prayers of petition. Among the ancient buildings near the Russian-Estonian border, the young people were open-minded, willing to find out. But they were jarred out of their willingness to believe when they saw that all must drink from the common cup that hung at the well head. "It's unsanitary!" "We can only drink bottled water!" "When was that cup washed?" "We don't know who used it before us!" Blinded by their own preconceptions, they let the opportunity escape.

WEEKDAY READINGS (Mo) Ephesians 4:32 — 5:8; (Tu) 5:21 – 33; (We) All Saints, see box; (Th) All Souls, see box; (Fr) Philippians 1:1 – 11; (Sa) 1:18 – 26

READING I *Deuteronomy 6:1–9*

Moses said to the people, Now this is the commandment — the statutes and the ordinances — that the LORD your God charged me to teach you to observe in the land that you are about to cross into and occupy, so that you and your children and your children's children, may fear the LORD your God all the days of your life, and keep all the decrees and the commandments of the LORD your God that I am commanding you, so that your days may be long. Hear therefore, O Israel, and observe them diligently, so that it may go well with you, and so that you may multiply greatly in a land flowing with milk and honey, as the LORD, the God of your ancestors, has promised you.

Hear, O Israel: The LORD is our God, the LORD alone. You shall love the LORD your God with all your heart, and with all your soul, and with all your might. Keep these words that I am commanding you today in your heart. Recite them to your children and talk about them when you are at home and when you are away, when you lie down and when you rise. Bind them as a sign on your hand, fix them as an emblem on your forehead, and write them on the doorposts of your house and on your gates.

READING II *Hebrews 7:23–28*

The priests of the first covenant were many in number, because they were prevented by death from continuing in office; but Jesus holds his priesthood permanently, because he continues forever. Consequently he is able for all time to save those who approach God through him, since he always lives to make intercession for them. For it was fitting that we should have such a high priest, holy, blameless, undefiled, separated from sinners, and exalted above the heavens. Unlike the other high priests, he has no need to offer sacrifices day after day, first for his own sins, and then for those of the people; this he did once for all when he offered himself. For the law appoints as high priests those who are subject to weakness, but the word of the oath, which came later than the law, appoints a Son who has been made perfect forever.

[Revised Common Lectionary: Hebrews 9:11–14]

GOSPEL *Mark 12:28–34*

One of the scribes came near and heard Jesus and the Sadducees disputing with one another, and seeing that Jesus answered them well, asked him, "Which commandment is the first of all?" Jesus answered, "The first is, 'Hear, O Israel: the Lord our God, the Lord is one; you shall love the Lord your God with all your heart, and with all your soul, and with all your mind, and with all your strength.' The second is this, 'You shall love your neighbor as yourself.' There is no other commandment greater than these."

Then the scribe said to Jesus, "You are right, Teacher; you have truly said that 'God is one, and besides God there is no other'; and 'to love God with all the heart, and with all the understanding, and with all the strength,' and 'to love one's neighbor as oneself,' — this is much more important than all whole burnt offerings and sacrifices." When Jesus saw that the scribe answered wisely, he said to him, "You are not far from the dominion of God." After that no one dared to ask him any question.

Thursday, November 9, 2000

THE DEDICATION OF THE LATERAN BASILICA IN ROME

Ezekiel 47:1–2,8–9, 12 *Saving water flowed from the temple.*

1 Corinthians 3:9–11, 16–17 *You are God's holy temple.*

John 2:13–22 *Zeal for God's house consumes me.*

Human flesh is God's dwelling place. In November, a season of ingathering, we assemble in the Spirit. Our own flesh and blood is becoming God's holy temple. All creation is becoming Jerusalem.

R E F L E C T I O N

Two weeks ago we heard a passage from the Letter to the Hebrews, in which Jesus was described as "a great high priest." At the celebration of our baptism, whether before the Second Vatican Council (1962 – 1965) or after, each of us was anointed as "priest, prophet, and king," and it is this baptismal priesthood that links us, the baptized, with the great high priesthood of Jesus Christ. The Letter to the Hebrews has a unique understanding of the connection between the priesthood of Jesus and the priesthood of the baptized.

Two aspects of the high priesthood of Jesus are highlighted in today's passage. First, Jesus Christ lives in the presence of God in order to make intercession as high priest on our behalf. He who was one of us in all things but sin (see Hebrews 4:15), is one with God and, having shared in our humanity, understands our condition and our weaknesses. Second, the reading proclaims that Jesus offered himself up as a sacrifice on our behalf, a sacrifice made once and for all.

In our parishes and worshiping communities we are the body of Christ, one with Jesus the high priest who makes intercession for us and offered himself up for our sins. By our baptism into the church, we have been united with him, and we are privileged to make intercession as he did and still does with the Father in heaven. While many think that the catechumens are dismissed from the liturgy only because they cannot yet approach the altar to share in the eucharist, they are dismissed also because they, as unbaptized, are not able to offer the intercessions. Making intercession is a privilege reserved for members of the priesthood of the baptized.

The intercessions in the liturgy can seem to be a kind of afterthought. But the assembly's role as intercessor for the community, for the church (local and universal), and for the world is an essential part of what we the baptized are called to do.

■ **Who writes the intercessions for your community's prayer in the Sunday assembly? Do the intercessions include the needs of your local community — for the sick, the dying, the dead — as well as intercessions for people who suffer elsewhere in the world? If not, and if you keep up with events and have the writing skills to do so, think about talking to the pastor about writing the prayers of the faithful for your parish. It is a behind-the-scenes task, but a very important one.**

PRACTICE OF FAITH

VISITING THE CEMETERY. Because we know that death is not the end of life, it is not morbid for Christians to visit the graves of their loved ones who have died. It is a good practice of faith to visit the cemetery in November, when the earth itself seems to be dying, and light and warmth are in short supply.

In some countries in Europe, tombstones have little basins in them to hold holy water, and people burn seven-day candles in red glass containers anchored to the grave. The water and the fire are reminders that in baptism, we die with Christ, and so are to be raised up with Christ, too.

Remember Mary Magdalene and the other Marys going to visit Christ's tomb. Confident that what they found we will find, make pilgrimages to the graves of your loved ones this month. (DP)

PRACTICE OF HOPE

ALL THE DAYS OF YOUR LIFE. One day, some of us took a hike. We didn't know exactly how far away our destination was. We walked steadily in the heat of the day, knowing we had to return by three o'clock. We saw some splendid sights, and all was green along the way. It was hot, though, and we began sweating. Walking uphill, I was breathing hard as the stronger walkers pulled ahead. One person suggested that we turn back since we were not sure how much longer it would take. But we decided not to turn back; we might be close, we thought. Minutes later, as we rounded a curve in the trail, we exulted in the ocean vista, a glorious cool breeze, and the fragrance of the sea air. (MP)

PRACTICE OF CHARITY

MINISTERS OF HEALTH. In the late 1970s, Granger Westburg, a Lutheran minister, taught medical residents about the necessity of a holistic approach to their work with patients. His belief that faith and health go hand in hand led him to a dream that became reality in the form of congregational-based health ministers or parish nurses. Twenty years later, parish nursing has spread across the country, in almost every religious denomination. Parish nurses serve as health educators, counselors, advocates, coordinators of volunteers in the church and proclaimers of the healing mission of Jesus Christ. To find out how your parish can provide this ministry, call the International Parish Nurse Resource Center at 800-556-5368.

WEEKDAY READINGS (Mo) Philippians 2:1 – 4; (Tu) 2:5 – 11; (We) 2:12 – 18; (Th) Dedication of Lateran Basilica, see box; (Fr) Philippians 3:17 — 4:1; (Sa) 4:10 – 19

READING I *1 Kings 17:8–16*

The word of the LORD came to Elijah, saying, "Go now to Zarephath, which belongs to Sidon, and live there; for I have commanded a widow there to feed you." So Elijah set out and went to Zarephath. When he came to the gate of the town, a widow was there gathering sticks; he called to her and said, "Bring me a little water in a vessel, so that I may drink." As she was going to bring it, he called to her and said, "Bring me a morsel of bread in your hand." But she said, "As the LORD your God lives, I have nothing baked, only a handful of meal in a jar, and a little oil in a jug; I am now gathering a couple of sticks, so that I may go home and prepare it for myself and my son, that we may eat it, and die."

Elijah said to her, "Do not be afraid; go and do as you have said; but first make me a little cake of it and bring it to me, and afterwards make something for yourself and your son. For thus says the LORD the God of Israel: The jar of meal will not be emptied and the jug of oil will not fail until the day that the LORD sends rain on the earth."

She went and did as Elijah said, so that she as well as he and her household ate for many days. The jar of meal was not emptied, neither did the jug of oil fail, according to the word of the LORD spoken by Elijah.

READING II *Hebrews 9:24–28*

Christ did not enter a sanctuary made by human hands, a mere copy of the true one, but he entered into heaven itself, now to appear in the presence of God on our behalf. Nor was it to offer himself again and again, as the high priest enters the Holy Place year after year with blood that is not his own; for then he would have had to suffer again and again since the foundation of the world.

But as it is, Christ has appeared once for all at the end of the age to remove sin by the sacrifice of himself. And just as it is appointed for mortals to die once, and after that the judgment, so Christ, having been offered once to bear the sins of many, will appear a second time, not to deal with sin, but to save those who are eagerly waiting for him.

GOSPEL *Mark 12:38–44*

As Jesus taught, he said, "Beware of the scribes, who like to walk around in long robes, and to be greeted with respect in the marketplaces, and to have the best seats in the synagogues and places of honor at banquets! They devour widows' houses and for the sake of appearance say long prayers. They will receive the greater condemnation."

Jesus sat down opposite the treasury, and watched the crowd putting money into the treasury. Many rich people put in large sums. A poor widow came and put in two small copper coins, which are worth a penny. Then Jesus called his disciples and said to them, "Truly I tell you, this poor widow has put in more than all those who are contributing to the treasury. For all of them have contributed out of their abundance; but she out of her poverty has put in everything she had, all she had to live on."

R E F L E C T I O N

The common element in the first reading and the gospel narrative is the presence of a widow. In the First Book of Kings we discover the prophet Elijah asking the widow for a little water and a morsel of bread. The widow and her son are so poor that they are close to starvation, but she shares what they have. In the gospel we see Jesus people-watching in the temple, and he sees a widow putting two copper coins "worth a penny" into the temple treasury. He praises the widow's generosity because she has given everything she has, even though it is so little. God's care for widows is apparent in the Hebrew scriptures, as is Jesus' in the New Testament.

The New Testament reveals that there was an official "order of widows" in some churches. In the First Letter of Timothy we find evidence of the enrollment of widows for ministry in the church: "Let a widow be put on the list if she is not less than sixty years old and has been married only once; she must be well attested for her good works, as one who has brought up children, shown hospitality, washed the saints' feet, helped the afflicted, and devoted herself to doing good in every way" (4:9 – 10). This follows the letter's description of the offices of bishop and deacon, whose job descriptions and qualifications are not that much different from those of the widow. Because the office of the widow is juxtaposed to that of the bishop and the deacon, we can only assume that, like those, it was a very important ministry in the early church.

In our own time and place, women typically outlive men by a number of years. There are many now-single older women who minister in our parishes, often making up most of the assembly for the daily liturgy. In parishes without resident priests, these widows are often the ones who keep the place going, updating visiting presiders when they arrive for eucharist. It seems that the office of widows is as vital today as it was in the early church.

■ **The widows in today's readings gave all they had for God's work. Giving generously, without thought of the cost, giving out of love — who do you know who gives like that? Is their generosity an echo of God's love? In what ways?**

PRACTICE OF FAITH

FAST FADES THE YEAR. Like the widow's flour and water in the first reading, the hours of daylight and the year are dwindling. Scripture and the season tell us that temporal things run out — provisions, time, money, life. Here we have three messages of complete giving: the last flour and oil of the widow of Zarephath, the death of Christ for humanity, and the total gift of the widow in the temple.

The lesson is consistent: Seek *first* the dominion of God and all else will be given besides. The message is the same to us: Withhold nothing. Our practice of faith calls us to seek out God's dominion in those who need us, especially the hungry, the lonely, the destitute. There is no shortage of needs, or of ways to respond.

PRACTICE OF HOPE

THE WIDOW. Jesus marveled at the generosity of the widow who gave but two coins, but in doing so gave everything she had. All she had left was hope. At first glance it may seem that this widow acted irresponsibly, giving up absolutely all she had. This is not prudent. How can she possibly be an example for us?

Each of us, however, has probably had a similar experience — not necessarily involving money, but involving how much we let go and commit ourselves completely to something we believe in, usually with no guarantees and only a lot of hope for success. There have been times we each have run on pure hope.

PRACTICE OF CHARITY

BUILD FOR THE PRESENT. Tears of joy flowed down Melissa's face. She held a shiny key in her trembling right hand and clutched her family Bible to her chest. Moments earlier she had unlocked the front door of her new home, which had been built with her own hands and those of more than fifty Habitat for Humanity volunteers. Surrounded by friends, family, new neighbors and Habitat volunteers, Melissa read aloud Psalm 127, "Unless the Lord build the house, they labor in vain who build." After the party, Melissa and her sons sat on the living room floor, soon to be crowded with packing boxes and furniture. They marveled again at the great good that can be accomplished when the Lord, with a little help from Habitat volunteers, builds a house. Locate the HFH affiliates in your area; help "the Lord build."

WEEKDAY READINGS (Mo) Titus 1:1 – 9; (Tu) 2:1 – 8, 11 – 14; (We) 3:1 – 7; (Th) Philemon 7 – 20; (Fr) 2 John 4 – 9; (Sa) 3 John 5 – 8

READING I *Daniel 12:1–3*

"At that time Michael, the great ruler, the protector of your people, shall arise. There shall be a time of anguish, such as has never occurred since nations first came into existence. But at that time your people shall be delivered, everyone who is found written in the book. Many of those who sleep in the dust of the earth shall awake, some to everlasting life, and some to shame and everlasting contempt. Those who are wise shall shine like the brightness of the sky, and those who lead many to righteousness, like the stars forever and ever."

READING II *Hebrews 10:11–25*

Every priest stands day after day at his service, offering again and again the same sacrifices that can never take away sins. But when Christ had offered for all time a single sacrifice for sins, "he sat down at the right hand of God," and since then has been waiting "until his enemies would be made a footstool for his feet." For by a single offering he has perfected for all time those who are sanctified.

And the Holy Spirit also testifies to us, for after saying, "This is the covenant that I will make with them after those days, says the Lord: I will put my laws in their hearts, and I will write them on their minds," then is added, "I will remember their sins and their lawless deeds no more." Where there is forgiveness of these, there is no longer any offering for sin.

Therefore, my friends, since we have confidence to enter the sanctuary by the blood of Jesus, by the new and living way that Christ opened for us through the curtain (that is, through his flesh), and since we have a great priest over the house of God, let us approach with a true heart in full assurance of faith, with our hearts sprinkled clean from an evil conscience and our bodies washed with pure water. Let us hold fast to the confession of our hope without wavering, for the one who has promised is faithful. And let us consider how to provoke one another to love and good deeds, not neglecting to meet together, as is the habit of some, but encouraging one another, and all the more as you see the Day approaching.

GOSPEL *Mark 13:24–32*

Jesus said: "In those days, after that suffering, the sun will be darkened, and the moon will not give its light, and the stars will be falling from heaven, and the powers in the heavens will be shaken. Then they will see 'the Son-of-Man coming in clouds' with great power and glory. Then the Son-of-Man will send out the angels, and gather his elect from the four winds, from the ends of the earth to the ends of heaven."

"From the fig tree learn its lesson: as soon as its branch becomes tender and puts forth its leaves, you know that summer is near. So also, when you see these things taking place, you know that he is near, at the very gates. Truly I tell you, this generation will not pass away until all these things have taken place. Heaven and earth will pass away, but my words will not pass away.

"But about that day or hour no one knows, neither the angels in heaven, nor the Son, but only the Father."

[Revised Common Lectionary: Mark 13:1–8]

Thursday, November 23, 2000

THANKSGIVING DAY (UNITED STATES)

Sirach 50:22–24 *Bless the God who has done wondrous things.*

1 Corinthians 1:3–9 *God's favor has been bestowed on us in Christ.*

Luke 17:11–19 *Give thanks to God.*

God has given us the earth, a land flowing with milk and honey. We show our thankfulness by being wise and selfless stewards of the earth and by sharing our gifts with one another.

R E F L E C T I O N

This passage from the Gospel of Mark comes from chapter 13, which is the very place in the gospel where the liturgical year began on the First Sunday of Advent one year ago. At that time the evangelist warned that "you will hear wars and rumors of wars" (13:7), but advised, "Do not be alarmed." Now we hear that "the sun will be darkened, the moon will not shed its light, stars will fall out of the skies," and so on. As we approach the end of this millennial year, we may hear predictions of doom from less reliable sources than Scripture. Keep the words of Christ from this gospel ever in your mind and heart, and do not be alarmed.

The evangelist is clear that these things will happen because the Son of Man is coming. But for those of us baptized in the faith, the coming of Christ is not something to be feared. In the community that gathers at the altar Sunday after Sunday, we have come to know the body of Christ; we have had our consciences formed by the word of God preached in the liturgy; we have let our bodies move, consciously or unconsciously, with the rhythm and postures of the assembly and its worship. We have been formed into the body of Christ, a body that is not so different from what we will find at Christ's coming at the end of time.

As with the end of our own lives, however, we do not know if the end of time is to happen today or years from now. What God asks us is that we be ready, that we live each day as if it were the last. And the best preparation for this end is the celebration of the liturgy.

■ **What do you think about the coming of the end of the world? What do you think about the coming of the end of your own life? Are these two inevitable events connected, or not? How does the church help you prepare for each of these ends?**

PRACTICE OF FAITH

COMING IN CLOUDS. Charles Wesley captured many of the images of the scriptures of these last weeks of the year in a beautiful hymn, "Lo, He Comes with Clouds Descending":

Lo, he comes with clouds descending
once for favored sinners slain.
Thousand, thousand saints attending
swell the triumph of his train.
Alleluia! Alleluia! Alleluia!
God appears on earth to reign.

Yea, amen, let all adore thee
high on thine eternal throne.
Savior, take the power and glory
claim the kingdom for thine own.
Lord, come quickly! Lord, come quickly!,
Lord come quickly!
Everlasting God, come down!

PRACTICE OF HOPE

WAITING IN JOYFUL HOPE. Jesus gave the disciples warnings and instructions about their future and the end of time. As Mark tells it, Jesus' vision was poetic, mystical. Early Christians lived in high expectation of the coming of Christ. Today's Christians hope to meet the Lord upon their death, while also believing that Christ will come again in glory at an unknown time in the future. A sound view is in this prayer: "Protect us from all anxiety as we wait in joyful hope for the coming of our Savior, Jesus Christ." (MP)

PRACTICE OF CHARITY

HUNGER FOR JUSTICE. It was a teachable moment. The high school youth group's three-day retreat began with a 24-hour fast and educational activities about the disparity between the hungry and the well-fed. Ted had been convinced that it would be impossible to go one day without food: "I'll die," he moaned. A few began to daydream about what would be served at the conclusion of the fast: pizza, French fries, ice cream, maybe brownies? To their astonishment, each was served a cup of water and a small bowl of rice or beans — and that would be their menu for the next two days. The learning was just beginning! Oxfam America raises funds to assist the hungry and educate the well-fed. Call 617-482-1211 for information.

WEEKDAY READINGS (Mo) Revelation 1:1 – 4, 2:1 – 5; (Tu) 3:1 – 6, 14 – 22; (We) 4:1 – 11; (Th) Thanksgiving, see box; (Fr) Revelation 10:8 – 11; (Sa) 11:4 – 12

READING I *Daniel 7:9–10, 13–14*

As I watched,
thrones were set in place,
    and an Ancient One sat down on the throne,
whose clothing was white as snow,
    the hair of whose head like pure wool;
whose throne was fiery flames,
    and its wheels were burning fire.
A stream of fire issued
    and flowed out from the presence of the
        Ancient of Days,
whom a thousand thousands served,
    and ten thousand times ten thousand stood
        in attendance.
The court sat in judgment,
    and the books were opened.
As I watched in the night visions,
I saw one like a human being
    coming with the clouds of heaven.
And he came to the Ancient One,
    before whom he was presented.
To him was given dominion
    and glory and kingship,
that all peoples, nations, and languages
    should serve him.
His dominion is an everlasting dominion
    that shall not pass away,
and his reign is one
    that shall never be destroyed.

READING II *Revelation 1:4b–8*

Grace to you and peace from the one who is and
who was and who is to come, and from the seven
spirits who are before God's throne, and from Jesus
Christ, the faithful witness, the firstborn of the dead,
and the ruler of the rulers of the earth. To the one who
loves us and freed us from our sins by his blood,
and made us to be a dominion, priests serving his
God and Father, to Jesus Christ be glory and dominion forever and ever. Amen. Look! He is coming
with the clouds; every eye will see him, even those
who pierced him; and on his account all the tribes of
the earth will wail. So it is to be. Amen.

"I am the Alpha and the Omega," says the Lord
God, who is and who was and who is to come, the
Almighty.

GOSPEL *John 18:33–37*

Pilate entered the headquarters again, summoned
Jesus, and asked him, "Are you the King of the
Jews?" Jesus answered, "Do you ask this on your
own, or did others tell you about me?" Pilate replied,
"I am not Jewish, am I? Your own nation and the
chief priests have handed you over to me. What
have you done?" Jesus answered, "My kingdom is
not from this world. If my kingdom were from this
world, my followers would be fighting to keep me
from being handed over to the Judeans. But as it is,
my kingdom is not from here." Pilate asked him, "So
you are a king?" Jesus answered, "You say that I am
a king. For this I was born, and for this I came into
the world, to testify to the truth. Everyone who
belongs to the truth listens to my voice."

R E F L E C T I O N

Scripture and the liturgy direct our thoughts about Jesus Christ to the past, the present and the future. But concentrating on any one of these to the exclusion of the others can lead to an unbalanced life.

Christians who look only to the past, in their own lives or in the life of Jesus of Nazareth, take the easiest route, for they can be merely passive spectators. They can keep a safe distance between themselves and God's reign, observing someone else's participation in the past rather than being active participants themselves. It is comparable, perhaps, to the difference between watching a sport and playing a sport, between passively watching a scripted life on TV and living a life.

Christians who concentrate only on the present are probably enthusiastic about their faith, eager to spread the good news. But if they are unaware of the history of Israel and the life of Jesus as known from the scriptures, and the teachings of the church throughout the centuries, then they have little foundation.

Christians who are eager for the second coming of Christ, not very mindful of the first coming or of the life of Christ today, are the ones who focus on the future. They probably do not participate actively in the liturgy, for the church in the present does not strike them as making much difference. They might spend more time looking to the heavens for signs of the second coming than looking at eye level for conditions that make life difficult for others here and now.

Healthy faith keeps the three time frames in balance: seeing the presence of God in the life of the incarnate Jesus of Nazareth and in the scriptures that are proclaimed in the liturgy; seeing the presence of God in the community gathered at the altar Sunday after Sunday, as well as in the world around us; soberly anticipating the end of the world and the end of our own life as we know it now.

■ **Lifelong Christians, perhaps, tend to be least attentive to the future. The readings remind us that God's reign will come, indeed is coming now. How are you committed to bringing the reign of God to the church and to the world?**

PRACTICE OF FAITH

CROWN OF GLORY. The year ends with the image of Christ crowned — first with thorns, then with the victor's laurel wreath, the evergreen crown of glory. No wonder that Christ the King Sunday leads to next week's First Sunday of Advent. After you finish celebrating Thanksgiving, prepare your Advent wreath. Whether you make or buy the evergreen circle, see it as a promise of the glory that awaits you. On your baptism day you were anointed with chrism, the royal oil that makes you another *christos,* another *anointed one.* You have the power to live faithfully and love fiercely. The crown of glory — Christ's very own — is promised you. On your baptism day a candle was lit from the Easter candle. As you light the first candle on your Advent wreath next weekend, know that Christ's light is in you. (DP)

PRACTICE OF HOPE

BELONGING. Today's feast stands as a pillar at the end of the church year, as another feast of Christ's kingship — the Epiphany — stands at the beginning of the year. Both feasts celebrate Christ as the "Alpha and the Omega, the first and the last, the beginning and the end." (Revelation 22:13) Because Christ is the way to the Father, our liturgical life revolves around the life of Christ. Year after year after year, we celebrate Christ's coming among us, his ministry, death, resurrection and gift of the Spirit. It is what we do; it is where we belong, year after year drawing ourselves ever closer to the Lord. (MP)

PRACTICE OF CHARITY

CHARITY AT HOME. Many of us have arranged to be with our families for this holiday weekend. Whether the Thanksgiving meal is shared with dozens of cousins, uncles and aunts, or just with a few close relatives, celebrating kinship is an integral part of the Christian experience. But tight scheduling and travel demands sometimes make the family gathering a frantic event, neither relaxing nor satisfying. Hindsight, as we travel home, can be harsh. "I should have talked more with Mom." "How did that turn into an argument?" "Where did the time go?" "Why couldn't we all get along?" As the new year begins and opportunities to share time with family abound, resolve to use them well. Focus on relationships that need special care. Practice the charity that we share with strangers with those we know well and love.

WEEKDAY READINGS (Mo) Revelation 14:1 – 3, 4 – 5; (Tu) 14:14 – 19; (We) 15:1 – 4; (Th) Romans 10:9 – 18; (Fr) Revelation 20:1 – 4, 11 – 21 (Sa) 22:1 – 7

Information on the License to Reprint from *At Home with the Word 2000*

The low bulk-rate prices of *At Home with the Word 2000* are intended to make quantities of the book affordable. Single copies are $7.00 each; 5–99 copies, $5.00 each; 100–499 copies, $4.00 each; 500 or more copies, $3.00 each. We encourage parishes to buy quantities of this book.

However, Liturgy Training Publications makes a simple reprint license available to parishes that would find it more practical to reproduce some parts of this book. Reflections (and questions), Practices, Prayers of the Season, and/or the holy day boxes can be duplicated for the parish bulletin or reproduced in other formats. These can be used every week or as often as the license-holder chooses. The page size of *At Home with the Word 2000* is 8 x 10 inches.

The license granted is for the period beginning with the First Sunday of Advent—November 28, 1999—through the solemnity of Christ the King—November 26, 2000.

Note also that the license does *not* cover the scriptures, psalms, or morning, evening and night prayer texts. See the acknowledgments page at the beginning of this book for the names and addresses of these copyright owners. Directions for obtaining permission to use these texts are given there.

The materials reprinted under license from LTP may not be sold and may be used only among the members of the community obtaining the license. The license may not be purchased by a diocese for use in its parishes.

No reprinting may be done by the parish until the license is signed by both parties and the fee is paid. Copies of the license agreement will be sent on request. The fee varies with the number of copies to be reproduced on a regular basis:

Up to 100 copies: $100
101 to 500 copies: $300
501 to 1000 copies: $500
More than 1000 copies: $800

For further information, call the reprint permissions department at 773-486-8970, ext. 268, or fax your request to 773-486-7094, att: reprint permissions.

Gifts of Prayer-Instruments of Peace

Use this series of pocket-sized prayer books to pray for and with those who are in need or to celebrate ministry of care in our lives. LTP's prayer books have a distinctive design that reflects the dignity of prayer and provide a means for family ritual and group prayer. These prayer books make excellent gifts and fit easily into most greeting cards. Give the enduring gift of prayer to yourself and loved ones.

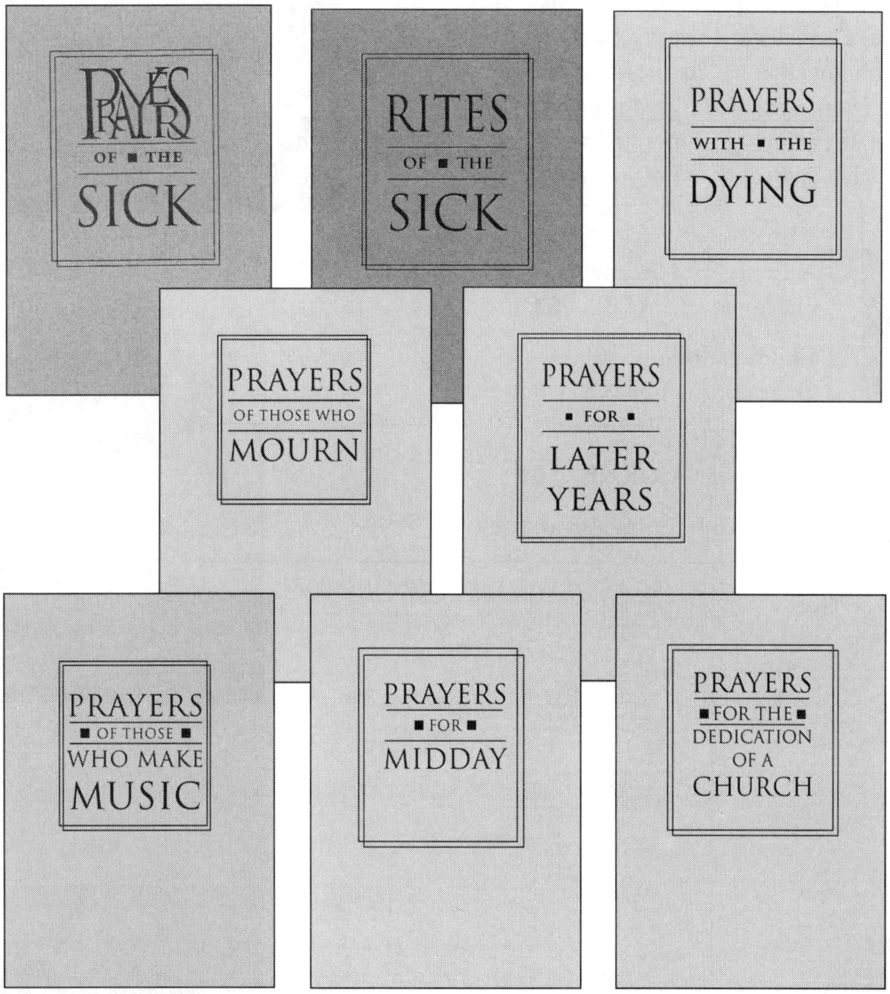

PRAYERBOOKS

PRAYERS OF THE SICK
Order code: SICKR **$4**

RITES OF THE SICK
Order code: RSICK **$4**

PRAYERS WITH THE DYING
Order code: DYING **$4**

PRAYERS OF THOSE WHO MOURN
Order code: MOURNR **$4**

PRAYERS FOR LATER YEARS
Order code: ELDER **$4**

PRAYERS OF THOSE WHO MAKE MUSIC
Order Code: MUSICR **$4**

PRAYERS FOR MIDDAY
Order code: MDAY **$4**

PRAYERS FOR THE DEDICATION OF A CHURCH
Order code: CHURCH **$5**

Ask about special quantity prices for large orders.

PRAY IN THE JUBILEE

PRAYERS FOR JUBILEE

Make 2000 a year of grace and blessing in your home or in all the households of your parish. This collection of prayers, scripture and songs focuses on a biblical approach to Jubilee: charity, justice, redemption, reconciliation and peace. You'll even find a short form of Morning, Evening and Night Prayer. Portable enough to carry with you every day and affordable enough to purchase for any size group.

Order code: PJUB

single copy: **$3** each
2–300 copies: **$2** each
301 or more: **$1.50** each

Listening to God's Word

by Eileen Drilling and Judy Rothfork

Initiation into the Christian life is fundamentally a sharing of faith. Whether passed from parent to child or from teacher to student, faith involves the whole family of God. The authors have put together an exciting approach to faith-sharing. Children will enjoy the time spent talking about God with an adult, and adults will be inspired by their child's growth in faith. This is an easy way to support our children in their relationship with God and for them to interiorize the gospel. It is an easy way for families to express verbally and ritually their experience of God and to strengthen their life together by sharing experiences, prayers and blessings. Although *Listening to God's Word* is designed for 8–12 year-olds, younger children will enjoy the stories and activities, and older children may use the Adult Journal or assist younger children.

Listening to God's Word is:
- intergenerational faith-sharing
- based in the Sunday gospels
- comprised of three resources
- activities with scripture and ritual

Use *Listening to God's Word* as a resource for:
- children's catechumenate
- sacramental preparation
- parish family programs
- faith formation in the home
- religion class
- vacation Bible school
- children's liturgy of the Word

YEAR B:

Activities and Stories
Order code: LCATB **$15**

Child's Journal
Order code: CJORNB **$5**

Adult's Journal
Order code: AJORNB **$5**

Year A and Year C also available.

ELEVENTH SUNDAY IN ORDINARY TIME

Jesus Sees Our Hearts

Based on Luke 7:36 – 50

Opening Question

Do you have any friends whom you did not like at first? What are some things that you like about them now?

Journal

See page 37, part 1 of your journal.

Story

Here is a story about a teacher who saw good in all of her students.

Sally's Gift

It was Mrs. Worthington's birthday, and the class had planned a surprise party for her. One of the parents decorated a special cake and there was plenty of punch and cookies, too. Even the principal stopped by to wish her well. Now everyone "ooh-ed" and "ahh-ed" as she unwrapped her presents.

Suddenly the class became silent as Mrs. Worthington picked up the last present. It was wrapped with wrinkled paper and had a few grease spots on it. Everyone knew it was from Sally. The teacher opened it carefully. She held up an old, worn teddy bear. No one "ooh-ed" or "ahh-ed" this time.

Mrs. Worthington smiled with delight. Hugging the bear she said, "I like this gift very much. I can tell this bear has been cherished and given lots of love. I'll keep it right by my books so I can see it every day."

Talk About the Story

Finish these sentences:

If I were the teacher, I would _______________________ .
If I were Sally, I would _______________________ .
If I were one of the students, I would _______________________ .

Scripture

Jesus finds goodness in everybody. Read Luke 7:36 – 50 to see what happened when Jesus visited Simon's house.

A reading from the holy gospel according to Luke

A Pharisee invited Jesus to have dinner with him. So Jesus went to the Pharisee's home and got ready to eat.

When a sinful woman in that town found out that Jesus was there, she bought an expensive bottle of perfume. Then she came and stood behind Jesus. She cried and started washing his feet with her tears and drying them with her hair. The woman kissed his feet and poured the perfume on them.

The Pharisee who had invited Jesus saw this and said to himself, "If this man really were a prophet, he would know what kind of woman is touching him! He would know that she is a sinner."

Jesus said to the Pharisee, "Simon, I have something to say to you."

"Teacher, what is it?" Simon replied.

Jesus told him, "Two people were in debt to a moneylender. One of them owed him five hundred silver coins, and the other owed him fifty. Since neither of them could pay him back, the moneylender said that they didn't have to pay him anything. Which one of them will like him most?"

Simon answered, "I suppose it would be the one who had owed more and didn't have to pay it back."

"You are right," Jesus said.

He turned toward the woman and said to Simon, "Have you noticed this woman? When I came into your home, you didn't give me any water so I could wash my feet. But she has washed my feet with her tears and dried them with her hair.

"You didn't greet me with a kiss, but from the time I came in, she has not stopped kissing my feet.

"You didn't even pour olive oil on my head, but she has poured expensive perfume on my feet.

"So I tell you that all her sins are forgiven, and that is why she has shown great love. But anyone who has been forgiven only a little will show only a little love."

Then Jesus said to the woman, "Your sins are forgiven."

Some other guests started saying to one another, "Who is this who dares to forgive sins?"

But Jesus told the woman, "Because of your faith, you are now saved. May God give you peace!"

The gospel of the Lord.

Reflection

If you were invited to Simon's party, what would you notice? What qualities would Jesus find in you?

Journal

See page 37, part 2 of your journal.

Prayer

Gather photos of people that you would have invited to Simon's party. Or make a list of people you would have wanted Jesus to meet at the party. Place the photos or list on the prayer table. Then pray:

God,
you sent your Son, Jesus, for everyone.
Thank you for accepting and loving us all.
Help us to respect and accept others in Jesus' name.
Amen.

92   Eleventh Sunday in Ordinary Time

Eleventh Sunday in Ordinary Time   93

Above: pages 94 & 95 from *Activities and Stories, Year C*

ORDER FROM YOUR BOOKSTORE OR FROM LTP:

LITURGY TRAINING PUBLICATIONS
1800 North Hermitage Avenue
Chicago IL 60622-1101

PHONE 1-800-933-1800   FAX 1-800-933-7094   E-MAIL orders@ltp.org